PRAISE FOR *LISTEN, WORLD!*

"A page-turning biography of Elsie Robinson (1883–1956), a prominent twentieth-century journalist and cartoonist. The account is enlivened with copious excerpts from Robinson's column and her memoir, all of which bring home her firebrand style. This entertaining account delivers."

—*Publishers Weekly*

"*Listen, World!* is the rarest of things—a lively piece of unknown history, a marvelous story of a woman's triumph, and a tremendous read. Scheeres and Gilbert have managed the trifecta, and we readers are the better for it."

—SUSAN ORLEAN, *New York Times*–bestselling author of *The Library Book*

"A riveting story about a woman who had nerve."

—JILL ABRAMSON, former executive editor, *New York Times*, and author of *Merchants of Truth*

"If you are a fan of spunky, spitfire heroines in the tradition of Hester Prynne, Elizabeth Bennett, and Jo March, you will love the true story of Elsie Robinson. Robinson was a maverick who chased wild dreams of adventure and independence instead of surrendering to her wealthy but soul-crushing husband—and ended up as one of the highest-paid, most-read writers in America. Like Elsie herself, *Listen, World!* is broadminded, sharp-witted, fast-paced, and funny. It reads like a breezy novel that lingers long after you've read the last page. I loved every word of it."

—DEBBY APPLEGATE, Pulitzer Prize–winning historian and author of *Madam*

"The long-forgotten 'most interesting woman in the world' comes vividly to life in this captivating new biography. The multitalented Elsie Robinson would have been a pioneering and estimable person had she lived today; that she became a revered journalistic and literary voice at a time when women were marginalized is testament to her force of nature. *Listen, World!* is an important read, particularly as we work to bolster women's overlooked place in history."

—LISA NAPOLI, author of *Susan, Linda, Nina & Cokie*

"Open this well-crafted and entertaining biography and it will become abundantly clear why Elsie Robinson was once one of this nation's most-celebrated and beloved columnists. Julia Scheeres and Allison Gilbert's teamwork resurrects the life and work of this dauntless twentieth-century newspaperwoman from her days toiling deep down in a gold mine to the heights of stardom in the Hearst newspaper galaxy. For decades, readers by the millions turned to Robinson for a dash of hope and a dose of encouragement. Now thanks to Scheeres and Gilbert, millions of twenty-first century readers can too."

—JAMES McGRATH MORRIS, author of *Pulitzer*

LISTEN, WORLD!

LISTEN, WORLD!

How the Intrepid **ELSIE ROBINSON** Became America's Most-Read Woman

JULIA SCHEERES
and
ALLISON GILBERT

SEAL PRESS
New York

Seal Press
Hachette Book Group
1290 Avenue of the Americas, New York, NY 10104
www.sealpress.com
@sealpress

Printed in the United States of America

First Edition: September 2022

Published by Seal Press, an imprint of Perseus Books, LLC, a subsidiary of
Hachette Book Group, Inc. The Seal Press name and logo is a trademark
of the Hachette Book Group.

The Hachette Speakers Bureau provides a wide range of authors for speaking events.
To find out more, go to www.hachettespeakersbureau.com or call (866) 376-6591.

The publisher is not responsible for websites (or their content) that are not owned
by the publisher.

Print book interior design by Jeff Williams

Library of Congress Cataloging-in-Publication Data

Names: Scheeres, Julia, author. | Gilbert, Allison, author.
Title: Listen, world! : how the intrepid Elsie Robinson became America's most-read
    woman / Julia Scheeres and Allison Gilbert.
Description: First edition. | New York : Seal Press, 2022. | Includes bibliographical
    references and index.
Identifiers: LCCN 2022002766 | ISBN 9781541674356 (hardcover) | ISBN 9781541674349
    (ebook)
Subjects: LCSH: Robinson, Elsie, 1883–1956. | Women authors—United States—Biogra-
    phy. | Women journalists—United States—Biography.
Classification: LCC PS3535.O254 Z86 2022 | DDC 818/.5209 [B]—dc23/eng/20220324

LC record available at https://lccn.loc.gov/2022002766

ISBNs: 9781541674356 (hardcover), 9781541674349 (ebook)

LSC-C

Printing 1, 2022

*To the two women I'd most want to have
dinner with. My mother, Lynn Tendler Bignell,
whom I miss supremely, and my muse, Elsie Robinson,
whom I never got to meet.*

—ALLISON GILBERT

*To my two amazing daughters, Tessa Liberty and
Davia Joy. May you live as intensely and creatively
as Elsie Robinson. I love you both forever.*

—JULIA SCHEERES

CONTENTS

AUTHORS' NOTE

THROUGHOUT THIS BOOK, WE INCORPORATE ELSIE Robinson's own words taken from her memoir, book of poetry, newspaper columns, interviews, and letters. These passages appear in italics and are referenced in the Notes. At times we've edited her prose for space and clarity.

INTRODUCTION

O N MARCH 4, 1940, ELSIE ROBINSON WROTE her boss the kind of scathing letter that she knew, in theory, could get her fired.

The famous columnist, whose opinions reached twenty million people a day and millions more through a vast syndication network, had just been offered a new contract at the same salary she'd been making for the past nine years. Outraged, she told her editor that the deal was *plain stupid*. When her editor failed to advocate on her behalf, she decided to go over his head and appeal directly to the head of the company they both worked for—America's most powerful publisher, William Randolph Hearst.[1]

"The Chief," as Hearst was called by those who worked for him, created the first media conglomerate in the world. By its 1930s height, he owned twenty-eight newspapers in nineteen cities; popular magazines including *Good Housekeeping* and *Cosmopolitan*; a radio network; and a film division. Elsie was emboldened by her stature within the Hearst empire. He'd hired her in 1924 and paid her more than any other woman writer. For more than fifteen years, her daily column, "Listen, World!," was devoured by Americans across the country who valued her take on everything from how to be happier to the spread of communism. Elsie knew her worth.[2]

Hearst sent one of his lieutenants, Abraham Merritt, a managing editor at one of his weeklies, to talk her down. Elsie wanted nothing to do with him.

> *Confidential*
> *Dear Chief:*
> *Your Mr. Merritt talked to me the other day. He seems pretty smart. I let loose at last and told him a few of the private opinions that have been stewing in me for nearly 20 years. He asked me if I would write them on paper. Of course I'll write them. Why should there be anything private in an organization like this?*

She listed her frustrations: her workload was crushing (in addition to her daily column, she wrote features and breaking news), she hadn't taken a vacation in a year, and yet, despite her dedication to her job, she was repeatedly denied a raise, not even given a modest bump.

After recounting her grievances, she launched into a criticism of the way Hearst was running his company, suggesting that he was losing his competitive and creative grip:

I knew you when you filled the whole horizon and licked twenty 20th Centuries. You didn't let anything stay stagnant for six years or six weeks. I'm not insulting you when I talk like this. I'm just remembering the glory that was Rome . . .[3]

Elsie had spent her entire career seizing opportunities and defying convention. In 1918, she noticed that the *Oakland Tribune* didn't have a children's section and convinced the paper to hire her to create one. She both wrote *and* illustrated the stories. "Aunt Elsie's Magazine" became a sensation, spawning Aunt Elsie clubs for kids across California. When she learned that parents were also fans of her work, she launched two popular advice columns geared at adults. In 1923, she scaled the much larger market of San Francisco with a third column, "Tell It to Elsie," for the *San Francisco Call and Post*.[4]

Elsie had always relied on her tremendous moxie to navigate life. In her early thirties, as a broke, single mom in the foothills of the Sierra Nevada, she'd talked her way into a gold mining camp where, for three years, she wore spiked boots and cheated death six hundred feet below the earth's surface, the only woman on a motley crew of prospectors, and spent evenings bent over a typewriter, trying to develop her skills as a writer.[5]

She remained just as fearless at fifty-six in her chastisement of The Chief—a man who lived on California's central coast in a castle sprawling enough to accommodate fifty to sixty overnight guests. She'd dealt with male bosses for her entire career and refused to be intimidated by them.[6]

If I hadn't improved on my stuff in nine years, I'd have been out on my ear in exactly eight years and eleven months, she had written her editor. *I know the comeback.* "But we give you a really staggering sum for a woman writer." *My answer is simple. I am not a columnist. I am a factory. You've not been getting a feature. You've been getting mass production for nearly twenty years.*

What happened next suggests she was either placated or promised a future pay increase. Perhaps both. We know she wasn't fired. Hearst continued to send her to cover the major stories for his papers, including the 1940 Democratic National Convention in Chicago, and he threw a luncheon in her honor at the lavish Warwick Hotel in New York.[7]

Elsie kept writing at a finger-numbing clip for another sixteen years, publishing as frequently as six days a week— producing approximately nine thousand columns and articles during her forty-year career. She was the most widely read female columnist of her day and reached double the number of current subscribers to the *New York Times*. She was also one of the first and only columnists in the country to draw her own blistering editorial cartoons to accompany her writing.[8]

In addition to journalism, she wrote short stories and poems that were published in national literary journals and collected in "best loved" anthologies.

During a time of rapidly changing mores—the years following World War I, during the Great Depression, and after World War II—she went from offering advice to mostly female readers to expanding her audience by sounding off on larger political topics and social trends. She tackled gender inequality more than a decade before Gloria Steinem was born: *I'm tired of hearing the differences of men and women emphasized and exploited,* she wrote in April 1922. *It has built a wicked wall between the sexes and it's time we knocked it down.* She denounced racism and anti-Semitism, condemned capital punishment, and advocated on behalf of immigrants.[9]

But she rarely wrote about herself in her columns. Save for a few mentions of her twenty-one-year-old son's death, she divulged little about her personal life. For that reason, this biography—the first of Elsie Robinson—reveals both her remarkable body of work and the heartbreaking and surprising paths she took to become one of the most prominent and powerful writers in America. She was lauded by her peers for giving "hope and inspiration to millions" and for being "one of the most interesting women in the world." One of the columns she launched would continue to be published for decades after her 1956 death, written by successors who kept up her brand and signature style.[10]

Nonetheless, despite her fame, today Elsie Robinson has largely been forgotten.

Her journey to journalistic stardom was arduous and unlikely. In 1903, at nineteen, she left her childhood home in frontier California to marry a wealthy widower in Vermont. Despite means and motherhood, she felt unsatisfied by conventional female roles and turned to writing and illustration first as a way to amuse her ailing young son and then, after she escaped her loveless marriage, as a way to forge an independent life.[11]

Her inspirational story still resonates, as women continue to fight against societal strictures in pursuit of their own versions of creative and professional fulfillment. There

couldn't be a better time to resurrect the dramatic life and
spectacular career of this twentieth-century heroine. With
this biography, we hope to restore Elsie Robinson to her
rightful place as a venerable American icon.

Chapter 1

BENICIA

PHOTO OF FIRST STREET IN 1900, THE SAME YEAR ELSIE ROBINSON graduated Benicia High School.

Courtesy of Benicia Historical Museum, Benicia, California.

T HERE WAS A LINE DIVIDING THE SINNERS FROM the saints in Benicia, and that line was F Street. Above F Street loomed St. Catherine's Convent, where nuns quietly worshipped behind high stone walls. Below F Street lay perdition: saloons, gambling parlors, and brothels where a large, transient population of men cavorted with an equally shifty population of "sporting women" eager to liberate them of their hard-won wages.[1]

As a teenage girl in the 1890s, Elsinore Justinia Robinson was intensely curious about both sides of town. Refined spirituality at one extreme, throbbing carnality at the other; a mere eleven blocks between them.

The ramshackle white clapboard home that Elsie shared with her parents and four siblings sat on a hill that was closer to the convent, but within earshot of the sin. She rose to consciousness each morning to the sweet peal of bells calling the virginal sisters to prayer. She fell asleep each night to the faint tinkle of dancehall mandolins and sporadic gunshots. And so it went throughout her girlhood, waking to God and falling asleep to the Devil. In the gray twilight hours, when her thoughts were solely her own, Elsie weighed the merits of each as she lay in her narrow bed. It didn't take much deliberation for her to reach a conclusion: the Devil was far more interesting.

A shocking confession? Not at all—a natural and most neces-sary one. Females are as lawless at heart, as intrigued by the for-bidden, as males. They are also as passionate, as rebellious. And, as you go down the scale, as vulgar and vicious.

Goodness, though it promised halos in heaven, certainly didn't offer a lively gal many breaks on earth. Bad Women, on the contrary, had practically unlimited freedom and fun.[2]

A lanky girl with large blue eyes and a mass of thick, dark blonde hair that she piled atop her head in a loose bun, Elsie invented excuses to go poking around below F Street, just to make her pulse race. For a restless, inquisitive teen, Benicia—a town of 2,300 perched on the edge of America's western frontier—was, at the turn of the twentieth century, a place of both titanic drama and astonishing human diversity.[3]

Located just thirty miles northeast of San Francisco, Benicia had long been a haven for dreamers and renegade souls. In the 1700s, when Spanish colonists rounded up Native Americans to force them to convert to Catholicism, the local Patwin tribe stayed fiercely independent and pro-vided a refuge for mission runaways. And it was in Benicia that the discovery of gold at John Sutter's mill was leaked to the world, starting a global stampede to California's Mother Lode. In 1848, one of Sutter's associates stopped by Von Pfister's General Store and Saloon on First Street, where—his discretion addled, perhaps, by too much ale— he pulled a handful of gleaming nuggets from his pocket and dazzled onlookers, unable to contain his giddy secret.[4]

Five years later, gold fever had more than tripled Cal-ifornia's population—from 93,000 people to 380,000—and

Benicia matured from a crude adobe settlement into a proper town of charming Victorians purchased as mail order kits from the East Coast and shipped around Chile's Cape Horn. Benicia's economy also evolved, from one that catered to gold prospectors and dealers into an independent manufacturing center.[5]

Situated along the sun-dappled waters of the Carquinez Strait—which connects California's great inland rivers to the San Francisco Bay and the Pacific Ocean—Benicia's waterfront factories churned out leather hides, flour, and tinned salmon, which were exported around the globe. Its shipyards built hundreds of yachts, brigantines, and schooners that were proudly launched from its waterfront docks. And a military outpost perched on its eastern bluff housed two hundred soldiers who galloped off periodically to engage in the brutal suppression of Native Americans as white settlers poured into the state's interior and claimed Indigenous land.

The 1860 census reflects the small town's startling diversity, with residents hailing from the United Kingdom, Belgium, Poland, Switzerland, Portugal, Hungary, China, Australia, Mexico, France, Germany, Canada, Spain, and Holland. By the time Elsie was born, in 1883, Benicia was a study in contradictions—a frontier village with a decidedly cosmopolitan flair.[6]

It was a town powered by muscle—the muscle of strapping young men of every hue and nationality: strutting, tattooed sailors and shipyard workers; black-bearded Greek fishermen; brawny Hawaiian stevedores who loaded grain onto scows in the nude, their broad backs gleaming with sweat.

All this raw virility did not go unnoticed by teenage Elsie.

I came from a land where the very earth quivered with desire.[7]

As a teenager—caught in that peculiar limbo between girlhood and womanhood—she found that many of the social protocols regulating her daily life had abruptly changed to telegraph her developing biology. In the 1890s, the length of a girl's skirt was determined by her age. A grade schooler's hem fell at the knee. At thirteen, a girl's hem was lowered to her ankles. At seventeen, when she was considered a woman in full, even her ankles were covered, concealing her entire leg from prurient male eyes. Elsie only reluctantly put aside the loose, knee-length dresses that allowed her to scramble up her front yard pepper tree to watch the sunset flare over the strait for long skirts that confined her movements and had to be lifted to climb stairs. Her hairstyle also changed: gone were the days of low ponytails tied with floppy bows; she now pulled it into a fussy, blowsy updo popularized by illustrator Charles Dana Gibson.[8]

These changes by turns irked and intrigued Elsie; the transformation of boys to men was not nearly as pronounced. The Victorian sensibilities of the time held that men and women were fundamentally different and must therefore behave and dress in ways that magnified these differences. According to *Godey's Lady's Book*, a popular monthly magazine, "true women" were "delicate and timid" beings who "required protection" and "possessed a sweet dependency."

In contrast, men were admired for their decisiveness and rugged individualism. These traits were distilled into fashion: women wore dresses in flowery calicos with ornate hats looking like frivolous baubles, while menswear was both practical and comfortable—dark, loose, and plain. The underlying message was not lost on Elsie: in women, appearance was exalted; in men, action.

The original woman was made of the same materials and for the same job as the original man. She didn't arrive with a blue ribbon tied around her big toe to indicate that she was of more delicate clay. Nope, she was just the other half of the working team.[9]

The transition to womanhood could be literally torturous for Victorian girls. Growing up in Ireland, Elsie's mother was fitted with a backboard—a wooden plank that was strapped to adolescent girls' backs to force them to maintain an erect posture. Teenage Elsie was fitted with another body-morphing contraption: the corset, a product of the era's fetish for tiny waists. You could interpret the corset as a metaphor for the repression of Victorian women, a worn cage that restricted their movement and put them on display like so many "exquisite slaves," as one writer put it. The shortness of breath induced by corsets spawned a need for "fainting rooms" and "fainting couches" and led to florid descriptions, in contemporary novels, of shallow-breathing, bosom-heaving heroines.[10]

Elsie described the arduous task of getting dressed each day in her 1934 memoir, *I Wanted Out!* First came a *stout, ribbed cotton undershirt that rolled around the hips like a life preserver. Then, underdrawers. And I mean underdrawers. No frivolous "scanties." Invincible garments that, at a pinch, could have served nicely for roofing. To be worn until the thermometer melted them off.*

Black cotton stockings, likewise resembling corrugated iron in weight and texture. They came three pairs for a dollar. Three pairs lasted you six months. Then they had shrunk to fit your little sister. Next, a whale-boned corset, armored like a war tank, reaching from armpit nearly to knee, to be laced until your tonsils cracked. I had a nineteen-inch waist. Where did I put my insides? You tell. Over the corset went a nice, long corset cover with, if necessary, many cold-starched ruffles to conceal nature's deficiency. Anything less than a bustling size 38 was considered a deficiency.

Then, quickly, more drawers. Cambric ones this time—big, balloony affairs, with enormous frilly flounces, and two sets of buttons so they wouldn't fall off.

(Anything more? My gracious, you're not tired already, are you? Why, we've hardly started. Now we come to the petticoats. And you might's well settle down and make yourself comfortable, for we're in for a good, long session.)

First—the flannel or crocheted wool petticoat. Knee length. Next, the plain, white, cotton petticoat. Shin length. Over this, another slightly fancier ruffled white petticoat, ankle length. Then, if you were Terribly Rich, a swishy taffeta. Or a Best Petticoat of white cambric, incredibly flounced, ruffled, tucked, with miles 'n' miles of eyelet embroidery, valenciennes lace insertion and edging and baby ribbon run through beading.

And now, at last, we can begin to get dressed!

Over the undershirt and the corset and the ruffled corset cover, went a starched shirtwaist—balloon sleeves—neckband like a man's. Next, the skirt. Skirts were lined, and interlined . . . stiffened with crinoline about the sweeping hem. Discreetly concealed by tape beneath the rear of the skirt, in case of more deficiencies, there was a small lump, somewhat larger than a grilled kidney . . . the bustle. Well-bred young ladies managed to keep this accessory in its proper place at the base of the spine. This was a feat beyond my undisciplined nature.

At last the Gibson Girl was dressed! Literary critics have remarked that during that period there was one outstanding feature in all novels—Virtue Always Triumphed. Well, stranger, I'm asking you—considering the handicaps, was it any wonder?[11]

Fully girded in her new underpinnings, teenage Elsie suddenly *looked* like a woman—or at least a caricature of one—and she was expected to modify her behavior accordingly. Gone were the languid days of childhood—the boisterous forays with classmates into downtown Benicia to stop by the butcher shop for free slices of bologna or to swipe watermelons from neighborhood gardens. She had a reputation as a "bad girl"—mouthy, impetuous, and hot-tempered. She roamed where she pleased. Sassed teachers. Got into fistfights. Spied on cockfights through fence knotholes. She much preferred the freewheeling company of boys, exasperated by what she saw as the cattiness and furtive scheming of her female classmates.

Now, by mere virtue of her sex, she was supposed to act "ladylike" and serve as an apprentice to her mother, learning the "womanly arts" of housekeeping in preparation for her own eventual marriage and pregnancy—the only acceptable life path for women at the time.

I'm sick of reading poetry about dear mother darning and scrubbing and drudging. That may be fine poetry, but it's a poor way to live. Mothering means something greater than the manufacturing of good soup. If your conception of a woman's highest duty is to be a vacuum cleaner, be one. But don't grumble thereafter if your family parks you behind the kitchen door. [12]

But none of the Victorian protocols regulating a teenage girl's dress, appearance, or behavior could put a damper on Elsie's raging curiosity. Again and again she was drawn to Benicia's main drag, First Street. The dirt thoroughfare was unshaded and deeply rutted, lined on both sides by elevated boardwalks. During the dry season, the sun baked First Street into a fine dust that was kicked up by horse hooves and wagon wheels and filigreed Elsie's long skirts in mocha-colored swirls; in the winter rainy season, First Street turned into mud that oozed over her dainty ankle boots and made it perilous to cross. In both seasons, onshore breezes often pushed the putrid stench of the tanneries up the street to assail the locals, who clamped perfumed hankies over their noses.

Flanking both sides of First Street were small stores, many with two-story false fronts to make them appear more successful than they actually were. The windows of Trautz's Pharmacy gleamed with jars of green and red liquids and elixirs touted to cure everything from "sluggish blood" to venereal disease. Rauhut's Dry Goods imported the latest fashions from the East Coast—stuffed parakeets sold as women's hat decorations, bolts of cotton printed with tiny pink rosebuds, silk taffeta parasols.[13]

As the newly corseted Elsie walked down the creaking boardwalks running errands for her mother—her bustle loose and bouncing jauntily on her hip—she was keenly aware of the adult world she was entering and still trying to figure out her place within it. Unlike the black-veiled nuns from St. Catherine's—who always traveled in pairs, kept their eyes trained straight ahead, and never ventured below F Street—Elsie didn't consider any part of Benicia off-limits. Etiquette books from the 1890s stated that it was "unbecoming" for women to walk alone in public places. If they couldn't find appropriate company, however, single women were advised to "walk slowly, do not turn your head to the right or left, unless you wish to walk that way, and avoid any gesture or word that will attract attention." In other words, make themselves as invisible as possible.[14]

This Elsie did not do. Not only did she roam around Benicia alone, she also was drawn to, again and again, the places that were verboten to girls. Places like Otto Singler's barber shop, where men waited for a shave and a haircut paging through the racy *Police Gazette*, reading lurid tales of Western gunslingers, and ogling engravings of burlesque dancers. Or any of the dozens of saloons concentrated at the foot of First Street, where the men reeked of rye and doffed their hats and raked their eyes over her pinched-waist figure. She felt the confused frisson of experiencing the animalistic male gaze for the first time, and the encounters charged and changed her. Before leaving home, she started dabbing cornstarch onto her face to conceal her pimples and pressing wet red crepe paper to her lips to color them. She knew to be discreet, however; only prostitutes—"painted ladies"—wore noticeable makeup.[15]

But in a town where men greatly outnumbered women, Elsie's graceful figure was bound to attract attention, regardless of how she held her head. You could practically smell the testosterone pulsing through Benicia's ecosystem—in the clip-clop of a cowboy's spurred heels on the elevated boardwalk and in the baritone laughter that tumbled over swinging saloon doors. She learned to swerve away from lurching drunks. To ignore the whispered come-ons of solitary mashers. To be watchful in an atmosphere that could explode into violence at any minute.

Once, going on a casual errand, rounding the corner, I came upon a scuffling crowd—saw a mob walk on a man's face. They opined he had it coming to him, the dirty—! What did he expect, using loaded dice in a friendly game? I stood there as long as there was anything to see, feeling hot and prickly sick. Then I proceeded on my errand for a perforated pasteboard to make a cross-work motto for the Church Fair. I saw nothing incongruous in the two incidents.[16]

The most forbidden place of all, however, was at the very tip of First Street—past the railroad depot, where the street jagged west and ended in a long pier that stretched out into the Carquinez Strait. There, in shacks built along the rotting piles and in the shabby houseboats anchored to them, Benicia's numerous prostitutes plied their trade.

Even in the wild and woolly Old West, prostitution was seen as a social evil. But a shortage of women had lured many "soiled doves" to California, where they lived separately from, and barely tolerated by, the striving middle class, which viewed sex workers as an affront to their efforts to bring respectability to the frontier.

Each night at sunset, Benicia's prostitutes emerged from their cribs.

Out across the swaying planks, teetering on their high heels, minced The Girls on their evening parade.

Bleached, bobbed hair—a certain sign of shame in a world of long tresses. Red-heeled slippers and silk stockings equally branding at a time when decent women walked in stout, ribbed cotton. Calcimined faces—lilac white above carmined lips, brightly blue about belladonnaed eyes. Rouge and bleach, garnet earrings, saucy slippers, "opera length" stockings, Jockey Club perfume— besides these they wore but one covering, a frilled Mother Hubbard of sheerest flowered muslin.

Fragile as glass against the sunset flare, down the plank they filed, their rounded bodies silhouetted in tinted sheaths— mandolins whining behind them—a circle of dark faces grinning before them.[17]

The low sun at their backs illuminated the fact that the women wore nothing beneath their thin dresses. No corsets, no petticoats, no bustles. They inhabited their bodies honestly, as nature intended—free of Victorian constriction or exaggeration—and moved with a brazen, earthy sensuality, their intentions shorn of any pretense.

Watching night after night, one could see the makings of the most spectacular pageant on earth. Swaggering, slouching, strutting, according to their nature or profession, out they came—those actors in America's last melodrama.[18]

It was this teasing interplay of the sexes that pulled hardest on Elsie's imagination. One afternoon, skulking about the wharf alone, she noticed that the door to one of the shacks was half open. She crept closer. She had only the vaguest idea of what happened in those dingy, kerosene lamp–lit rooms. No one talked of sex in her circles. Nobody even said the word aloud. Above the noise of the tidal slosh came other sounds—utterances and murmurs. New sounds. She glanced about discreetly to make sure nobody was watching her, then peered through the door. There, in the murky interior, a naked couple writhed on a thin mattress. She turned and rushed away, cheeks aflame. So that was sex. It was only a glimpse, but the image made her question everything she'd been taught about the differences between women's and men's "essential natures."

We are all, in fundamental and inextricable ways, products of the places that raise us. *For most of us there is no love on earth like the bonds that bind us to the little town where we were born.*[19] A distinguishing characteristic of the American frontier was an ambivalence toward authority and social decorum. A scholar visiting Benicia in 1915—years after Elsie had moved away—would gripe that the town was a place of "unrestrained liberty," where children lingered in the doorways of dance halls to gape at carousing adults.[20]

But it was precisely Benicia's independent and bohemian nature that shaped Elsie's character. The freedom to contemplate opposing lifestyles at close proximity—the convent novice versus the saloon girl, the banker versus the bandit, the preacher versus the gambler—would equip her with a radical empathy and open-mindedness that would someday vault her to fame as a syndicated columnist, fiction writer, journalist, and poet.

I have known a diversity of people in my day. Miners and stevedores, writers and taxi drivers, janitors and jailbirds, deacons, murderers, gentlemen of leisure and the more obvious kind of pickpockets, gamblers, common Bill Browns—scores of them, and the women of their kind, from prostitute to nun. . . . And whatever the surface, something was there, unspoiled. And always, sooner or later, that beauty spoke.[21]

But as a teenager at the brink of the twentieth century, roaming about a Western town in a tight corset and absorbing life through wide eyes, Elsie had no idea that the most epic drama she'd witness would be that of her very own life.

Chapter 2

HOME

ELSIE AS A TEENAGER IN 1901.

*Photo courtesy of Northfield Mount Hermon Archives,
Gill, Massachusetts.*

P ERCHED ON THE EDGE OF AN OVERGROWN field of mustard grass, the Robinson house, at what is now 1305 West Second Street, was the magnet that always drew Elsie back up the hill at the end of the day. Home represented everything that First Street did not: safety, order, and above all—family.[1]

Everywhere in the 1880's American life centered around homes. This omnipotence of homes was due to one simple fact— in a world still largely unmechanized they were practically our only social centers, frequently our industrial, educational and medical centers as well. Presently this was to change. Within the next twenty years the machine age, with its countless gadgets for amusement and transportation, was to invade the home, challenge its power, destroy its privacy. But in the '80's family life was still walled within the home as closely as a chicken in the shell. And so, though my eyes were eagerly staring beyond the cypress hedge, and my pigeon-toed feet scrambling over the picket fence, home was still my horizon.[2]

Elsie's mother, born Elizabeth Pearson to a monied family in Ireland, immigrated to the United States as a twenty-one-year-old, where she met and soon married Alexander Robinson. In the early 1870s, the newlyweds had moved to California, part of a massive wave of fortune-seekers lured by the Golden State's promise of abundant opportunities and easy wealth.[3]

But the couple's milk-and-honey fantasies never quite played out. They purchased their home in Benicia unfinished, and over the decades that they lived in it, they were never able to scrape enough money together to complete it. Alexander only found intermittent employment—sometimes as a city surveyor, sometimes as a superintendent for the water company—but nothing that provided a steady, reliable income.[4]

When Elsie was a baby, he permanently mangled one of his fingers.

I suppose he was working overtime as usual—perhaps was groggy with weariness. For some reason, he fumbled—and his hand was caught in the swiftly moving machinery. A flash of steel—and half the finger dangled from the bone.[5]

Unable to afford a doctor, he wrapped the two pieces of his finger together and jury-rigged a homemade splint; he managed to save the finger, but it would forever be deformed.

The couple had five children in sixteen years (Paul in 1875; Winifred roughly two years later; Elsie in 1883; Phil in 1885; and Mardele in 1891). The family made do, using packing boxes as bureaus, eating crude meals of fried salt pork and cornbread laced with molasses. Elizabeth was a deeply religious woman who was given to long, moody silences. Elsie would come to believe that her mother's taciturn nature *hid an intensely rebellious and dramatic inner life* that a stifling sense of propriety prevented her expressing. Elizabeth never took to the arduous role of frontier wife and faced the daily onslaught of household chores with a resigned efficiency.[6]

Her rebellion against sordidness of any sort was almost a religion with her. Yet it was dignified to the plane of a spiritual protest. You felt it in the way she held her head, firmed her lips. Never once in all her life did I hear her whine. Though often I heard her storm![7]

Elizabeth didn't mollycoddle her children—in that era, few mothers did—and as a child, Elsie didn't feel particularly close to her. But there was one activity that drew mother and daughter together like no other: gardening. When the Robinsons moved onto the Benicia property, the yard was as *bare as a bleached skull*. But slowly and assiduously, Elizabeth transformed the barren land into a private Eden. Every January—the wettest, darkest time of year in Benicia—seed catalogs, often running more than a hundred pages, began to arrive at the Robinson household, and with them, the promise of paradise.[8]

As she held the thick catalogs in her calloused hands, Elizabeth's gray eyes would brighten; her whole being seemed to lighten. The catalog covers featured glorious, full-color illustrations of fat English roses, dainty petunias, giant dahlias. In an era before photography undermined advertising hyperbole, the hand-drawn illustrations also marketed a fantasy: asparagus were drawn as fat as zucchini, tomatoes as big as softballs, camellia bushes produced more blossoms than leaves. The prose was just as overwrought:

the "finest roses in all of existence," the "most prolific watermelon ever planted!" But it was a fantasy within reach of a frugal housewife like Elizabeth—a packet of seeds, light and compact, only cost three to five cents each, including shipping.[9]

At the end of a gloomy winter day, Elizabeth sat at the dining room table studying the pages of the seed catalogs by the light of a pungent kerosene lamp, her fountain pen circling and scribbling. Elsie often sat at her mother's elbow just to absorb Elizabeth's rare contentment and share her mirth at the overblown descriptions of common vegetables. Elizabeth would happily go without a new dress to spend money on a rare rose.

Each heart knows its own needs. Each heart seeks its own expression and compensation for its loneliness.[10]

Elizabeth's garden stood as a refined counterpoise to the coarse frontier town, recalling, on a very minor scale, the magnificent estate gardens of her native Ulster. After completing her long list of household chores with pinched resentment, she could gladly retire to her garden to spend hours bent over the mud, yanking out bull thistles and bindweed and pressing seeds and bulbs into the ground, her fingers stained with dark clay. As the weeks passed, she'd feel a deep satisfaction as the seedlings broke free of the heavy soil and grew, by miraculous transmutation, into vegetables and fruit for her table and cheery bouquets for her parlor.

A woman's garden, in the 1800s, was more than just another corner of the household she was responsible for

tending. A woman's garden provided a refuge from an un-
equal society—an interstitial space just outside the confines
of home—where she was allowed to be both creator and
ruler.

Likewise, a daughter could enter this matriarchal realm
to act out her own escapist reveries. The garden was a place
where Elsie could find relief from the intense pressure on
Victorian girls to always "be good" and project "sweetness
and light"—pressures that trained girls to smother their
impulses and desires. A good girl was a happy girl—or
one who forced herself to project happiness. The role of
a sixteen-year-old daughter, a columnist explained, was to
"make the sunshine of the home, to bring cheer and joyous-
ness into it."[11]

*A garden wasn't just flowers to a girl in the '80's. It was
everything she'd heard of Indian raids, covered wagons, [and]
Andersen's and Grimm's Fairy Tales. It was dens, lairs, teepees,
gold mines—long dreams in the green caverns and tunnels under
the figs, loquats and olives where jeweled bugs and great, spangled
worms feasted on the fallen fruit.*[12]

Boys, meanwhile, were allowed a fuller range of emotions—including anger. Boys who didn't fight with their
peers were considered unnatural; indignation was seen as
the root of fearlessness in men. Children's stories depicted
girls as sweet and timid while boys were shown struggling
to control their tempers. Boys who exhibited fear were
called "sissies"—a derisive term for a cowardly boy that, before the 1880s, was simply an affectionate term for "sister."[13]

Reading provided another way for girls to escape these asphyxiating gender norms, allowing them access to worlds and emotions they were barred from exploring or expressing in their daily lives. Victorian girls devoured adventure tales featuring (male) protagonists who fought pirates (*Treasure Island*), sailed the Mississippi (*The Adventures of Tom Sawyer*), or solved crimes (*Sherlock Holmes*). Immersed in a harrowing story, girls could, for a brief moment, be genderless and free.

I read everything I could lay my hands on. Anything about humans was grist for my mill. In our shabby hodge-podge of a home, we had two things which will transform life for any sensitive, intelligent child—an abundance of flowers and of books. My mother and father read ceaselessly. Unnoticed, squatting in the dark corners of the big, untidy rooms—hiding in the thickets of mustard or wedged high in the crotch of the pepper tree, I followed the book trail, gobbling words greedily, though nine times out of ten I hadn't the slightest notion what they were all about.

By twelve I had read Dickens, most of Thackeray, all of Shakespeare. Of the last I could make little meaning but got from it in some mysterious way a great sense of splendid fury. I was in love with words—hungered for them as other children hunger for candy. For hours I would sit simply saying words aloud—page after page of fine words—crying and flaming to the flow of them, stalking up and down repeating them, with gestures. I have had much the same experience in the few operas I have heard—feeling the throb and leap of the human heart beneath the noble sweep of music, even though it was all in a foreign language.[14]

Elsie must have recognized herself in the protagonist of Louisa May Alcott's 1868 novel *Little Women*, Jo March, a girl who also resented—and bucked—gender norms. "It's bad enough to be a girl, anyway," Jo says in *Little Women*. "I like boys' games, and work, and manners. I can't get over my disappointment in not being a boy." Jo's character would be embraced by generations of girls who admired her brash independence and perhaps wished for a little of it themselves.[15]

Luckily, Elsie's autonomous streak was encouraged by her father, who didn't differentiate in his treatment of his daughters and sons—all the Robinson kids were expected to work hard, be honest, and not whine or tattle on each other.

As a teenager, Elsie's guilty pleasures included reading the novels of Margaret Wolfe Hungerford, who wrote under the pen name "The Duchess." Hungerford, who coined the phrase "beauty is in the eye of the beholder," specialized in unconventional female protagonists, women who were sultry, worldly, and independent—and yet were deeply desired by men. *I longed to be a LOVELY TEMPTRESS with Marvelous Red Hair and Violet Eyes whom Men Couldn't Resist.*[16]

Novels featuring such brazen women rankled conservatives, who warned parents that allowing their daughters to read the "wrong" type of literature could lead to a life of debauchery. "This intemperate craving for sensational fiction weakens the mental grasp, destroys the love of good reading, the power of sober and rational thinking, takes away all relish from the realities of life, breeds discontent and indolence and selfishness, and makes the one who is addicted to it a weak, frivolous, petulant, miserable being," wrote Congregational minister Washington Gladden in 1900. "I see girls all around me in whom these results are working themselves out, steadily and fatally."[17]

Although many parents censored their daughters' reading materials—scanning books for references to anti-Christian sentiment or the "generative process"—Elsie's bibliophile parents allowed her great latitude in her literary choices.[18]

She already knew a thing or two about the "generative process"—that searing glance into the shack along the wharf—and about the type of female physique that quickened men's pulses. She'd seen such a woman, in her full carnal glory, one day when she passed a saloon and bent down to look under the batwing door.

Scrooching, I could see an enormous painting of a "nekkid" lady with a large, bulging, very pink tummy and bosom and masses of bright orange hair, lying, full length, front face, on rumpled plush. Still scrooching, I prayed earnestly that God would give me a shape like that.[19]

Elsie's voracious reading habit, curiosity about the world, and desire to express herself freely prompted her to start writing and illustrating her own stories.

As early as I can remember, I wrote. Not with any idea of being a writer. I was trying to get something out of me which I could release in no other way. After it was done I showed the thing to nobody. Just threw it away. The fun was over. When I wasn't writing, I drew—for the same reason. Groping at something—trying

*to make it on my own. And all the time I was speculating. Trying
to understand what this strange performance was all about. Why
were people what they were?*[20]

She shared her love of literature—both high- and
lowbrow—with her older sister Winifred, who was studying philosophy at UC Berkeley. Education was another area
where the Robinsons treated their daughters and sons as
equals. Many East Coast colleges barred female applicants
for decades; Harvard refused to allow women to live on its
storied campus until 1972. In the West, however, colleges had
admitted women on an equal basis with men since 1870.[21]

Nevertheless, many Americans thought educating girls
beyond high school was a waste of time and money: If a
woman's destiny was to become a wife and mother, they
reasoned, why bother educating her? Conservatives worried
that degreed women would compete with men for jobs. Lib-
erals were hardly more enlightened, countering that women
should attend college just so they could raise smarter (male)
children. The question of what women themselves wanted
was rarely considered.

When Winnie returned to Benicia on weekends or holidays, she regaled Elsie with stories of college life—about
her studies of Socrates and Rousseau, about handsome Cal
boys, about military balls and football games and student
pranks. As Winnie spoke, it was easy for Elsie to idolize her
sister's life—and to imagine her future self walking down
UC Berkeley's elegant corridors, arms full of books, head
full of belletristic thoughts, one of a small number of young
women among young men in brown corduroy suits.

But when Elsie was a junior in high school, her college aspirations were shaken by a seemingly minor incident: her mother couldn't afford to sew her an Easter dress. At the time, waltzing into church on Easter morning in a frilly new dress was an essential part of the holiday ritual. The custom traced back to early Christians, who donned fresh linen tunics on the anniversary of Christ's resurrection from the dead to symbolize their own "new life"—a renewed dedication to their religious principles and efforts to lead a life without sin. Over the centuries, the tradition evolved into something darkly superstitious: believers *must* wear new Easter clothes or risk bad luck for the rest of the year, a sentiment captured in a popular couplet:

At Easter let your clothes be new,

Or else be sure you will it rue.[22]

In years past, Elizabeth had spent hours at the dining room table transforming one of Elsie's everyday dresses into a spectacular new confection.

All through the day—and far into the night—there'd be the clunketey-clunk of the scissors against the scarred wood . . . and the thud of the sewing machine treadle beating the floor . . . and the flash of the needle, slipping endlessly through the fingers that were rough with their pricking, year in, year out. Long after we'd gone protesting to bed, we'd hear the fury of it going on, like an army of banners . . . and the rank smell of the coal-oil lamp would be thickening through the house, and its dim light falling over her valiant figure.[23]

The next morning, Elsie would rush downstairs to view her mother's handiwork, the old dress unrecognizable with

the fanciful addition of beading, ribbons, flounces, shirr-
ing, and silk flowers. A leghorn hat, wreathed with flowers
plucked fresh from the garden—pink roses, daisies, butter-
cups—would complete the look.

In 1899, however, Elizabeth solemnly informed Elsie
that she couldn't afford to make her a new Easter dress; the
family's finances were too tight to spend on such fripperies.
And there was worse news, much worse: the Robinsons
couldn't afford to send Elsie to college—a brutal blow to a
girl already lit from within by visions of herself as a scholar.

As she sat in the lily-scented church sanctuary that Easter morning, wearing a familiar gingham dress and watching her classmates sashay down the aisle in new frocks, it
was more than jealousy that bit her heart; it was anxiety,
spiked with fear.

*I didn't care about the dress itself. But suddenly I faced the
insecurity of life—like a sleep walker wakened at the edge of a
precipice. I saw the abyss beneath my dreaming feet. I have never
lost sight of it since! With that shock, came general realization.
Soon I would be graduated from High School. Then what? There
was no money for me to go to college. There was no money to keep
me at home. Life seemed rushing at me from every side—churning within me—with startled eyes, I saw that everything had
changed.*[24]

At Winnie's graduation from UC Berkeley the year before, she sat with her family under a large tent and watched
her big sister stride across a stage to claim her sheepskin. She
was filled with a mixture of pride and excitement, glimpsing

her own future in Winnie's achievement. Now that her col-
legiate dreams had been snuffed out, dread about her future
life consumed her.[25]

At her graduation ceremony on June 21, 1900, she was
one of eleven seniors. Surely her parents and siblings were
sitting high in their chairs, happy to celebrate Elsie's educational milestone. For the graduating girls, however, the
cheerful event masked a dark reality: they had crossed an
invisible threshold into an overtly sexualized world. From
now on, Elsie, and all the other rosy-faced female graduates, would be seen not as heady pursuers of knowledge but
as nubile young women, measured and judged in terms of
their marriageability and child-producing capabilities.[26]

*Lacking the education to teach, there was practically only one
respectable opportunity ahead—Marriage. Society in the '90's
was still very explicit on that point. And the west—wildly unconventional as it might be in the conduct of its men—was ultra
conservative in its attitude toward women. It recognized but two
types . . . Good Women . . . Bad Women.*

*A Good Woman was a Wife, Mother, or a Dear Old Maid
with a Secret Sorrow. Lady missionaries and school teachers were
respectable but evidently unsuccessful souls. Commercial work for
women hardly existed and was strictly taboo, save under gravest
urgency. Girls who went into it—even into nursing—were always
under suspicion.*[27]

And when that day arrived—when you finally became a
young bride—you relinquished much of your identity and
power. Even though wives were slowly being allowed to

own property and sign legal contracts (by 1900, every state had passed legislation granting married women some measure of control over their assets), only your husband was permitted to have a say in the way the world was run by voting at the polls.[28]

The place to find the actual standing of the old fashioned home is not in the poetry books, but in the law books of a nation. The law books of this particular nation reveal that for much of the time the wife's status in the home was just about on par with the bossy cow's. And not always as good.[29]

The tremendous pressure for young women to find a husband and have children was relentless and multidirectional, coming from their families, peers, religious leaders, and popular media—advertisements, songs, and magazine articles. Even literature's most famous tomboy, Jo March, eventually bowed to gender norms and got married. And even though Elsie graduated in the first year of the new century, very little had changed for women since archaic humans first implemented a gendered division of labor. Gender roles and expectations, in 1900, still seemed to be set in stone. The graduating boys, of course, had an almost endless range of options open to them, including careers, college, or travel.

It isn't any more "normal" for the average young woman to find complete satisfaction within the four walls of her home than it would be for the average young man. All these distinctions and barriers which have arisen between men and women are wrong. Men and women aren't primarily Hes and Shes with separate

and distinct niches in life. Men and women are, primarily, just
PEOPLE—with identical impulses, identical interests.[30]

At seventeen, Elsie wasn't savvy enough to articulate these thoughts. Even if she had been able to express her opinions, her words would have fallen on dismissive ears. Her formal education was now complete, and a new primary objective was thrust upon her: to find a husband and set up a house of her own.

Late one night, unable to sleep and fretting about her future, Elsie decided to take her case directly to God. The house was silent as she slipped from bed, tiptoed downstairs, and walked out the front door in her nightgown.

Our house lay on the outskirts of the town. Beyond our house, on a still higher hill, at the end of a sinister, weed-tangled road, was the Graveyard. I was scared pink of the Graveyard. But, by my youthful reasoning, it was only the proper place to make my bargain with God and midnight must be the time.[31]

Heart thudding, she climbed an overgrown slope filled with mildewed tombstones spaced at body-length intervals. Here were the graves of Benicia's founding fathers, its barkeeps and preachers, its prostitutes and tannery workers. The graves of women who'd died in childbirth and children who'd died in infancy. All the vast iterations of human life.

She kept climbing until she reached the highest point—a clearing where, she figured, she would be more visible to God. In the distance, between the trunks of towering eucalyptus, the Carquinez Strait glimmered darkly.

It was increasingly evident that life didn't always go as one desired. Certain people plainly lost out in the shuffle. I had no intention of letting that happen to me. God at least should be reminded of my presence. I went to meet my God and told Him what I wanted. Covered with confidence, and goose-pimples, I informed God that I wanted to Know Life. I wouldn't ask to have fun, and be rich and beautiful. But I must find out everything about Life—feel all there was to be felt. In short—I wanted God to Give Me The Works.[32]

It was a big ask. Perhaps the biggest. As a seventeen-year-old girl from a poor frontier family in 1900, every card was stacked against her.

Chapter 3

ROMANCE

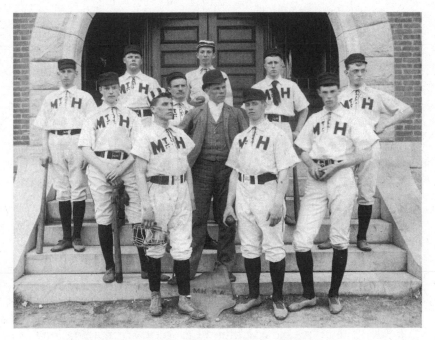

ELSIE'S FUTURE HUSBAND, CHRISTIE CROWELL
(front, holding baseball), in 1890.

*Photo courtesy of Northfield Mount Hermon Archives,
Gill, Massachusetts.*

T HE ANSWER TO ELSIE'S MIDNIGHT PLEA APP-
eared in church one Sunday morning—not in
the form of a divine message, but in the shape
of a visiting worshipper.

The white-steepled Congregational Church was a mere
two blocks away from the Robinson house. Every Sunday
morning and every Sunday evening, Mrs. Robinson faithfully herded her progeny down the dirt street and through
its doors, hoping a proximity to God would infuse her five
children with a deep, abiding morality. (Mr. Robinson did
not bow to this pressure to worship collectively, but stayed
home, enjoying the rare solitude of a quiet house.)

The congregation only had seventy-three members,
and the pastor was a recent seminary graduate named Bur-
ton M. Palmer, who hailed from a line of Congregational
preachers stretching back more than two hundred years.[1]

But even Reverend Palmer's youthful enthusiasm for the
Word failed to capture Elsie's attention for long. As he stood
behind the pulpit parsing biblical esoterica or reading long
sections from a King James Bible, her mind drifted. On clear
mornings, when the sun pierced the tall stained-glass windows and cast jeweled beams over the pews, she'd probably
fidget, playing a little game to pass time by trying to catch

the candied light in her white gloves. But if her mother noticed, she'd throw Elsie a scalding look: as a young lady in
the marriage market, her every movement, word, and fa-
cial expression was supposed to be poised and unchildlike.
But who among us steps over the threshold from childhood
into adulthood without wavering? Introit to postlude, Elsie's mind wandered, and of late, it kept rounding the same
alarming thought: she needed to find a husband. But how?
And who? There were only three boys in her graduating class
at Benicia High and none of them had expressed interest in
her. She'd always felt like an outsider in her hometown, seen
as an odd bird—too brash, too opinionated.

*I wasn't an orthodox young woman. I wasn't even a popu-
lar one. Most of my playmates considered me "kinda funny," and
were at no pains to hide it! The boys who had swiped melons with
me at ten now found me too tall and far too "smarty" for their bud-
ding male egotism. Such was the toll of the unfeminine courage
and curiosity my father had bred into me. I was lonely and longed
for companionship with the girls but we could establish no common interest. They thought me queer. I thought them silly. I had
no place in their picture. Yet I would have to have a place in that
picture if I married. There was no other picture for me.*[2]

In a small church a stranger stands out, and on this particular Sunday morning, a visitor sat by himself in a front
pew, gazing at Reverend Palmer with stooped shoulders.
Elsie craned her neck to peer through the thicket of wom-
en's hats—all those bows and gauzy poufs and desiccated
parakeets—for a better view. When the organ launched into

a hymn and everyone stood, the visitor rose, tall and lean in a dark jacket. Under a thick shock of sandy blond hair, his face was young, but his demeanor severe. He looked as if he'd had all the joy socked out of him. And yet he was handsome. His very unfamiliarity held a mysterious and appealing quality that drew her attention to him again and again throughout the service.

Reverend Palmer introduced the visitor as a close personal friend, Christie Crowell. They had been classmates at a religious boarding school called Mount Hermon in western Massachusetts. Mr. Crowell, a Vermont native, would be staying with Reverend Palmer for several months that winter.

After the service, as the faithful filed out of the sanctuary into the bright morning, Elsie saw the stranger face-on for the first time. His eyes drew her in; they were dark blue with slight bruise-like hollows beneath them, bringing a strange pallor to his thin face. When Reverend Palmer presented her to him, Christie held himself rigidly, but his doleful eyes stayed on her, absorbing this vivid, flush-cheeked Western girl as if she were an exotic species. He wasn't accustomed to women like this, women who boldly held his gaze and offered unrestrained smiles and conversation.

He was ten years older: twenty-seven to Elsie's seventeen. She'd soon learn the reason for his mournful demeanor: he'd come to California to recover from the shock of losing his wife, who had died nine months after they were married. Here was a moody, haunted figure reminiscent of the mysterious Mr. Rochester, the love interest of the titular character in Charlotte Bronte's *Jane Eyre*, a man much more complicated, and therefore more interesting, than the boys her age in Benicia.[3]

Sickly and a Widower—was there ever a girl who didn't adore Tragedy? He was reasonably good-looking and had about him a sort of snooty sadness that made our local youths seem crude goofs. Wasn't all that the answer to a maiden's prayer?[4]

Just as Mr. Rochester had his Thornfield Hall, Mr. Crowell also had a manor, with an equally pretentious name— "Lindenhurst" (linden tree grove) in Brattleboro, Vermont. Christie described his home to Elsie with quiet pride as she plied him with questions. Lindenhurst—with its thirty-seven rooms, two towers, and servants' quarters—was far grander than any building in Benicia. Christie Crowell was a very, very rich man. This fact alone made him as exotic to Elsie as her ebullience was to him.[5]

She began looking forward to church, spending hours primping in front of the mirror, cinching her corset ever tighter, teasing her hair into ever-higher updos, dabbing carmine crepe paper on her lips. These efforts did not go unnoticed by Christie.

Courting rituals were still preordained at the dawn of the twentieth century. Men pursued; women waited to be pursued. Dating was a chaste affair with much angst spent on the question of kissing. How old should a girl be before accepting a dry peck on the lips from an amorous suitor? *Detroit News* columnist Nancy Brown proclaimed that even a seventeen-year-old girl should keep her lips unsullied. "The right kind of girl does not allow promiscuous kissing," she wrote in 1919. "The right kind of girl . . . should not always (be) thinking of kissing." What boys really sought in a future wife was modesty, conservatives declared; only girls who fastidiously guarded their chastity and reputations would win a beau's lifelong admiration and love.[6]

There was little opportunity, at least among middle and upper classes, for hormones to surge into action because teenage couples were rarely left alone.

A man courted a potential mate by formally calling on her at her parents' home. The couple sat in the parlor, chatting awkwardly under the watchful eyes of the young woman's mother and sometimes her brothers. Each comment and gesture was considered, calibrated, and loaded with meaning. There were rules that governed everything from appropriate conversation topics (the focus, young women were told, should always be on the gentleman caller and *his* interests) to chaperonage (the mother stayed in the room on the first visit, but if she lingered there on subsequent visits, it usually meant that she did not approve of the match and would not welcome further visits). If a man met the mother's approval (and she drifted off into another part of the house to let the young couple chat semi-privately), it was a good sign. The couple would gradually be given greater freedom to spend time alone together until the man proposed, with his full understanding, given the time he'd invested in these elaborate rituals, that his offer would be accepted. To follow these unspoken rules was considered a reflection of "good breeding." The end game was always marriage. There was no such thing as a casual romance.

When Christie began calling on her, Elsie bowed to convention and followed the protocols, which she'd later denounce as unnatural:

One of the healthiest signs of the present age is the fact that the young people are no longer regarding each other's most trivial acts as signs of "serious intentions." There is really a great deal of work for men and women to do together outside the business of matrimony. It isn't pure or idealistic to insist that young people should be guarded from each other until the love-making time arrives. It shoves humanity down to the level of the gophers and toads whose only association comes through mating.[7]

Elsie's parents certainly deemed Christie suitable husband material: he came from a devout Christian home, had been vetted by their pastor, and had abundant financial resources to care for their daughter. As the spring rains turned Benicia's hills electric green in 1901, the couple was permitted to stroll outside together without chaperones.

Elsie felt the season's renewal on a bone-deep level. Her concerns about the future were now anchored in this tall, taciturn Prince Charming. When she addressed him as "Mr. Crowell," he told her to call him Christie. As they walked down Benicia's streets or down pathways cutting through the surrounding fields—the sun-dazzled strait winking in the distance, orange poppies blooming at their feet—Christie was somber and restrained, so Elsie filled the silence with nervous chatter.

Slowly, she drew him out. In a choked voice, he told her the story of his wife, Louisa, a petite brunette with clear blue eyes and a round child's face. They'd met at boarding school. Louisa, or "Lulu," studied at the sister school of the academy he'd attended with Reverend Palmer, called Northfield Seminary.

Their June 1898 wedding, held outdoors at Louisa's childhood home in Hackensack, New Jersey, was officiated by Louisa's father, a Reformed church pastor. After a short honeymoon on Block Island, off the coast of Rhode Island, the newlyweds moved into Lindenhurst with Christie's parents. A few months later, Louisa began to feel exhausted. They assumed, joyfully, that she was with child.[8]

But she failed to gain weight and her discomfort intensified. The couple's excitement turned to anguish when an X-ray found a malignant tumor in her abdomen. Her parents insisted Louisa return to New Jersey to be treated at the new, state-of-the-art Hackensack Hospital, whose founder, Dr. David St. John, personally supervised her treatment. She underwent a long, risky surgery to remove the tumor and seemed to be recovering when she took a turn for the worse. She died on April 8, 1899, only twenty-four years old.[9]

A devastated Christie accompanied his wife's body two hundred miles by train from Hackensack to Brattleboro, where she was buried in the Crowell family plot. Lindenhurst became, per the customs of the era, a funeral parlor.

The Crowells hung a wreath tied with black ribbons on the front door to reflect their state of mourning, drew the blinds, and turned inward in their sorrow.[10]

Louisa's death was the latest in a string of tragedies to befall the Crowell household. When Christie was ten, his eleven-month-old brother Ralph died of bronchial fever. And then there was his brother Herbert, a mere thirteen months younger than Christie. As a teen, Herbert had been briefly institutionalized for exhibiting an "unnatural mental state," but improved enough to enroll at Mount Hermon, where he joined the school paper and was known around campus for his outlandish pranks.[11]

His upward trajectory ended in the spring of 1896, when Herbert was twenty-two and just a month shy of graduating. One Wednesday night, he walked to the room of the school's athletic starter—the boy who indicated the start of track meets by firing blanks from a revolver—where a group of boys were making lemonade. Herbert joined them before casually asking the starter where he kept the revolver. After learning it was in the dresser, Herbert retrieved it and—as the other boys continued to merrily make their lemonade—sat in a chair and replaced the empty cartridge with a loaded one. He pressed the gun to his heart and pulled the trigger. It took the other boys a few minutes to realize it wasn't just another of Herbert's practical jokes.

His suicide was reported in sordid detail on the front pages of the local Brattleboro papers, adding a deep layer of shame to the family's lacerating pain. For the devout Crowell family, having a son take his own life—a sin, according to

the Bible—in such an extravagant and public fashion stig-
matized the entire household.[12]

As Christie related his woes, Elsie cried and held his
hand, wondering how one person could contain such a
crushing load of grief. Christie had come to Benicia trying
to outrun his misery, only to find it resided within him like
an extra organ. Elsie, so different from the demure society
women Christie knew back East, was a welcome distraction.
Her sheer vitality pushed away his lonely despair when they
were together. He saw in her a clean slate, another chance
at living.

For her part, Elsie saw Christie both as a wounded soul
in need of a woman's attention and a ticket out—out of
Benicia and out of the unappealing option of selecting a
husband from among the local roughnecks. That he was
wealthy—to a girl who'd experienced financial insecurity
and times of hunger—was also a boon.

*I believed he was the answer for my need of many things. An
answer to that incoherent need for "out" into a wider, richer experience. An answer to my young loneliness and bewilderment—my
secret humiliation at my own clumsiness and unpopularity—
my desire for a dignified and orderly life—my equally poignant
desire to put something over on my snooty classmates!*

*So many "answers" to hang upon one person. In all his days
he had never known such joyous free living, such independent
action as he saw in that visit to the west. He was like a shiv-
ering, ragged child sticking his nose against a lighted window
behind which blazed a gorgeous Christmas tree. In me—in my*

rowdy young impudence, my laughing slang, my sudden un-
restrained tenderness for anyone or anything that excited my
emotions, he saw the embodiment of all this western happiness,
freedom and strength. He thought he wanted me—feeling that I
could give him all that warmth and confidence which his grim
environment had denied him. I was the wildest creature he had
ever seen. He was the tamest in all my experience. We discoursed
together about life. We agreed that no one had ever understood
either of us.[13]

As they shared stories of heartache and hope, the awkward stiffness of new acquaintanceship fell away. One day
when they were out strolling, Christie leaned into Elsie and
kissed her on the mouth. He then asked her the question
she'd been waiting for. Her joyous answer came without
hesitation: yes, more than anything, she wanted to be his
wife.

Upon returning home after his proposal, she found she
was overcome with emotion.

I went out into the mustard fields and crept deep into the
thick, sweet darkness that lay between the stalks and lay there for
hours, shaking with fear, crying with loneliness—laughing with
triumph. I had wanted out. I was on my way![14]

※

ELSIE'S PARENTS WELCOMED the news. *My exhausted mother*
drew a deep breath of relief. But there was a catch: Christie's
parents. They'd ascertained from his letters home what
Christie already knew to be true: Elsie lacked refinement.

She didn't have the demeanor of a proper New England wife. She had no idea how to run a household. Her emotions were sloppy and uncontained. And she was still a *teenager*. The last thing George Emerson Crowell and Mary Spencer Crowell wanted was another motive for familial shame, embarrassment, or pity.[15]

Christie spent many nights at his inkwell composing impassioned arguments to his parents about why he wanted to marry Elsie and waited achingly for their responses—it took a week to mail a letter cross-country by train and another week to send one back. He had been widowed for less than two years, and his parents must have worried that he was not thinking rationally about the long-term implications of bringing this Californian—about whom they knew nothing other than what their enamored son told them—into the family.[16]

After months of epistolary discussion, the Crowells set down their terms. Christie could marry Elsie on one condition: she first spend a year at the same boarding school that Louisa attended, Northfield Seminary, the sister school of his alma mater, Mount Hermon. At Northfield, she would receive instruction in household management, elocution, and the Bible, among other classes that would transform her into a fitting bride for their son. Northfield was less than twenty miles from Lindenhurst, which would give the Crowells ample opportunity to become acquainted with their son's fiancée.

Elsie accepted this stipulation and quickly gathered her materials for the Northfield application, including her high school transcript and letters of recommendation. Her recommenders were unstinting in their praise. An "A" student, her high school principal extolled her "unusually bright mind." Reverend Palmer wrote that she had "promising talent in the lines of sketching and English work."[17]

As she formulated her own letter to school administrators in March 1901, she was keenly aware of Northfield's Christian foundation—and knew precisely what they wanted to hear.

As to my purpose in life and especially my motives for wishing to attend Northfield Seminary, I can simply state this. I wish, with God's help, to lead the most upright, strong and influential Christian life possible and with this end in view, I wish to place myself under just such influence as I believe this school to possess. . . . I can promise that if I am permitted to enter this school I will faithfully undertake any work laid down for me and to the best of my ability prove myself worthy of the privileges offered me.

Her mother filled out a questionnaire in which she noted Elsie's preference for literature and art courses. Asked if her daughter was "fitting herself for any special work," Mrs. Robinson answered that Elsie hoped Northfield could help her attain "the highest type of womanhood." Asked whether her daughter had "any bad companionships or bad habits," Mrs. Robinson wrote that Elsie had only one character flaw: "impatience."

The Robinsons mailed the application and then waited for a reply over the course of several anxious months. Elsie's life hung in the balance as a school three thousand miles away weighed her merits as a student, and in doing so, determined her future.

Finally, in late June, she received an acceptance letter from the head of the school. She could breathe deeply again; if everything went according to plan, she would emerge from Northfield after a year, polished enough to take on the Crowell family name.

Chapter 4

NORTHFIELD

ELSIE WAS ASSIGNED TO REVELL HALL,
the larger building seen in this photo, circa 1890.

*Image courtesy of Northfield Mount Hermon Archives,
Gill, Massachusetts.*

T HE TRAIN LINKING CALIFORNIA TO THE REST of America had long been a source of wonder for Elsie.

Often at night as a child I woke to hear that shrill, arrogant cry—over the roaring of the wind, the lashing of the rain, the whisper of the fog—and wondered what lay beyond in the land from which it came.[1]

The 1,900-mile transcontinental railroad, completed in 1869, had been an epic feat of engineering. More than twenty thousand railroad workers, most of them Chinese immigrants, blasted tunnels through granite mountains, assembled bridges over soaring river canyons, and endured the sweltering monotony of the Great Plains. When the last steel stake was driven into the track in Promontory Summit, Utah, America was finally united by a single thoroughfare. Overnight, a cross-country journey that took months on horseback could be made in less than a week.

At the small railroad depot at the end of First Street, Elsie had often watched porters unload parcels shipped from distant cities: the latest fashions from New York, silverware forged in Midwestern factories. Barrels of whiskey and maple syrup. Crates of books and magazines. Bundles of mail from distant friends and family.

But the transcontinental railroad did more than bring people and products to California. It also erased the frontier, changing the very essence of the "Wild West." New ideas were imported, among them the East Coast notions of respectability. The era of hard-living, hard-drinking desperados began to wane. Members of the Woman's Christian Temperance Union, a teetotaling import from Ohio, began to protest the dozens of saloons on Benicia's First Street, barging through the swinging doors to stage "pray-ins" for the whiskey-logged souls inside. The sheriff found he could no longer turn a blind eye to personal vendettas or mob justice; he was now expected to enforce the law.

With respectability, Benicia had grown colorless and dull. This taming of her hometown made Elsie even more impatient to see what else America had to offer. And so, on a bright, late-summer day in 1901, she waited at the First Street train depot to board the Southern Pacific's #4 *Atlantic Express* to Chicago on her way to Northfield Seminary.[2]

She'd never traveled more than thirty miles away from Benicia, and never alone. *China seemed nearer, more comprehensible to Californians of the 1890's than Vermont.* Now she was moving across the country, away from everything she knew, to begin a life among strangers.[3]

Christie had preceded her, returning to his parents' home in Vermont. He was the only person she knew on the East Coast, which surely made her a bit uneasy. Standing on the platform, Elsie churned with both anticipation and apprehension; sweat soaked her corset and shirtwaist despite the cool onshore breeze. Her family and friends took turns embracing her and wishing her success in a teary send-off, and then she stepped into the train car alone.

Rigidly I sat down on the stiff, wicker-covered seat—a thin, clumsy, staring child in a brown mohair dress with a "golf cape" suspended from my narrow young shoulders. My hands were covered with brown silk gloves. The palms, clenched tightly, were black with terrified perspiration. My cheeks, red with excitement at first, whitened. Presently, through the gathering grime, tears dripped on to my high-boned "choker" collar. But I did not move. The roar of the engine, the rock and rack of the flat wheels over the uneven road bed, the rattle of the cinders against the small, blurred windows, the reek of the aging lunches, mingled in a sort of shell-shock on my senses.[4]

Beside her sat a large, wicker "telescope basket," containing her clothing as well as six days' worth of food. While dining cars were available on premiere trains, the train Elsie took wouldn't have one until three days later, when one was added in Nebraska. Travelers, instead, could leave the train for a hasty, and not particularly good, meal at passing depots or pack their own food, choosing slow-to-spoil items such as hard-boiled eggs, meat and fruit pies, salted ham, and sourdough rolls, which they ate over newspaper spread on their laps. Ever mindful of household finances, Elsie's mother had helped her pack her own provisions for the trip.[5]

Outside the clattering windows, America streamed by like an animated postcard. Elsie gazed upon landscapes she'd only read about—the spires of the Sierra Nevada

and the Rocky Mountains, the glassy expanse of the Great
Salt Lake, the undulating wheatgrass that covered the vast,
sparsely populated Great Plains. The ephemera of long-ago
pioneers—the sun-bleached skeletons of dead oxen; abandoned covered wagons; solitary, wind-scoured tombstones—
allowed her to fix herself within the grand wheel of time.
She felt modern as the train effortlessly swept her across
the country. The days passed slowly as the brass chandeliers
swayed and creaked overhead. Passengers read, paced the
aisles, played cards. Porters patrolled the aisle to check in
with "Ladies and Children and those unused to traveling
alone." The Pullman tourist sleeping car came with seats
that unfolded into berths; passengers pulled curtains shut
for privacy.[6]

Elsie befriended a young Chinese man in her section
who claimed to be a "highbinder"—part of a Chinese gang
whose members bound their long braids on top of their
heads to prevent them from being grabbed during fights and
carried concealed hatchets as weapons. Elsie knew what a
highbinder was; coverage of violent tongs, or gangs, in San
Francisco's Chinatown dominated papers throughout the
Bay Area. Ever inquisitive, she asked the man for proof of
his claim. He raised his tunic just enough to reveal a hatchet
tucked into his waistband, much to Elsie's delight.

It was a swell hatchet. At last, I felt, I was seeing life.[7]

Four days later, the train reached Chicago, a metropolis
of cement and glass that bristled toward every horizon.
Elsie craned her neck to survey the amber-lit skyscrapers

as they raked the heavens. A booming industrial center of 1.7 million souls and six train stations, most newcomers found Chicago immense and intimidating. When the *Atlantic Express* arrived at the Chicago & North-Western depot—a mammoth five-story brick structure along the Chicago River that served nearly a hundred trains a day— Elsie's anxiety spiked again; the station seethed with bodies and noise. She grabbed her basket and pushed her way through the crowd with *the dumb terror of caged cattle*. She followed the current of people to an exit and then waited in line for a buggy to take her a few blocks to Dearborn station, where she transferred to another train line for the rest of the journey east, landing her in Buffalo, New York. From there, the last leg of Elsie's trip required three more trains.[8]

Finally, six long days after leaving California, as the rising sun pierced the train's dusty windows, Elsie approached her destination.

We were running beside the shining sweep of a wide river— the Connecticut—and everything was covered with picture-card trees and little houses and we were at Northfield.[9]

Situated in northern Massachusetts, Northfield was a quaint town of tidy saltbox colonials and sprawling green yards. It exuded orderliness and calm. Elsie stepped off the train—self-conscious in her wrinkled muslin dress, hair greasy after days of not bathing—and was surely greeted by Christie. He came bearing somber news that made her mood shift from nervous anticipation to a state of vigilance: the entire town of Northfield was under quarantine due to an outbreak of deadly scarlet fever. Caused by the same bacteria that leads to strep throat and named after the bright red rash it produces on the skin of the afflicted, scarlet fever spread easily through coughing and carried a mortality rate of up to 25 percent in some areas. Symptoms included a sore throat, fever, headaches, rash, and swollen lymph nodes, and infected households were required to post notices on their front doors warning neighbors to "Keep Out." Local schools, including Northfield Seminary, postponed classes to curb the outbreak.[10]

There was also dire news on the national front. An anarchist had shot President William McKinley in the abdomen while the president visited the World's Fair in Buffalo. Although McKinley was rushed into surgery, his wounds developed gangrene, which slowly poisoned his blood. After days of front-page newspaper updates, McKinley died on Saturday, September 14—Elsie's first weekend at Northfield—and Vice President Theodore Roosevelt was sworn in as the nation's twenty-sixth president. McKinley's body was transported back to Washington, DC, in a funeral train draped in black cloth as mourners along the route tossed flowers onto the tracks. At Northfield, the student boarders sobbed openly. It was a strange and not particularly auspicious beginning to Elsie's New England adventure.[11]

With classes delayed because of scarlet fever, Elsie tried to get her bearings on the 250-acre campus. Her dormitory,

Revell Hall, was an ivy-covered, red-brick residence built in high Victorian Gothic style, with dramatic pointed arches and dormers that recalled an elegant church—fitting for a religious school like Northfield. The first floor had formal sitting rooms furnished with plush chairs, a piano, and elegantly draped windows looking out onto a grass tennis court. The bedrooms were on the second floor.[12]

There were about two dozen girls in Revell. Elsie quickly found she stuck out—a loud, brash Californian among East Coast girls who spoke in soft, diffident tones and held their hands over their mouths when they laughed. She had no interest in joining "The King's Daughters," a campus club whose members strived to be "true and pure in thought, word, and deed" and "uniformly unselfish, cheerful, and helpful." To Elsie, pure thoughts were boring thoughts; she'd been to the end of First Street, and its vibrant carnality still pulsed at the corners of her mind.[13]

Pure thoughts, however, were the only thoughts allowed to be expressed at Northfield Seminary, which had one overarching purpose: waking young people "to lives of Christian usefulness."

Northfield and its brother school, Mount Hermon, were founded by the world-renowned revivalist Dwight L. Moody, a Northfield native who envisioned his institutions as training centers for lay evangelists who would spread Christianity across the globe. The focus of Mount Hermon, the boys' school, was on creating religious leaders. Northfield's focus was on producing godly wives and mothers who could braise a leg of mutton *and* recite from the book of Proverbs by heart.[14]

It wasn't until Elsie paged through the school handbook that she felt the full chill of New England puritanism descend on her.

Northfield believed in an Actual Devil and a Personal but Peevish God. It was Biblically literal, to the last whiff of brimstone. Practically every human function or desire was held to be evil. Christianity—as presented by the faculty of 1901—was a dour affair. We couldn't dance. We couldn't go to shows. We couldn't party with young men. Sunday afternoons were supposed to be spent in our rooms, writing letters or reading elevating Works. Occasionally it was permissible to take a walk, but only if accompanied by one of the teachers. The wisecracker who wrote—"To the pure all things are impure," might have graduated from Northfield.[15]

Yet students still found ways to have fun—sledding and ice skating in winter, attending corn roasts in the fall, holding chess and checkers competitions. The sexes mingled, but only under the watchful eyes of chaperones. Twice a year, Northfield students walked to Mount Hermon to watch boys participate in a field day. The girls weren't allowed to partake in the athletic events but were there to applaud and cheer on male contestants, a fact that grated on Elsie's nerves.

I don't know who first called women "the weaker sex" but I'll bet it was a man.[16]

Elsie's classes—among them "Cookery" and "Household Science"—forced her to engage in the domestic drudgery that her mother loathed and that she herself had mostly avoided during her childhood. Northfield students were also required to do all the cooking and cleaning in their dormitories—and to undertake these chores "cheerfully." The handbook explained that this extra work would help female students develop "efficiency in a department where every woman ought to be efficient. But more than this, it develops character; and nothing the girls have to do is a better test of character than this domestic work."[17]

To keep their charges in line—and their virtue intact—Northfield administrators kept students on a tight schedule. Elsie was busy from the moment she woke at 6:15 a.m. to the moment she stretched out on her mattress at 9:30 p.m. In the elegant Stone Hall at the center of campus, a bell rang to signal the beginning and end of each school period. All day long it tolled as Elsie rushed from morning worship to the Recitation Hall to Talcott Library and back to Revell Hall again. Students were permitted only twenty minutes of free time each evening, which they were to spend alone, in their rooms. "This ensures to everyone at least one short period of such privacy each day for the highest uses," the handbook explained.

For a young woman accustomed to copious amounts of free time, the rigid schedule was the cruelest sort of shock.

I was miserable. Desolate and desperate beyond all description. And fighting mad . . . a trapped wildcat. This dour Puritan Jehovah! This sour and all-pervading Sense of Sin! These people who seemingly lived but to suffer . . . whose thoughts were bent on Sacrifice and Hard Labor . . . who shuffled through life like

a chain-gang, never rebelling, never rejoicing, never adventuring!
All the vitality in me rose in revolt against such a God and such a
people. If this be the way to enter Heaven, I wanted to raise Hell.
And proceeded to do so. I cried. I swore. I hurled books through
windows.

But there I was. And there I stayed. Do something about it?
What could I do? Run away? Where could I run? I had $5 a month
"spending money" which also had to cover school supplies. And
I didn't know a soul, save my fiancé and his family, within 3000
miles. Life was a one-way street for Nice Girls in 1901.[18]

She felt fortunate to have an escape from school in the
form of her dashing beau, who lived about an hour away.
Sometimes she took the train to Brattleboro for visits, but
sometimes, weather permitting, Christie retrieved her from
Northfield in his family buggy. Whenever his carriage arrived at Revell Hall and she dashed out the door to greet him
(he wasn't permitted inside), she could sense her envious
cottage mates spying on her behind the heavy velvet curtains. Because they were engaged, the couple was allowed
to take unchaperoned buggy rides and hold hands in public.
But Elsie was disappointed that the secret, passionate kiss
they shared in Benicia—the one that sealed their romance,
and their future together—was so infrequently repeated.
Now that Christie was back in his native New England, he'd
become more mindful of protocols and appearances—and
more formal toward her.[19]

Even after they'd trotted away from campus, Christie's
stiff mannerisms rarely softened. While Elsie chatted about
Northfield—the quirks of her dorm mates, the demands of

her teachers, the endless chores—Christie was mainly silent. The ten-year age gap sometimes felt like an unbridgeable chasm. Elsie was a schoolgirl again at nineteen and Christie was a twenty-nine-year-old businessman with his own surveying company, a man who spent his days measuring property boundaries, drawing maps, and negotiating with clients.

He'd grow a bit more animated after they safely crossed the double-decker bridge spanning the Connecticut River; a train track crossed the top level, carriages used the bottom level. The passage was often terrifying: whenever a train thundered overhead, smoke billowing, sparks showering, the horses would startle and threaten to bolt. Successfully over the bridge, breathing a little easier, they traveled another fourteen miles north before arriving in Brattleboro. With 6,600 residents, Brattleboro was twice the size of Benicia and one hundred years older, originally chartered as a fort to protect English colonists from Native American incursions.[20]

As Christie turned the buggy up Main Street, Elsie noted the handsome two- and three-story brick buildings—not a false façade in sight—that housed banks, hotels, churches, and shops selling books, toys, and tobacco. Over the ground-level shops were private offices of lawyers and doctors. An electric trolley ran down the middle of the street. The sidewalks were not made of creaky wood but of smooth cement, which was swept clean each morning by merchants. And the streets were filled with families, not shifty-eyed, solitary men and rouged women in bleached bobs. While Christie pointed out this or that landmark, Elsie noticed what Brattleboro didn't have—there were no saloons, gambling parlors, or dance halls. And there were certainly no bordellos. Where Benicia permitted uncorked hedonism, Brattleboro exuded moral rectitude and order.[21]

One of the more imposing symbols of that righteousness was the 140-foot spire of the First Baptist Church that loomed over the middle of Main Street, where the Crowells were long-standing members. Christie had served on the church's Board of Trustees and was part of a quartet that sang during services. His first wife, Louisa, had taught Sunday School at First Baptist—it was also the place where her memorial service was held. The church would soon become a regular fixture in Elsie's life as well, since she was expected to take on her husband's churchgoing customs and religious views. It was all so much to absorb, including the stories Christie had begun to share about his family's storied past.[22]

The Crowells claimed to be descendants of Oliver Cromwell, the bloodthirsty seventeenth-century English general and politician—a man so reviled by the time of his death in 1658 that his enemies exhumed, hanged, and finally beheaded his body. The Brattleboro Crowells maintained that when their ancestors immigrated to the United States, they'd flipped the middle "m" of Cromwell to "w," perhaps to sidestep the stigma of the Cromwell name—but by the late 1800s, they had fully embraced the association.[23]

Christie's father, George Crowell, did have one solid commonality with Oliver Cromwell: both men possessed an almost preternatural drive to succeed in life. At thirteen, George dropped out of school to help on his family's New Hampshire farm until the Civil War broke out, at which time he joined the Union Army and traveled to Louisiana to fight the Confederates. While he was gone, his father died and George inherited the family farm, along with a heavy mortgage. He decided to go into journalism to pay off the debt, moving to Brattleboro in 1866 to become the agricultural editor at the *Vermont Record and Farmer.* Living on a salary of $15 a week, he slept in the newspaper office, subsisted on milk and bread, and managed to reduce his expenses to $10 a month. In this penny-pinching fashion, he saved $50 a month toward paying off the farm's debt.

It was at the *Record and Farmer* that George made an astute, and ultimately very lucrative observation: one of the paper's most popular sections was a column dealing with domestic affairs called "The Household." The recipes printed in the column, in particular, were a hit with readers. He wondered if a publication focused solely on running a home would be successful, and in 1868, he launched *The Household,* a monthly newspaper divided into sections mirroring "the various departments of a well-ordered New England household" including "The Veranda," "The Library," "The Parlor," "The Kitchen," "The Dining Room," and "The Nursery."[24]

For five difficult years, he continued to live like a pauper while he tried to boost his readership. His gamble paid off: by the time he sold the paper, in 1890, *The Household* had eighty thousand subscribers spread across every state and several countries and had inspired a spin-off, *Good House-keeping* magazine, still extant today.[25]

George Crowell's vision and dogged persistence had made his family tremendously affluent. He then diversified his wealth into other income-producing holdings, including residential real estate, the town's single water system, a factory that made cider jelly and cucumber pickles, and another factory that produced cottage organs—piano-sized organs that could fit in the parlor of a family home.

As they trotted down Main Street, Christie pointed out the elegant brick building where, for many years, *The Household* kept its offices, alongside the Cheney & Clapp Bookstore.

When they reached High Street, Christie turned the horses onto the broad, upward-sloping road, where they rode shaded by massive locust and sugar maple trees, past stately, black-shuttered colonials. At the top of a hill, they reached an expansive park behind a white picket fence. As they drew closer, a three-story, Queen Anne–style mansion—complete with turrets and a cupola—came into view, situated quite a way back from the road. The two long arches spanning the second-floor window frames looked uncannily like raised eyebrows.

This was Lindenhurst. Upon seeing the Crowell mansion for the first time, Elsie must have felt a rush of disbelief, good fortune, and even pride: after she became Mrs. Christie B. Crowell, it would belong to her as well.

A wide veranda wrapped around the entire front of the house, and as Elsie walked over it toward the massive double door entryway, it all must have felt a bit surreal. She tried not to gape as Christie gave her a tour, yet in her mind, she kept a running count of every extravagance, the better to note it in a letter home to her family:

Fifteen fireplaces—including one on the first-floor landing of the main staircase. Massive gas chandeliers throughout. Twelve types of exotic wood to make the fretwork, paneling, and columns, including Tennessee ash, sycamore, western cherry, mahogany, mottled whitewood, and cypress. A closet just for furs. Another just for linens. A library. A school room. A "sunrise room," which faced east and had its own balcony. A large wine cellar—that did not contain a single bottle of fermented grape juice, of course, because the Crowells equated drinking alcohol with sin.

The kitchen consisted of four rooms, each dedicated to a different task—cooking, prepping, cold storage, and a bank of sinks for washing dinnerware. And perhaps the most astonishing discovery of all: a staff of servants who lived in rooms above the kitchen.

Thirty years later, after the Crowells hit hard times during the Great Depression and could no longer afford mortgage payments, the bank would raze Lindenhurst, which the *Brattleboro Reformer* would then describe as "one of the largest and most pretentious dwellings in Southeastern Vermont."[26]

But in 1901, as the newly engaged pair explored the long hallways, the Crowells still prospered; servants in uniform scuttled by carrying piles of fresh laundry or buckets of soapy water, deferentially greeting "Master Crowell."

Christie's mother supervised the staff's labors from the parlor, summoning them via an elaborate call system of numbered pulleys that connected to bells inside their rooms. It was strange for Elsie to witness this ranking of humanity by wealth, this stark division into servant and master. Christie had grown up extraordinarily privileged; she'd known days of bitter hunger. She had learned, soon after arriving in New England, that rich families normally married within their social class to preserve their status and fortunes—which explained why some of the people she'd met had reacted so coldly to her engagement. She was a cipher from the uncivilized West, a commoner; clearly they thought Christie was marrying down by choosing her as his new bride.

In California, nobody cared about your past—it didn't matter who your parents were, or how much status your family had before moving to the Golden State. California gave people a clean slate. What mattered most was individual merit: what you did with the cards life dealt you, not some inherited privilege.

But there was more than class dividing Christie and Elsie. Although the fireplace mantel in Lindenhurst's reception hall was emblazoned with the word "Welcome" in prominent relief letters, Elsie didn't feel the word was directed at her, not even from her future husband.

Sometimes when she was alone with Christie, a throb of eros, that irrepressible sap of youth, would rush through her and she'd press herself against his tall, lean body, inhaling his musk, seeking out his eyes, his lips, his hands. The fact that he'd been married—that he already possessed intimate knowledge of a woman's body—excited her. But whenever Elsie surged toward him with ardor, Christie stiffened and gently pushed her away. Granted, there was little privacy at Lindenhurst. Since they weren't married yet, the pair slept on separate floors in bedrooms that were linked by long, creaky hallways. Downstairs, the Crowells had installed window-paned doors in the public rooms; you never knew when you'd look up to find Mrs. Crowell peering through the glass, checking to make sure your actions were above reproach.

After several visits to Lindenhurst, Elsie began to dread her time there, especially if she stayed for dinner. In the Robinson household, supper was an ebullient affair. Elsie's family held forth loudly and passionately about everything from politics to weekend plans. Sometimes the spirited conversation led to arguments that ended with her mother launching plates across the room and her father scudding out the door. At Lindenhurst, as Elsie sat at the baronial dinner table—a massive gas chandelier hissing faintly overhead, coolness emanating from the wood floor at her feet—she became increasingly aware of the frosty hauteur of the family she was marrying into. She tried to remember her table manners—no slouching, no elbows, napkin draped over her lap, the "correct way" to use a knife, a fork. *Each careless gesture was regarded with grim disapproval that, to me, seemed all out of proportion with the offense.* She tried to act like them, to tone herself down.

If Christie felt she was being too unrestrained, he'd shoot her a biting look, or even shush her—as if she were a mere child—and his reprimand would make her cheeks burn with shame.[27]

They tried to be kind to me. I tried to be cordial to them. Neither of us succeeded. It was plain that they felt that their son had laid a dreadful burden upon them by bringing this outlander into their midst.[28]

Elsie was beginning to understand the dimensions of the box she'd consigned herself to with her betrothal to Christie. The Crowells saw her as a companion for their son and a future mother to his children, nothing more. They were fundamentally uninterested in her as a person; they cared nothing about her opinions, her passions, her hopes or dreams.

She often returned to Revell Hall dejected and tamped down. The one place she found solace, during those days of growing dread, was in her writing. She used the precious twenty minutes of "silent time" at the end of each day to express herself fully and freely on the page.

A story had bloomed in her mind—a tale about California, about fate and love, about another woman who was manacled by her sex, but in a different way. The story, "Twixt Fish Alley and the Joss-House," was set in San Francisco's Chinatown, a neighborhood that was rife with crime—the most egregious being the sexual slavery of young women and girls who were kidnapped in China and sold in San Francisco. Fish Alley was a real street, and "Joss houses" were Chinese temples.[29]

The protagonist was an enslaved girl, Pun Yee—petite, fresh-faced, with *wondrous black eyes*—who lives in an underground cellar with other enslaved women and girls. Pun Yee's predicament is distressing: running errands in Chinatown one morning, she exchanges a long, meaningful look with a young fishmonger, and for a moment, the electric potential of love leaps between them. But it's hopeless. The girl has already been sold, we soon learn, to an older man, an *opulent barber*. Her life, her destiny, is not her own.

It's impossible to read the story and not see reflections of Elsie's own situation. Her future had also been determined by a culture that insisted women were the weaker sex, not smart enough to vote or lead or engage in intellectual pursuits, but whose best use was as sexual vessels and baby-makers. Girls were brought up to believe that their loftiest aspiration should be to become a servile helpmeet to the husband who ruled them: bondage in a more abstract, and socially acceptable, form.

Elsie found that as she immersed herself in the fictional world of Pun Yee, everything else receded—her worries about the future, her unhappiness at Northfield. The story took over her mind completely; there was only the heartbeat of her creation and the scratch of her pencil nub across the page. She worked out the beats of the story as she walked between classes, did chores, and lay in bed at night, polishing, adding details, sharpening the core, teasing out the ending. Writing was an antidote to everything that felt wrong in her life—all of her resentment, powerlessness, and disappointment. She was building a world, word by word, over which she alone had total dominion. It felt good—it felt great—to be in control of this one small thing.

Her year at Northfield drew to a close. On June 14, 1902, the school paper, *The Hermonite*, dedicated a special issue to graduating "senior maidens." Each graduate had her portrait published, and these all looked startlingly similar: each young woman twisted her hair into a chignon, each wore a white shirtdress with a stiff, detachable collar. Under the portraits ran brief interviews about the graduates' future plans, which ranged from working as private tutors to joining the growing fleet of missionaries bound for Africa. One student, Mildred Scranton, was off to Mount Holyoke College. Because Elsie didn't graduate—her Northfield year was meant to hone her demeanor and housekeeping skills, not her résumé—her portrait wasn't published in *The Hermonite*. Nor were her future plans, which had been dictated long before she stepped foot in Massachusetts.

But on the very last page of the school paper, after a platitudinous essay that ended, "And going out from Northfield we shall never forget the greatest lesson of all—that the meaning of life is loving, cheerful service," Elsie's name did appear—as the author of the story about Pun Yee. At two full pages, "Twixt Fish Alley and the Joss-House" occupied more space than any of the breezy senior profiles.

Elsie never learned to be of "cheerful service" at Northfield. Nor did she achieve the wifely polish that the Crowells had hoped for. The wisdom she acquired there, however, was far more valuable: she learned to use her literary talents as a counterweight to the existential despair of being a woman in a man's world. On the page, she made the rules, she bent fate, she righted wrongs. This exhilarating discovery of creation and self-expression would become a balm for her during troubled times for the rest of her life.

I started writing for exactly the same reason that a starving man starts eating—to save my life.[30]

Chapter 5

MARRIAGE

OFF FOR THE EAST
TO BECOME A BRIDE

Miss Elsmore J. Robinson.

ELSIE POSES FOR her wedding announcement photo, published in the *San Francisco Bulletin* on March 12, 1903. Note the misspelling of Elsie's first name in the caption.

WHEN ELSIE RETURNED TO CALIFORNIA, ALL it took was one whiff of Benicia's briny tide, one glimpse of her mother's Edenic garden, one afternoon of freedom strolling down loud, lusty First Street to confirm that marrying Christie would be a colossal mistake. She belonged to California.

She asked her mother to break off the engagement. Elizabeth refused. It was a matter of honor: Elsie had told Christie she'd marry him and now she must keep her word. Elsie begged. She shouted. She sulked. But Mrs. Robinson stood firm: Elsie would go through with the marriage and become Mrs. C. B. Crowell.

Why did I stand for it? Why didn't I break it myself? Astounded, disgusted, any modern girl is bound to ask those questions. Where was that hell-cat spunk of mine? What had happened to all my revolutionary ideas?

I can only answer—that was a different world. Why do we do the things we do? We think we do them because of some quality within ourselves. Far oftener we do them because of some condition in the world we inhabit. Poor as we were, it was a matter of honor, not of money, that I keep my promise. But I felt as plainly as any girl of my generation the economic pressure that molded my fate. If I didn't go back to Vermont, where did I go?[1]

Elsie spent that winter flinging herself at pleasure, attending dances and parties, roaming wherever and whenever she pleased. She was just nineteen, but her days of carefree living were numbered. She was in a glowing, liminal space between sheltered daughter and duty-laden wife, fully her own person for the first time yet freighted with a sharp awareness that her self-rule would soon end—and perhaps for forever.

The wedding preparations were of no interest to her. When a seamstress came to the house and draped a shroud of cold white silk over her shoulders to take measurements for her dress, it took everything within her not to shrug the material, that cold weight of her destiny, onto the floor. Her parents could not afford to travel to Brattleboro for the ceremony, but they did put money aside to pay for a simple dress, which her mother then embellished with flounces and bows and a row of delicate buttons down the back of the bodice.

Soon—too soon—winter passed. The wedding was scheduled for March 20, 1903. An announcement was published in the *San Francisco Bulletin* along with a large studio portrait of Elsie in her dress—the white flounces forming a capelette of sorts around her shoulders and rows of tiny ruffles adding girth to her bust. She is shown in profile, unsmiling, staring dully into the distance. "Off for the East to Become a Bride," announced the headline. The subheadline continued, "Vermont Business Man Has Won One of California's Fair Daughters Who Now Leaves Her Home at Benicia to Join Him." The same announcement was re-printed, sans photo, in the *Vermont Phoenix*. The wheels had been set in motion; there was no stopping them.[2]

On the morning of her departure, she tried to hide her bitter tears from the numerous townsfolk who came to the train depot to bid her farewell and wish her a long life of happiness and prosperity. During the journey east-ward, she distracted herself by striking up a flirtation with a young salesman, introducing herself as *Esmeralda Du Barry*—the alias tantalizing on her lips and in his ear, likely inspired by one of the steamy romance novels that she loved and that her in-laws would have found so déclassé and sinful.

When she left Benicia, wildflowers carpeted the hills surrounding the town. When she arrived in Brattleboro six days later, the sky was slate gray, the ground still crusted in snow. Christie was waiting for her on the platform. For sev-eral long seconds, the young couple eyed each other warily.

There we were, we two—come from the ends of the earth to marry each other. The stark truth rose before us. We were strang-ers. Not even congenial strangers—yet horribly, incredibly, we would marry each other and become husband and wife! And he didn't want to do it. Ignorant as I was of men and their expres-sion, I knew that much . . . he didn't want to do it.

But hadn't we planned marriage? Bewildered, we thought we had—and could not reach down to the saving fact that we hadn't. Two other people, living in another world, had planned this mar-riage. A frightened man, a restless girl, had planned it.

She—because she wanted to find life.

He—because he wanted to get away from it.

They had thought they had discovered their answers in each other—and so had called that brief excitement love. But it wasn't love. Actually, those two had never seen each other at all. They had only seen their own needs, their own dreams. And now, we two were up against the consequences.[3]

She started to say something to him, but a lump formed in her throat and instead she began to cry. "Now, now, Elsinore," Christie said, mortified at the curious looks Elsie's noisy sobs drew from passersby. Her formal name in his mouth only made things worse. Nobody ever called her "Elsinore" but the Crowells.

At some point during the cross-country trip, she'd become separated from the trunk containing her trousseau. She hoped it would remain lost; that way the wedding would be delayed. But alas, the trunk showed up two days later and was brought to Lindenhurst. The dress was badly wrinkled. She thrust it onto a hanger and stuffed it into an armoire in the grand bedroom she'd been assigned on the third floor, whose windows overlooked an expanse of dead grass and skeletal trees—a landscape as bleak as she felt.

The wedding day arrived. A Friday. In the afternoon, Elsie walked up the two flights of stairs to her room to dress for the ceremony. Alone in her room, she stepped out of her day dress and stood in front of a standing mirror to yank on her corset laces, trying to compress her ribs and abdomen to fit into the gown's nineteen-inch waistline. When she fetched it from the armoire, she was dismayed to find it was still wrinkled. She felt too shy, too out of place, to ask for an iron.

It was growing late. The watery light, grayish-white as the melting snow, sifted a little over the ornate window sills, leaving a central core of darkness. Outside the wind was rising in a long wail. I was late. I was always late. They hated lateness. I must hurry.

My hands were shaking. Nothing went right. But I hurried. Endless buttons, hooks, clasps. It would have been nice if someone offered to help. Oh, I'd never get the hooks all right. There—I knew it! The ones in the middle were wrong! Wouldn't meet! And the pearl button on my slipper had broken off entirely![4]

Her mother had helped her dress for her wedding portrait, her gentle hands patting her hair into place, aglow with pride at her grown-up daughter. Her mother had also been there when her big sister Winnie married, helping her dress and adding to the buoyant mood of the day. Winnie's wedding had been so sunny with promise, a celebration of love. *How wonderful it would be to be standing in the middle of all that, laughing, and the man you loved waiting for you to come!*[5]

Remembering her absent family only made her loneliness more acute.

Suddenly I flung myself headlong against that alien bed— with my flounces in a great tumble all about me—And I was praying as I had never prayed in my life before—gasping, twisting my cold, skinny little hands—whispering—"Please . . . please . . . please God—" I stopped. What did I want "please God" to do?

I didn't know. It didn't matter, anyway. There was nothing that God, or anyone else could do.

Silently I stumbled to my feet. My dress was still unhooked. My pompadour was all askew—with yellow wisps tumbling down. But I did not care.[6]

Downstairs, the Crowells and their moneyed friends waited in the parlor, the one with the word "Welcome" carved into the mantel. She slowly descended the two flights of stairs, gripping the balustrade to steady herself, the hem of white silk sweeping the steps. The murmuring from the parlor grew louder. As she walked down the hall and into the room, she forced her lips into a smile. There was Christie in a black, double-breasted long coat, standing with his parents. When he turned his head to watch her enter, she could tell by the set of his jaw that he was irritated by her tardiness.[7]

The man I was to marry came across the room and took my hand. There were no flowers, no smiles—only the rising wail of the wind. I tried to look at the minister—tried to speak solemnly. But my breath caught. With a shaking sob I promised to love, honor and obey, until death do us part.

Still shaking, I looked at this man whose ring I wore, whose wife—within the last second—I had become. The room was still and gray. Shyly, through a great wonder, I saw, for the first time— my husband!

What did he see? I shall never know. Probably only an awkward, inept girl—her wedding dress half hooked, her wedding slipper gaping with a missing button—her tumbled hair slipping over tear-wet eyes, swollen red nose.

Limply he held my hand. Awkwardly he pecked my cheek. Then turned away—back to his mother. I was married. I was filled with a vast bewilderment, a mounting misery which, for the first time in my life, I was unable to express. In the meantime, I went ahead, making what I hoped were the right gestures—fitting myself, outwardly, into this new scene.[8]

Elsie accepted the cordial felicitations from Christie's family, acutely aware of their dim view of her—the second wife, the California upstart, the strange girl from the unknown family who was marrying above her station. How she must have wished for a few sips of California's fermented grape juice to make the joyless evening more tolerable.

As Christie conferred with his mother, another event now loomed in her mind: the conjugal act. All she knew of sex was that lusty transaction between the sailor and prostitute in Benicia. She assumed married sex was different somehow.

Like most Victorian brides, she was wholly unprepared for her wedding night. It was considered a mother's duty to explain the cycle of menstruation to her adolescent daughter, but that's where conversations about reproduction started and ended. Doctors, preachers, and parents shared a common fear that if teenagers were too familiar with the mechanics of sex, there would be nothing to prevent them from testing them out. Better to keep them ignorant. As a result, some girls worried that kissing or even holding hands with a boy during their period could get them pregnant. Others didn't realize that there were genital differences between the sexes. Teenagers who took their surging hormones into their own hands—so to speak—were condemned as immoral and warned that masturbation, the so-called "secret vice," could lead to invalidism and even insanity.[9]

This puritanical aversion to carnal pleasure extended to the marriage bed. Newlyweds were told that too much sex could "weaken the intellect" and "drain their physical powers." The Victorian anti-sex furor reached a crescendo in 1873, when Congress passed the Comstock Law, making it illegal to send "obscene materials"—anything from naked photographs to birth control information to racy personal letters—through the US mail.[10]

As a result of this information vacuum, most brides were shocked by their first sexual encounter, according to a groundbreaking survey conducted by Stanford physician Clelia Mosher in the late 1890s. One young woman was so spooked by the sight of her groom's erect penis that she bolted and ran back to her parents' home (only to be promptly returned to her husband and told to behave). For many brides, their first sexual experience was essentially rape, with their husbands—ignorant of the delicate workings of female pleasure—forcibly exerting their connubial "rights."[11]

It had been assumed—mainly by doctors, who were overwhelmingly male—that "well-bred" women endured, rather than enjoyed, sex. This view dovetailed with the Victorian idea that women were more "high-minded" than men. Mosher's pioneering study challenged this assumption: After wives grew accustomed to "the marital relation," Mosher found, they did find sex pleasurable—especially if

their husbands touched them in a way that encouraged mutual bliss. "It sweeps you out of everything that is every day,"
one enthusiastic young wife told Mosher.

Faced with a dearth of information, young women
turned to other women for knowledge, seeking out married
friends for some sense of what to expect. A brave women's
rights crusader named Ida Craddock defied the Comstock
law in 1902—the year before Elsie married—by publishing
a how-to guide called *The Wedding Night*, which gave couples advice on how to navigate their first sexual experience.
Craddock was particularly concerned with the quandary of
the bride: "She, who has never bared more than her throat
and shoulders and arms to the world, now finds that her
whole body, especially those parts which she has all her life
been taught it was immodest to fail to keep covered, are no
longer to be her own private property; she must share their
privacy with this man." To make the bride's experience less
harrowing, she gave detailed instructions to the groom,
even mentioning the clitoris—an organ widely ignored by
male doctors—as an erogenous zone. "A woman's orgasm
is as important for her health as a man's is for his. And the
bridegroom who hastens through the act without giving
the bride the necessary half-hour or hour to come to her
own climax, is . . . acting selfishly."[12]

Months before Elsie's wedding, Craddock was arrested
by Anthony Comstock himself—the powerful head of the
New York Society for the Suppression of Vice for whom
the repressive Comstock law was named. Facing a lengthy

prison sentence and public scorn, Craddock, forty-five, took her own life by slashing her wrists.

Having been ensconced in the godly confines of North-field Seminary and having grown up with a mother who would never dare discuss such things, Elsie was likely oblivious to Comstock's crusades against sex education and "evil pictures" and Craddock's attempts at enlightenment.[13]

But on her last night in Benicia, Elsie managed to work up the courage to ask her mother what she should expect.

It was late—the house still—when the terror came on me suddenly. I went slowly, stumbling, down the hall to my mother's room.

I wonder if she knew I was coming. She was standing, looking out at the plum tree. For a long moment we stood there, not touching each other, staring out together.

Then I tried to speak. But my tongue moved like a thick rope in my throat and my lips seemed made of wood. At last it came—in a sort of gasping whisper—

"Mother— Mother, tell me—about marriage—" I did not know. Nice girls didn't. But now—

She did not answer. She tried—but the words would not come. Her face flamed—her head went high—and then suddenly, I, her great girl, was in her arms—and she was sitting in her rocking-chair, holding me, hushing me.[14]

On her first married night, Elsie lay awake, waiting for Christie's footfall upon the stairs. But he didn't come to her. Not that night. Nor the next. And rarely thereafter. He remained in his childhood room and, during the day, still treated her with formal affection.

She suspected his lack of desire was related to Lindenhurst's ghosts. Three times the black wreath of mourning
had hung on the mansion's front door. Three times the undertaker selected the appropriate color badge: white for the
baby, a black-and-white rosette for Christie's brother Herbert and for Louisa. Christie had been ten when his infant
brother passed away, a young man of twenty-three and
twenty-six, respectively, when his brother and wife died.[15]

The ghostly presence that most haunted Elsie, of course,
was Louisa's. Christie and Louisa had lived in Lindenhurst
for nine months as newlyweds—it was where their exhila-
rated assumption that she was expecting a child turned to
horror, where Louisa had transmogrified from a dewy bride
into a withering invalid. Perhaps the lingering scars of that
experience kept Christie from Elsie's door. Or worse yet—
perhaps he still pined for his first wife.

After all, Louisa had been the perfect match for Christie in many ways. At Northfield and Mount Hermon, they
were both well-known—Christie the captain of the baseball team, Louisa the president of her class. Where Elsie
detested Northfield's regimentation, Louisa embraced it—
after graduating, she even became president of its alumni
association. And like Christie, Louisa hailed from a pious
family. While Elsie's father avoided church, Louisa's father, Reverend Nathaniel Van Arsdale, not only officiated
her and Christie's wedding, he was also an editor of the
Christian Intelligencer, the official newspaper of the Reformed Church. And what a wedding it had been: in stark
contrast to her own perfunctory ceremony, Christie's first

wedding had been a showy affair, complete with grooms-men, bridesmaids in matching green-and-white organdy dresses, ushers, and basketfuls of white and pink roses. Louisa's obituary called her an exemplar of "purity and nobility," a woman "not in the least self-assertive." How could Elsie, who had intense feelings and opinions about everything, compete? Perhaps, she thought, if she and Christie moved out of Lindenhurst—if they got away from his prickly family and the insuperable bar set by Louisa— her husband would change.[16]

I had seen other brides and grooms. It is true that in public their demeanor was dignified, demure. But one felt that behind this discreet mask, there were ecstatic raptures, intriguing revolts. Or were there?[17]

As long as she and Christie were imprisoned by Linden-hurst's gloom, their every interaction keenly watched by his parents, she felt she'd never know.

But then, a windfall: one of the Crowells' many rental homes in Brattleboro was vacated. It was a modest clap-board house—two stories, four bedrooms—at 13 Myrtle Street, a few blocks from Lindenhurst. With Elsie's urging, Christie talked his parents into letting them move into it, and Elsie breathed a sigh of relief.

After being occupied by a series of tenants, the house was in poor shape—the walls grungy, the wide pine-plank flooring scuffed and stained. Elsie set about making it her own. In a storeroom, she found a roll of oyster-white wall-paper stamped with bunches of gold-leaf cherries and used it to paper the living room. She painted a set of high-backed

Windsor chairs gleaming black. Bought unbleached muslin and stitched up curtains. Rubbed boiled linseed oil into the wooden floor until it shone like a mirror. Cut old stockings and cotton sacks into strips and braided them into rag rugs. Little by little, room by room, she converted the place into a cozy home. As a finishing touch, she gathered marigolds from the dooryard and placed them in a blue mixing bowl on the kitchen table.

When Mrs. Crowell sent over some mismatched, cast-off tables and chairs that she'd pulled from the basement at Lindenhurst, Elsie sent them back. She didn't want hand-outs from that ghost-tainted place. But the furniture rejection put her at odds, once again, with her mother-in-law. Increasingly Elsie had found excuses not to visit her in-laws at Lindenhurst, where her guard was always up and she still felt like an intruder.

For weeks she waited for her husband to praise her efforts. But he didn't seem to notice the changes unless she pointed them out. When he came home from surveying each evening, she had dinner ready and rushed to the door to greet him. She'd been alone all day and longed for company. To her great dismay, he remained aloof. She kept waiting for him to pay her a compliment, for a kind word. But they ate dinner in near silence and slept in separate beds. She kept waiting for him to rise from his mattress and come to where she lay. She kept waiting for him to touch her the way a husband was supposed to touch a wife, the way he'd touched Louisa. She lay in her nightgown, freshly bathed, her body nearly electric with desire for him, for his caresses. She watched the moonlight sift through the trees on the other side of the window until his heavy breathing told her the obvious. Night after night, the same scene played out.

Nothing ever happened. But more and more I was consumed with the idea that something should. These empty hours, this cool, uncommunicative return at nightfall, was this all there was to marriage?

What did I know of men and women and married life? Nothing. But I had seen spring come racing, naked and glorious across the wilderness, buds in her hair, lambs at her breast, a million tiny calves and colts, puppies, kittens and baby birds, toddling, tumbling, wobbling, scampering after.

There were no seasons or reasons for mating in those swooping skies and sprawling hills and swelling tides of my youth. Spring, summer, autumn, winter, was one long bacchanal. All through the day, the roses opened, heavy with pollen . . . the bees staggered, drunk with honey . . . the doves cooed and called—yearning, ecstatic. All through the night there was a whispering and low laughing . . . the throb of guitars . . . the scent of fruit . . . far off, full-throated, a coyote's mating cry.

What did I know of love? Nothing. Everything! I was born of it. Bred in it. Ready for it. What else should there be but to go on from that warm, sweet, innocent girl dreaming into the sweeter, madder surrender of a woman to a man?

Yes—it was true—we still seemed strangers. But what did that matter? The earth was hard and reluctant after the summer drought. The earth was like an alien stranger—rigid, locked. But with the first rain, overnight, she was laughing and soft—and twinkling with a loveliness of green release.

And could we not . . . we two . . . could we not . . .[18]

She poured herself into domesticity, thinking she'd win Christie's affection that way. Although she'd hated the housewife-in-training militarism of Northfield, she now embraced it.

Gesture by gesture, I learned to "keep house." I made my own soap, concocted cough medicine, baked endless mountains of bread, rolls and pastries, crammed hundreds of jars, crocks, glasses and bottles with preserves, conserves, jams, jellies, marmalades, pickles and fruit juices, boiled fruit puddings and hung the dark, rich, chunky bags in a row along the woodshed ceiling, to be cut down in winter when desired, thawed out, reheated.

I had never sewed. But "machine stitching" was still anathema in a well-kept Vermont home. Even the lowliest dish-rag was hemmed by hand. Mile after mile, I toiled along endless hems with almost invisible stitches . . . learned to draft patterns, to cut and tailor, make perfect buttonholes, insert gussets. All my husband's shirts I made—every garment of my own, even my suits and overcoats.[19]

By the time Elsie moved into the Myrtle Street house, the industrial revolution had transformed American households—and women's lives. Products whose fabrication had consumed women's daily routines for millennia could now be purchased at the store, including soap, bread, clothing, canned beans, and fish. But to people like the Crowells, whose *The Household* had glorified old-fashioned homemaking, buying "ready-made" was lazy; wives were judged by their handmade abilities. Elsie did her best to conform to their expectations.[20]

For a time, the novelty of any new task, distracted me. But always, as soon as my hands became accustomed to the new rhythm, back came that old, nagging questioning. We had been married weeks, months—why did we still seem strangers? Why did he caress me so seldom—act so guilty when he did? Why was he always trying to repress my laughter, my impulsive affection? Was I a mystery to him, too? Was he, perhaps, as lonely and bewildered as I? Sitting across the "center table" from him at night—dutifully darning his socks—lying, rigidly awake in my twin bed at night, while he snored lustily a yard away, I studied his face—wondered. Those sensitive, finely modeled, intelligent features—those reserved, dark blue eyes—that sensitive full mouth which, save in sleep, was so rigidly tightened—was I never to know what lay behind their locked door?

Sometimes I tried to ask him. But the bred-in-the-bone Vermonter, even to this day, has a horror of words. To him they are not a natural means of expression but lewd lapses from self-control.[21]

Christie found excuses to stay away from home. In addition to singing in the men's quartet at church, he played in the YMCA baseball league, showed his buff cochins at regional poultry shows, and attended meeting after meeting at the Masons' lodge.[22]

Elsie's loneliness grew by the day. She had no idea how to articulate her disappointment to her husband. Popular advice columnists seemed to suggest unhappiness was part and parcel of wifehood. "No matter how much a wife may suffer, she must learn to control herself, and to bear as much as possible with her husband's weaknesses," wrote the ever-popular Ruth Ashmore of the *Ladies' Home Journal*. If a husband leaves his dirty socks on the floor, they should be picked up without protest. A wife's main objective was to avoid quarrels, Ashmore advised, and if the couple did argue, the wife should promptly apologize and promise her husband never to provoke him again. "It is the only way that one can become a good wife, and a happy one," Ashmore concluded.[23]

The kind of housekeeping which polishes the furniture and lets a human grin grow dingy is an abominable kind of housekeeping. Jenny has given herself over to the functions of a machine—cooking, cleaning, sewing. And she has forgotten the functions of humanity—laughing, dreaming, risking, adventuring, making experiments. She has put scalloped paper on all the shelves in the house, but she has left her own spirit as dusty and bare as the woodshed.[24]

The term "good wife" was Victorian code for only one thing: subservience. The husband was the undisputed ruler of the household, per a society founded on the Bible. Ephesians 5:22–23 commanded, "Wives, submit yourselves unto your own husbands, as unto the Lord. For the husband is the head of the wife, even as Christ is the head of the church." Elsie had grown up hearing that passage, but until she was married, had given the verse little thought. She wondered if Christie would always treat her as a subordinate, if that was the nature of marriage.

Alone in a strange town, dejected and lonely beyond imagining, Elsie fell into a funk. A *slow, steady poisoning of unhappiness* made it a chore for her to rise from bed each morning. She barely ate. She stopped trying to engage her husband at the dinner table and resigned herself to the poisonous silence, the only sound the scritch of elm branches against the window, the scrape of forks on plates. At night, she clamped her pillow over her head to muffle the steady drone of his snores, angry and resentful.[25]

Months passed. Finally, Christie noticed that his bride had become gaunt and withdrawn and grew worried for the health of *this* wife.

Elsie may have been plagued by "neurasthenia," a nervous disorder that emerged in the late 1800s among isolated and overburdened American housewives. Symptoms included irritability, insomnia, precipitous weight loss, and a general malaise—all of which, doctors warned, could snowball into a full-blown mental breakdown. Patent medicine hucksters targeted housewives suffering from the disorder, selling them addictive and often dangerous tonics that contained morphine, cocaine, even strychnine—a substance commonly used in rat poison.[26]

Christie booked an appointment with a doctor in Boston. As the doctor examined her, she lay on the table balling her fists with near-paralyzing modesty. Afterward, he called Christie back into the room. There was nothing wrong with Elsie's body, he told them; she was a perfectly healthy young woman. He then eyed them both and shook his head with dismay. "What's the matter with you two youngsters?" he asked. "What this girl needs is a baby."

A baby! . . . What else was he saying—and what was my husband answering? I do not know. I remember only my heart was leaping as though it would leave my body.[27]

She was euphoric. It took a doctor's orders to bridge the physical divide between Elsie and Christie. Around their first-year anniversary, Elsie discovered she was pregnant.

Chapter 6

AWAKENING

A FAMILY PHOTO OF ELSIE'S SON,
George Alexander Crowell, circa 1907.

Image courtesy of Robin Lovering, Elsie's great-nephew.

E LSIE HAD ALL THE CLASSIC SYMPTOMS OF pregnancy: sore breasts, nausea, exhaustion— and a pressing fear of death. In 1904, one in thirty American women died in childbirth, and the joyous antici-pation of motherhood was tinged with stomach-clenching worry. Some pregnant women went so far as to write out their wills, stating their preferred name for the baby and dis-tributing jewelry. Elsie was one of them.[1]

I knew I was going to die. I even wrote elaborate farewell letters to my friends. I willed my graduation beads to my sister, Winnie. With all the heroic resignation of an early Christian martyr marching to the lions, I told my husband that I wouldn't mind if he married again.[2]

Childbirth-related deaths were so common that they fostered a new field of postmortem photography. The dev-astated husband would summon a photographer to capture one last image, a *memento mori*, of his dead wife, laid out on fresh bed linens, often with her stillborn babe at her side— one life cut short, the other never begun.

Even if you survived childbirth, there was a not-insignificant chance that the process would leave you per-manently maimed. Forceps and other instruments used by doctors to speed delivery could cause tears between your vagina and bladder or rectum, the worst cases resulting in urinary or fecal incontinence. Women who lived with this malodorous condition were often ostracized by relatives and friends. There was also the possibility of cervical damage, resulting in a prolapsed uterus, which would make it difficult for you to have sex or even walk. For many women who suffered from such birth-related trauma, one doctor wrote, "death would be a welcome visitor."[3]

Doctors were part of the problem; they were overwhelmingly male and treated obstetrics as a lesser field of medical practice. Some worried about offending the Victorian sensibilities of female patients by being too candid about the birth process and therefore withheld useful information. Instead, they advised mothers-to-be not to dwell on delivery dangers—lest their anxiety produce morose or anxious children—and to focus on "reading good books, looking at beautiful pictures, and listening to delightful music."[4]

A book written by a female gynecologist in 1886 offered far more practical advice. Dr. Alice B. Stockham, the fifth American woman to obtain a medical degree, published *Tokology: A Book for Every Woman* to fill the information void. ("Tokology" refers to the study of childbirth, midwifery, and obstetrics.) Written in lay terms that the average woman could understand, *Tokology* was brazenly direct because Stockham believed that only by educating themselves would women reduce their chances of childbirth-related death or permanent injury. A mother of two children herself, Stockham dedicated her book to "all women who, following the lessons herein taught, will be saved the sufferings peculiar to their sex."[5]

Tokology included detailed illustrations of the female reproductive system and of embryonic development. Stockham urged women to stay limber for the rigors of labor by staying active—regularly climbing stairs, gardening, and doing stretches. But her most consequential advice was for women to be relentlessly proactive about their own healthcare.

"Protest positively and persistently," Stockham told the reader, if a doctor tried to expedite delivery by giving her a labor-inducing herb such as black cohosh or a fungus called ergot (both of which could cause fatal uterine ruptures) or if the doctor tried to use forceps to forcibly pull out the baby, which could tear the vaginal walls. She recommended patience and hot sitz baths instead. "Better wait for nature than suffer the effects that are sure to follow," she advised. *Tokology* sold more than two hundred thousand copies, was passed from friend to friend and mother to daughter, and helped establish the value of women's health in American medicine.[6]

Pregnancy also posed a curious social problem for prudish Victorians. Although they venerated motherhood, a woman's growing belly was blatant proof of sex and they couldn't quite reconcile the lofty ideal of feminine purity and high-mindedness with a crude, carnal act. As Elsie wrote, *it wasn't even nice to discuss one's condition.*[7]

The extreme solution, for mothers-to-be in the middle and upper classes, was to hide their pregnancies altogether. Around the fourth month, when a corset could no longer suppress their swelling abdomens, middle- and upper-class women were expected to go into "confinement" and generally stay home until the baby was born. Elsie followed this custom, only leaving home to attend church services. If she'd been in Benicia, she could have maintained a social life by receiving friends and family members at her home. But in Brattleboro, where she had no close connections, she was alone all day and frequently in the evenings as well. *Life that had been narrow and silent enough before now closed around me in a veritable Black Hole.*[8]

Bored, restless, and increasingly unsettled as her pregnancy progressed, she began to leave the house under cover of darkness. If she walked to either end of Myrtle Street, she could enter the woods and stroll unseen beneath towering sugar maples and chestnuts as the cicadas chirred overhead. As the baby grew inside her, she held fast to the hope that its irrefutable presence would uncork some new tenderness in her husband, that he would awaken to *all that married romance should imply; gay planning, brave adventuring—the dear delight of making a home—the pride and wonder and fun of making a family.*[9]

She didn't write to tell her mother that she was "in a family way" until late in her pregnancy, *so bound were we both by the vicious false modesty of our times.* Her mother's response was tempered by the same reserve; she *did not write one page of the practical information or sane reassurance I so greatly needed.* She didn't even discuss the pregnancy with the one other person who had the most vested interest in its successful outcome—Christie.[10]

How did my husband feel about it all? I do not know. There was such a terror of life upon him that I suspect he hardly dared feel at all. Since he was a child, emotion—outside of religious or filial expression—had been branded as a dubious indulgence, probably shameful, bordering on sin. What did he think, that pale, slender man of thirty, who came and went like a stranger through the house during the waiting days? Was he happy and proud that at last he was taking a normal part in man life? Or was he abashed and appalled at the prospect of any experience which might disturb the dusty order of his shadow world?[11]

Yet there were *touches of joy,* Elsie would later reflect, *as sweet and swift as the flash of a bird's wing.* One afternoon, she came into the kitchen and found Christie bent over the table, working on a cradle.[12]

The light came dimly through the thick, wavy glass. I stood leaning against the door. He did not know I was there. I can feel the frame behind me yet—my fingers gripping the worn boards lest I move. I wanted to move. I wanted to rush to him . . . to dance and laugh and shout and whisper gay young foolishness. But, though his hand moved lovingly over the bits of wood, his eyes were closed doors.

The Crowells arranged for a midwife to attend the birth. At the time, 50 percent of women still delivered at home, although a growing number opted to give birth at a hospital, where they'd have access to modern equipment, trained staff, and painkillers that made the experience less harrowing. Doctors gave women morphine to put them into a "twilight sleep" at the beginning of labor, chloroform to alleviate the sharp pain of crowning, and scopolamine—an amnesia-causing drug—to erase the memory of suffering.[13]

But biblical literalists such as the Crowells believed that any type of intervention that dulled labor pain ran counter to God's will. "In sorrow thou shalt bring forth children," decreed Genesis 3:16. It was Eve's curse: the original woman defied God by eating from the forbidden tree of knowledge in Eden, and therefore God punished her, and every subsequent generation of women ad infinitum, with agony in childbirth.

Most women wanted their mothers present for the birth of their child, especially their first. Who better than your own, experienced, mother to calm you down, talk you through the process, and rub olive oil onto the small of your back when the labor pains started? But Elsie's mother did not come to Brattleboro as Elsie's time approached, likely due to the same financial constraints that kept her away on Elsie's wedding day.[14]

Elsie's contractions began the first week of December 1904. They lasted for days. The midwife—*a little, fat, futile woman*—was called, and as Elsie paced the upstairs hallway, the midwife trailed behind her, fussing and gurgling advice. As her labor pains grew sharper, Elsie pushed the midwife away and tried to focus on the internal gears of her body. Sleet pelted the windows. She wished, more than ever, she was among her own people in California. She walked faster and faster, trying to evade and shake off the pain.[15]

Presently, it wasn't I who was walking. . . . The pain was walking . . . swinging back and forth like a monstrous pendulum. And I was spiked to the pain—swinging with the pain.

Then, vaguely, far off, I heard someone screaming, hour after hour. . . . One day? Two? It didn't matter. Time had stopped . . . space had vanished . . . there were no hours, no walls, no people—

Only the screaming, going on and on in the darkness—And,
strangely, the sound of my husband—that cold man—sobbing—
Then suddenly—silence—
And, in the silence, a tiny, bleating cry!
I struggled to my elbow, hands fumbling through the darkness,
and clutched him to me, laughed and cried and mumbled at his
tiny hands.[16]

⁂

ELSIE WAS GLAD it was a boy. Boys could do more in life. Be
more in life. Perhaps, she thought, she could experience a
bit of this male freedom vicariously as his mother.

Born December 4, 1904, they called him George Alexander Crowell: George after Christie's father, Alexander
after her own. All throughout that snowy New England
winter, Elsie bundled her infant son against her chest, rel-
ishing the miracle of his existence, *a small, pink blur against*
my heart. She sang to him, rocked him, murmured into
the warm crown of his head, kissed his delicate fingers
and smooth cheeks. She'd finally found a worthy recep-
tacle for her affection, one who returned the sentiment
in toothless, drooly grins. *He had come! My little boy had*
come![17]

But her relief at surviving childbirth and giving birth
to a baby with a healthy squall was short-lived. For her son
had inherited his father's weak lungs. Christie's asthma attacks were severe, especially in the cold winter months.
But the disease was much worse for little George, whose
tiny airways constricted more quickly. As he grew into

toddlerhood, his breathing issues became even more pronounced.[18]

He was so lovely—my darling! A thistledown baby . . . tumbled gilt curls, dark-lashed violet eyes . . . slender body, swift and light as wind across the grass—Gay, too! Bubbling laughter, adorable puppy clowning—And then, just as the whole of me sang with the sweet, small joy of him, those sudden silences, as though a skeleton hand gripped his throat and my heart in one agony—that long, gasping, wheeze . . . that ghastly, strangling, dimming of the eyes—Oh, God! was there—is there—no prayer to lift such misery from the heartbroken mothers and the helpless babies who must live through that?[19]

His fragility was even more worrisome because the two leading causes of death in the United States were respiratory diseases—tuberculosis and pneumonia. For an asthmatic child, a case of either could prove fatal.[20]

Asthma remedies for children were scarce, mostly ineffective, and sometimes dangerous; a few contained cocaine or arsenic. Over time, Elsie came to believe that permanent relief for George would never be found in Brattleboro. Researchers already knew the most likely culprits of asthma attacks: allergies and other environmental triggers. In 1908, a prominent pediatrician named L. Emmett Holt posited that the best treatment was to "send the child at once to a warm, dry climate" for "at least three to four years." The belief that temperate climates were the healthiest prompted the creation of sanatoriums throughout the West offering "climatic prevention" to clients seeking relief from everything from "throat troubles" to rheumatism and lung ailments, including asthma.[21]

Elsie raised the idea of returning to California with Christie. They'd discussed it before, when they were courting. "Some day we'll ranch," Christie had promised. Now, given George's precarious health, the move seemed imperative. She'd already figured out a job for Christie, should he want it—her older brother Paul worked as a surveyor for an electric company that was building a hydroelectric dam in the Sierra Nevada. She was certain that Christie, also a surveyor, could join the same project. It seemed like a perfect solution.[22]

If only we could get away from the humid summers, the raw winters of Vermont, back to the vast, healing air of the west— perhaps he would be well. I was frantic to go. To go at once![23]

But Christie hemmed and hawed. Moving to California would mean starting from scratch, without the free residence and stature that being a Crowell in Brattleboro afforded. The topic became a thorn between the couple. One day Elsie cornered her husband and demanded an answer: Was he willing to move for the sake of their son's health, or not?

He averted his eyes and paused before responding. "I can't. It would mean deserting the family."[24]

As his words sank in, a chill swept through her—a sudden, unmistakable understanding of where she stood in his life.

But aren't we your family? she asked. It was hard to choke out the question.

He only stared—shut his jaw stubbornly, turned and walked away. He knew the answer—so did I—why bother to put it into words?

She now had confirmation of something she'd long suspected: Christie's loyalty would always be to his parents. She—his wife, the mother of his child—would always come in a distant second.

I want to be fair with him. He must have loved his boy—longed for his healing. And yet—he was utterly unable to break the bond to Brattleboro, to his family.[25]

The conversation was a tipping point for their marriage. Having a baby had not improved their relationship as she had hoped. Emotional damage—avoidance, anger, resentment—had festered between them for years, but now their mutual disdain was out in the open, uttered and acknowledged.

The battle lines were drawn. Her anger and sorrow turned into resolve: if Christie chose his parents—*his mother*—over her, she would choose her son over him.

Even the tragedy of our boy's ill health could not draw us together. We both grieved—then the inevitable difference in attitudes occurred. He took the problem as a cross to be borne—I took it as a battle to be won.[26]

Elsie was twenty-one when George was born and her life path seemed poured in concrete: wifehood, motherhood, housekeeping, church. Silent evenings—silent years—with an emotionally barren man who treated her with a mixture of patriarchal disdain and exasperation, a husband who, at the slightest sign of high emotion, turned on his heel and walked up the street to his mother.

Had I been of softer stuff, I would have taken the count. We would have gone on together, through the years, in one of those ghastly sadistic marital feuds—spending our strength in torturing and being tortured. But certain things made it impossible for me to accept such a fate. Fundamentally, of course, the elements in my own blood steadied and stiffened me . . . the bulldog stubbornness of the British, the die-fightin' fury of the Irish, and an invincible optimism I had absorbed from that passionate pageant of the pioneers. But mainly it was my love of the boy—I couldn't—wouldn't give up my hope for him![27]

She made a decision: she would give every ounce of her affection to her son and no longer expect any warmth from her spouse. Yet she still felt confused and wounded by Christie's attitude toward her. Why was he so prickly toward her and so affectionate with his mother? Why had he found her so alluring during their long strolls in Benicia but now barely looked at her?

Her questions drove her to Brattleboro's public library, where she found herself in the stacks of nonfiction books. The shelves of neatly arranged hardbacks, the titles on their spines filigreed in gold, contained free and precious knowledge for people like Elsie who couldn't afford to attend college or who were barred from higher education because of their sex or race.

She snapped up any book she could find on the growing field of psychoanalysis. Among the bestsellers of the time was Sigmund Freud's groundbreaking *The Psychopathology of Everyday Life*, which examined unconscious thought and impulses, including free will and repressed ideas and tendencies.

I read, read, read. Psychology, sociology, anthropology—everything I could lay my hands on. [28]

She struggled with erudite concepts and stilted language.

I yawned, fidgeted, bored to tears by the big words, the stuffy writing. Tried to apply what I had read to the lives I knew.

She attempted to break down complex theories into simple English, which she recorded in a notebook.

I thought how I'd have written it—simply, in small, strong, easy words, in the slangy vernacular of the people.

Writing down her observations and thoughts became a daily exercise for her during those solitary, aching years. She'd push her anger and sorrow onto the page, pencil scraping, thoughts roiling, until she'd expressed herself fully and felt a little relief from the violent churn of her emotions. Keeping this journal, she would later say, kept her sane in the sterile bubble of her marriage, providing a silent confidant that absorbed her mental burdens.

I only wanted one thing—to understand people, to grasp life, to make some ordered pattern out of all this seeming waste and confusion. So, steadily, I observed life as it came and went in my little street, thought about it, set down what I thought. And thereby unwittingly built a bridge between my isolated cell and the vast world of human beings.[29]

She hid her notebook in a place Christie would not look and sometimes even burned pages after writing them.

But something remained—inside me. Truth remained. I was learning to read the truth, think the truth, face the truth.[30]

Throughout her marriage, Elsie never complained to her family about her relationship with her husband. *Decent, spunky people kept their troubles to themselves as a matter of course.* Her parents continued to believe that Christie was a good catch; as a member of the Crowell family, Elsie would never be plagued by the financial concerns that dogged the Robinson household.[31]

But money couldn't heal her marriage—or her son, whose asthma attacks left her feeling scared and desperate.

Since Christie refused to move to California, she weighed her options for finding other means to return to the place that she never stopped thinking of as home. Perhaps, she thought, her parents could afford to buy two third-class train tickets back to California for her and George.

For the boy's sake, I would do anything. I would write, ask, beg—they'd find a way for us to come.[32]

⁕

BEFORE ELSIE COULD broach the topic with her father, however, she received devastating news: at age sixty-five, Alexander Robinson had died "after a fit of coughing"— most likely tuberculosis. It was January 1907. Five months later, she was again blindsided by grief: her older brother Paul, the surveyor, contracted typhoid fever from contaminated water in the Sierra Nevada and also died. He was only thirty-three.[33]

The two deaths gutted her. Her mind reeled back to an image of her father and Paul in Benicia, on the night their home was electrified. The family had gathered in the living room at twilight, where a single, naked lightbulb dangled by a black cord from the ceiling. Paul had reached up to turn on the current and white light flashed into the dim room, illuminating the family's awed, upturned faces.

We sat watching this strange and wonderful thing which had come to us.

The other children went to bed. They did not notice me, sitting back in the shadows, my eyes trapped—like some young jungle animal's—by that globed fire.

And my father and brother sat talking about it, late into the night.

Electricity—what was it? Nobody knew, they said. Power. But what was power?

Across the years, I see my two men—their thin faces strained with the intensity of their thought, their thick mops of hair tumbling above their searching eyes. Of all they said I can only remember one thing—and the pause that followed.

"But suppose, dad—suppose we—all men—are made of this stuff too? Suppose it's Life! Then—how about death? This doesn't stop—if the bulb breaks. This goes on . . . somewhere. Then if we're made of this—!" Their eyes stared at each other—The room filled with a great hush.[34]

That mystical moment would prompt Paul to study engineering at UC Berkeley and reverberate within Elsie for the rest of her life whenever she turned on a light. She desperately wanted to believe that her dad and Paul also lived on, *somewhere.* After she put George down for the night and settled on the sofa with a library book, the electric halo cast onto the page by the lamplight made her feel a little closer to both of them.

The Brattleboro library had also become a source of joy for George. Among the classics published in the early years of the twentieth century were the Tom Swift adventure

series and Jack London's *The Call of the Wild* and *White Fang*.
Frances Hodgson Burnett's *The Secret Garden*, with its depiction of a lonely, sick boy who is ultimately healed by the
regenerative power of love—and a beautiful garden—must
have struck a deep chord with both Elsie and George.

George attended High Street School—a minute's walk
from home—where his teacher was Christie's older sister.
But his asthma flare-ups often caused him to miss school,
especially in the winter months, and Elsie kept piles of children's magazines at his bedside to entertain him during his
sick days, including the magazine she had loved as a girl, *St.
Nicholas*.[35]

But it was a new, subscription-based newsletter called
John Martin's Letters that quickly became George's favorite.
Sent to children by mail and published by a former greeting
card designer named Morgan van Roorbach Shepard, *John
Martin's Letters* was full of whimsical illustrations, riddles,
stories, and word games aimed at five- to ten-year-olds. In
1910, when George was nearly six, he would have received
Letter Number 9 (eight pages in all) and been entertained by
the continuing escapades of a runaway boy who crosses
paths with a sea serpent and a "Moorish Pirate Man." In an
era before radio, television, or the internet, when there was
little to keep a sick child occupied—especially during the
long, brutally cold New England winters—George would
spend hours devouring the newsletter, amused by the tales
of talking animals.[36]

One day, on a whim, Elsie picked up a pencil and started
crafting an original story for George, returning to a hobby

that had kept her occupied during the long lazy hours of her girlhood. Writing in her neat, tight cursive, she addressed the stories to "Dear Boy," mimicking the style of *John Martin's Letters*. One of her early tales featured an eight-year-old boy who gets lost in the woods at night and encounters a bear. At first he is fearful, but the bear is of the friendly sort and introduces the boy to a range of woodland creatures.

Hist! That's the way adventure stories always begin, and as this is to be a very adventurey story you must hist as hard as ever you can. Close your eyes and listen until the wind howls three times—Now where are you? Not in a room at all. But out in the far woods. The trees are rocking overhead.[37]

She populated the page margins with drawings of playful animals and children with paper doll–like articulated limbs. She read her story to George as they sat on the sofa under the golden beam of the lamplight, taking in his delight, his laughter, his admiration. Her creation was a distracting balm for them both.

She wrote another story, and then another. She began to wonder, shyly at first, if her stories were good enough to be published in *John Martin's Letters*. She mailed the story about the lost boy to van Roorbach Shepard's office in New York City, and to her astonishment, van Roorbach Shepard wrote back, saying he'd like to publish the story—and asking if she had more work he could publish. She began to write for *John Martin's Letters* on a regular basis in 1911, using the pen name "Comfy Lady."[38]

Emboldened by this success, she began to express her creativity in other ways.

Life didn't stop being interesting for men, just because they were married. Men went on being other things besides husbands. Why must married women be only wives?[39]

She joined the local community theater troupe. When the *Vermont Phoenix* published an article on a play the troupe was performing, it ran a glamour shot of Elsie in a shoulder-baring dress, her wide-brimmed hat tipped coquettishly on her head. Her in-laws were scandalized; the Crowell women wore their dresses buttoned all the way up, they did not show flesh. *I wore only gray chambray for weekdays, black taffeta or wool for Sundays. Gray and white was permissible. Dark blue was conceded.* When she was twenty-two, her mother had sent her a rose-colored flannel outfit—a long skirt with matching button-down jacket. *I loved that suit! I whooped over it . . . Kissed it!* But soon it mysteriously disappeared from her wardrobe, forcing her once again into sartorial conformity.[40]

As Elsie pursued interludes of autonomy and adventure, she grew more resentful at the limitations society imposed on her for the crime of being born female. These sentiments prompted her to join the local chapter of the Federation of Women's Clubs, which were precursors to the feminist consciousness-raising groups of the 1960s. Members networked and advocated for social justice causes, including women's right to vote and attend universities on equal footing with men.[41]

As she became bolder in her rebellion against the Crowells and everything they stood for, her demeanor changed in sometimes shocking ways.

I had been a cry-baby. Now the tears dried and I stared ahead, straight and hard. I had been chinless. Now I grew a chin of which Dempsey himself could have been proud. And a temper that was a honey! For years I had been watching, analyzing, enduring. Now—t'hell with that! I was going to show action! Bam!—away went every pretense of meekness. Boom!—Crash! China broke— furniture splintered to the right and the left of me. I heaved the washtub and clothes wringer down the back stairs. I pitched the darning into the fire. With whoops—and adjectives I had learned listening in on stevedores twenty years before.

Amazed, horrified, my sedate relatives surveyed this new harridan. What on earth had come over Elsinore, all of a sudden? Nothing had come over Elsinore all of a sudden. Nothing comes over any of us "all of a sudden." We are the harvest of seeds we sow. Secretly for years I had rebelled, rioted, cussed 'em out. Now I was merely doing in the open what I had done in secret. Easy enough now, with our modern knowledge of psychology, to understand what had happened. I had "cracked up" under the strain of work, worry, monotony and the futility of my life. I was in the grip of hysteria. But to my Puritan kin, considering all problems in terms of theology, I was possessed with devils.[42]

Elsie's feelings of slow strangulation were brilliantly captured in Kate Chopin's scandalous novel, *The Awakening*. Published in 1899, the novel portrays a young married mother who rejects convention and forges her own path toward self-discovery and erotic freedom. But the American public wasn't ready for such a gutsy female character. After critics decried *The Awakening* as "unwholesome," libraries banned it and Chopin's publisher canceled her next book.

Chopin fell into obscurity and was only rediscovered by feminists in the 1970s.

Faced with Elsie's insurrection, Christie had no choice but to take out a newspaper ad for "a reliable girl" to do the housework his wife refused to do.

That little, quiet cottage under the New England elms . . . like many another quiet cottage of those times . . . became a hell on earth. I had always—from the Puritan viewpoint—been a queer, brooding or boisterous creature, apt, at any time, to do the strangest things. Now I did even stranger ones. Laughed, hard and wild, where before I had not dared to smile. Sneered, openly, where before I had cringed. Talked . . . famished for words . . . to anyone who would listen. To strange women. And—utterly abominable— to men! Walked, frantic for freedom . . . anywhere, everywhere, blind to where I went.

And now—like the monotonous yammering of a mad man— one desire and one only went on and on, in my frantic mind, in my feverish flesh—I wanted out! I wanted out! I wanted out.[43]

Her out would once again present itself as a twist of fate. Except this time, she didn't stumble upon the answer to her most urgent desire at church—but at a mental hospital.

Chapter 7

ART

FOLLOWING HER SUCCESS WITH *JOHN MARTIN'S LETTERS*,
Elsie began drawing illustrations for children's books. This one
appeared in *Behind the Garden Wall*, Paul Elder and Company, 1913.

HIS NAME WAS ROBERT WALLACE. WHEN ELSIE met him, he was forty and an inpatient at the Brattleboro Retreat, formerly known as the Vermont Asylum for the Insane.

Robert Wallace was the opposite of Christie Crowell in every way—a darkly handsome flaneur where Christie was a tightly wound moralist; verbose and earthy, where Christie was restrained and decorous. Wallace was also a man who deeply enjoyed—and sought out—the company of women.[1]

Like Christie, Robert was born with a silver spoon in his mouth. His father was a self-made millionaire who'd immigrated from Scotland at twenty-five and cofounded an upscale, eight-story department store called Forbes & Wallace in Springfield, Massachusetts.

At the time that his life crumpled, Robert was a well-paid and well-liked manager in his father's store and lived in a stately home with his wife, three young children, and two live-in servants. But his emotional troubles ran deep. His mother died of a fatal postpartum infection when he was eleven, and each of his three younger siblings died before age five. His father remarried in a union that produced five more children. At seventeen, Robert was poised to attend Yale when he suffered a mental breakdown, brought on, a psychiatrist would later surmise, by excessive consumption of alcohol and tobacco. Nonetheless, he was able to bounce back enough to marry and work full-time at the department store—until he had a falling out with his father, who accused Robert of "squandering vast sums of money" and fired him.[2]

For years, Robert's wife—who was the head of the Forbes & Wallace millinery fitting room, where she helped women choose among the latest trends in lavishly decorated toques, turbans, and hats—put up with Wallace's erratic behavior. This included his daytime drunks on juniper-flavored Holland gin, chain-smoking through dinner, and frequent absences in which he spent time with other women. After losing his department store job, Robert read about a gold boom in Ontario, Canada. Seeing an opportunity to "strike it rich" with no experience and what seemed like relatively little effort, he moved his family to a Canadian gold mine and set up shop as a dealer. When the mine dried up a year and a half later, he was still trying to get a toehold in the business. Fed up with her husband's antics, his wife and three children boarded a ship to Paris, and Robert returned to Springfield, alone, where he once again became financially dependent on his father. The implosion of his mental health after his return was swift; he dressed and acted erratically and drank his meals. On September 19, 1911, encouraged by his father, he checked himself into the Brattleboro Retreat.

The retreat was avant-garde in its treatment of the mentally ill. In contrast to the demeaning and punitive practices employed at other asylums—including shackling patients

and locking them in isolation cells—Brattleboro Retreat patients were given private bedrooms and had a fair amount
of autonomy. Patients enrolled in continuing education
classes, worked in the facility's expansive gardens, and
tended to cows in its dairy. High-functioning patients were
even allowed to leave the campus on their own to mingle
with the townspeople.[3]

After interviewing Robert over the course of several
days, the residential psychiatrist recorded a diagnosis: Robert Wallace, he wrote, was a "constitutional psychopath."
Based on Robert's history of carousing, the psychiatrist
also suspected Robert suffered from "general paresis" or
neurosyphilis—a dementia caused when the bacteria that
causes syphilis, *Treponema pallidum*, infects the brain and
erodes one's sense of reality. Indeed, he noted, Robert exhibited classic neurosyphilis symptoms, including a loss of
social inhibitions, grandiose delusions, impaired judgment,
and bouts of melancholia.[4]

While he was living at the retreat, Robert began writing
a book of rhyming-verse stories for his three children, whom
he hadn't seen in more than a year. Titled *Behind the Garden
Wall*, the book is narrated by an insomniac, as Robert himself was, who is kept awake by the racket of insects in his
garden. One sleepless night, the narrator is visited by an elf
who hands him a key "as clear as glass" that enables him to
decipher the "babblings of each blossom, bug and bird" and
grants him entry into a whimsical world where mosquitoes
play baseball and crickets rescue ants from burning stumps.
No doubt Robert hoped that the book would be a way for

him to win the respect and admiration of his young children in a way he'd never quite managed to do in day-to-day life.[5]

But what is a children's book without pictures? It is only half complete. Robert inquired after local illustrators and was told of Elsie's work—perhaps from Christie himself, as both men were Masons and likely attended the same lodge meetings. For Elsie, it was a perfect opportunity: a satisfying, creative endeavor that would keep her occupied for months. She quickly agreed to work with Robert and the duo set a schedule. Every morning, Robert left the asylum and headed toward Myrtle Street, reaching Elsie's front door in fifteen minutes.

Unless eight-year-old George was too ill to go to school, they were alone. They worked at the kitchen table, Elsie sketching, Robert tweaking his prose and asking for Elsie's opinions.

Christie was fond of Robert and trusted him as a fellow Mason. After all, two of the guiding principles of the fraternal organization were "brotherly love" and "relief"—or helping people in need. Perhaps Christie also hoped that the project would improve his wife's mood and restore a sense of calm to his household.[6]

At first, Elsie was a bit guarded around this strange, dark-eyed man. She knew only the broadest outlines of his backstory. But the routine of a shared objective, the hammering out of an artistic vision, helped her overcome her reservations. She began to look forward to his visits. Unlike Christie, Robert loved to talk and was full of starry-eyed plans and enthusiasm for the future—despite his unfortunate past. It was odd to have this cheerful patter in the house, arousing to be alone with a man who was not her husband.

It was the first break in the morbid monotony of years of isolation. At first, I was silent, distrustful—not daring to believe that that house could hold normal, happy chatter. He thought me sullen. He came daily, bringing the manuscript, taking the drawings as they were finished.[7]

After noticing Robert routinely lumbering up the sidewalk to 13 Myrtle—to spend hours alone with Mrs. Christie Crowell—the neighbors began to gossip.

"Look at her!" they whispered—sharp eyes peering from every primly shuttered window, every neatly trimmed shrubbery or a seemingly empty street.

"Look at her!" the party-line telephones tingled, the backyard fences buzzed.

"Look at her! Didn't we say she'd come to this? One of those queer westerners."[8]

Elsie didn't give a damn what the neighbors thought of her. Nothing could turn her away from a relationship that had sparked her back to vibrancy.

Life seemed especially perilous to them both—a sense that was underlined when the RMS *Titanic* sank on April 15, 1912, after striking an iceberg on its maiden voyage from England to New York, killing more than 1,500 passengers. The outsized saga had caught the entire world by the throat. The *Vermont Phoenix* published daily updates on the "most terrible marine disaster ever known," including the harrowing accounts of survivors.[9]

Perhaps Elsie and Robert saw parallels to their own lives in the tragedy. The *Titanic* passengers had strolled up the gangway into the largest, most expensive ship ever built bristling with excitement, cheered by a throng, acutely aware of their significance and good fortune—only to perish in the icy waters of the Atlantic Ocean. Elsie and Robert had also sailed into their respective marriages buoyed by their families' enthusiasm and hope but now found themselves adrift and disillusioned.

As they continued working together, Elsie regaled Robert with tales of her beloved California, of growing up in a place that valued gumption and independent thought over surnames and piety. Robert was intrigued; California seemed the antithesis of the old-money, rule-bound environment he'd been raised in. Likewise, Robert stoked Elsie's ambitions with his own unbroken trust in a better time to come.

How about that richer life you wanted for yourself? Who was the blame because you failed to attain it?

How have you acted when opportunity came your way? Did you grab it with both fists, fearless of consequences?[10]

As the shadows cast by the towering elms on the wood-plank floor marked the passage of the days and weeks and months, the initial awkwardness between the pair melted into intimacy. Elsie began to confide in Robert, to tell him of her loveless marriage, of her loneliness, and Robert responded with empathy and kindness.

Perhaps his own tragic breakdown had taught him wisdom— helped him understand the alternating sullenness and wildness of this strange, gaunt creature who talked and laughed and cried and whispered at him, all in one breath, across the drawing board.

His face became wonderfully gentle as he watched me those days, as he tried to help me.[11]

An erotic undercurrent started coursing between them. Elsie was attention-starved and existentially bored. Robert was woman-starved and worldly. As the leaves turned gold and spiraled to the ground, as the evenings grew dimmer and colder, Elsie grew increasingly aware that her newfound happiness had an expiration date. The drawings for the book were almost complete. She dreaded the end of such a fulfilling endeavor—and of Robert's companionship.

But perhaps Elsie and Robert didn't need to part ways. Perhaps they could alter their fates and continue the artistic delight of their partnership. Robert's wife had already made it clear that she would continue being his spouse on paper only. From France, she had moved on to Switzerland, where she had enrolled their children in school. Robert and Elsie began to discuss. To suggest. To plot. To find a way to continue their collaboration . . . their relationship, which had since become something far more charged than friendship. Elsie's father was dead. So was her brother. She had a growing cognizance of her own mortality. Like the passengers on the *Titanic*, she had one life to live, one very precious life.

You may not be tragically unhappy—yet you aren't quite satisfied with your life, are you? Secretly you're rather sorry for yourself, feel you've never had as good a chance as the Other Fellow. BUT WHOSE FAULT IS IT? STOP AND THINK. HAVE YOU TREATED THE CHANCES THAT DID COME YOUR WAY?

Have you been willing to take chances, run risks, make changes, as that man or woman whom you envy?[12]

Elsie wanted to leave Vermont, feeling pulled toward California more than ever. For George's health, yes, but also from a deep-seated urge to be with her mother and surviving siblings—the people who so unsparingly loved and needed her. On the heels of the deaths of Paul and her father came more blows. That March, her sister Winifred's husband—the owner of a successful stationery store in San Francisco and the father of their two children—had killed himself by overdosing on morphine. Afterward, Winnie suffered a nervous breakdown that left her so weak that she was forced to use a wheelchair. And then her brother Phil, a recent Stanford graduate, suffered a freak accident in Chile, where he was working on a project to string power lines across the Andes. As he was inspecting a water boiler that was leaking gas, a coworker lit a match so they could better view the mechanism and the gas ignited, exploding the boiler and leaving Phil critically injured. He returned to California a broken man. Her family needed her. Her ailing son needed her. Elsie needed, wanted out.[13]

Quietly, Elsie and Robert hatched a plan.

Robert would do the talking. He had a silver tongue and an easy camaraderie with Christie, his fellow Mason, who still thought of Robert as a charity case, not an equal—and certainly not a romantic rival.

One Saturday afternoon that fall, Robert invited Christie to play a game of chess in the parlor, as a ruse to have a conversation with him. Elsie sat across the room, sketching and watching the two men face off over the wooden chess-board, struggling to keep her pencil from shaking. Robert glanced at her then turned to Christie.

He told Christie he might go to California, or Australia, or perhaps Alaska, to "try and forget and begin over." He twirled a chessman indifferently between his fingers.[14]

A long moment—that was like a tightening, trembling wire—then, coolly, casually, he said those words which were to change our lives.

"Your wife hasn't seemed well lately—If you'd like to send the boy and her out with me, for a visit to her mother— No expense to you, of course. I owe you both much more than that for your kindness, and the book—"

Christie agreed to Robert's proposition; it would do Elsie good to visit her kinfolk in California. When she heard her husband say she was free to go, she stood to put on the best performance of her short community-theater acting career.

I smiled. In a small, indifferent voice I said—"That would be nice." Still smiling, I walked quietly out of the room—quietly through the hall—through the dining room, kitchen and out to the place where my little lad sat, white face languid, fumbling at his toys—then with him in my arms, ran headlong into the woods—shouting for joy![15]

On October 14, 1912, she filed a "Petition and Citation for Guardian of Insane" at the probate court in downtown Brattleboro, promising to look after Robert. It was not a responsibility to be taken lightly. Vermont's public statutes contained dozens of clauses related to guardianship, which

Elsie now had to learn and follow. Each year, until the guardianship concluded, she would be required to file a detailed report summarizing Robert's progress and condition, including a description of his health, medical care, residence, and employment; an explanation of how she carried out her duties as guardian; and her opinion as to Robert's continued need of supervision.

Robert's bond was set for $2,500, a sum paid for by Christie's own father to assure the court that Elsie would have enough money to care for him.[16]

On November 1, Robert moved out of the Brattleboro Retreat, much to the dismay of the staff. "His discharge was not advised," his psychiatrist noted before adding, in a clear tone of disapproval, that "while on parole, nearly all of [Robert's] time was spent in this woman's [Elsie's] company."[17]

Meanwhile, at 13 Myrtle Street, Elsie packed up her belongings—the last letters from her father and brother, a few treasured books—burning with the secret knowledge that she and George were about to leave the little house forever.

What did I think as I went down that quiet street for the last time? I didn't think anything. We never do—in the great moments of our lives. Words, then, mean as little to us as they do to the dead or the newly born. But I felt—I felt an enormous desolation—in which there was no time, no space, through which I walked blindly, senselessly, on and on, and on—

I remember walking. And the strangeness of my feet, lifting, falling, lifting, falling. I remember the blankness of the silent

*houses—a blankness that hid, I knew, a living wall of eyes. I re-
member, just once, turning slowly . . . starting to look back . . .*

*Then I felt my little son's thin hand, and saw his troubled face
looking up into mine, and I turned and went on.*[18]

⁕

BY DEFYING DEEPLY entrenched cultural mores and choosing to forgo financial security to pursue her own self-
fulfillment, Elsie was taking ownership of her life in a way
that few women of the era dared contemplate. It's unclear
where Robert lived once they reached California, but pre-
sumably, because Elsie was his guardian, he lodged with the
Robinson family, now living in Berkeley.[19]

After finishing *Behind the Garden Wall*, the duo worked
on a second children's book. *Within the Deep Dark Woods*
featured the misadventures of a pet guinea pig named Gus,
who rides a Fourth of July rocket into a thicket of trees and
is taken in by forest creatures. Both books were printed in
the summer of 1913 by small San Francisco presses and received favorable reviews. Robert dedicated *Behind the Garden Wall* to his children, Janet, Dudley, and Dorcas. Elsie
dedicated *Within the Deep Dark Woods* to her son George.[20]

Elsie's growing portfolio helped her find subsequent
work. She illustrated two more books for young readers
that were published in 1914.[21]

Christie came to visit in 1915 and took his family to the
World's Fair in San Francisco. They watched demonstra-
tions of new technologies, including cars, airplanes, telephones, film, and cow-milking machines. The Sun-Maid

raisin girl, donning her trademark red sun bonnet, boarded a low-flying plane and pelted the crowd with the dehydrated fruit. The Underwood Typewriter company showed an eighteen-foot-high, fourteen-ton typewriter. Long lines formed for one of the most popular exhibits, "Stella," a full-sized nude painting of a woman reclining on a sofa, viewable to fairgoers for ten cents a head. As souvenirs, Christie bought George a suit and Elsie a vase.[22]

Despite the excitement of the fair, Christie's visit was fraught. Elsie had never outright told her husband that she wasn't returning to Brattleboro; she just knew it to be true in her heart. In letters, she kept finding excuses for prolonging their stay. It was clear that Elsie wasn't just "visiting her mother." Three years had passed. He pressed her to return to Brattleboro.

Would I come home? The request was not enthusiastic—the answer obvious. The boy could not survive removal. We tried to talk, but there was nothing to say. What could we say? I asked him again to come west—take a ranch. He answered again that it was impossible—he "couldn't leave The Family."[23]

Although Christie infrequently, and with great reluctance, sent her money, it wasn't enough to cover her living expenses. This withholding of funds was clearly an attempt to force her back to Vermont.

Elsie failed to find regular work after finishing the two readers, and George continued to suffer. She had thought that the more moderate weather of the Bay Area would be easier for him to breathe and was crestfallen when he still had coughing fits. Sometimes he spent the day in bed and

Elsie did what she could to bring him comfort, massaging his chest and burning jimson weed to decrease the inflammation of his airways. The rainy winter months, when coal and wood smoke hung heavy in the damp air, were the worst. *The boy sickened. His bones showed sharp beneath his blue skin.*[24]

To make matters worse, and despite their guardianship arrangement, Robert had decamped for the foothills of the Sierra Nevada, again caught up in gold fever and the fantasy of striking it rich. He'd even persuaded Elsie's brother Phil to join him in the adventure.

Elsie was concerned that Robert was chasing yet another delusion that would end in failure, as it had in Canada. But he proved her wrong: In August 1915, he and Phil struck gold in a deserted mine, a pocket of ore worth an estimated $500–$1,000. The find prompted the two men to take over the claim, certain they'd find more.[25]

The mine was in a rural area, Robert wrote Elsie, on the outskirts of an old boom town called Hornitos. The area was bone dry, the sun merciless, and the labor backbreaking. But his tone was jubilant; this was the big break he'd been waiting for. Very soon, he assured her, he'd be a rich man and all her day-to-day penuries would end—never again would she have to worry about being able to afford George's medicine.

Elsie viewed the news as a boon of a more immediate sort for George: the dry air of the California foothills, away from the foggy bay, was just what her son needed.

The more she thought about it, the more solid her decision became. She and George would pick up stakes and join Robert and Phil in the gold mines.

Only one obstacle barring you from Success, holding you back from Happiness . . . FEAR. Indecision can bankrupt you. Completely safe lives are completely dead ones.

You are as vital as your curiosity. As young as your own restlessness. As strong as your own courage.

If you want to really grow, really live—CUT OUT THE CAUTION AND THE CODDLING AND TAKE CHANCES—

You can't win unless you risk. If you risk, you land in many a mudhole. But you also achieve a mountaintop now and then. And for the sake of one mountaintop you should be willing to endure a million mudholes.

Human existence was never intended to be safe and sane.

Power and wisdom are the fruits of danger rather than of safety; of adventure, rather than of inertia; of restlessness, rebellion, hardship and discomfort, rather than resignation and comfort.[26]

These optimistic lines were surely easier to write in retrospect, for her path ahead would indeed be riddled with many mudholes.

Chapter 8

HORNITOS

PHOTO OF HORNITOS IN 1917,
during the period Elsie and George lived there.

*Image courtesy of Mariposa Museum and History Center,
Mariposa, California.*

TUCKED INTO THE REMOTE SIERRA NEVADA foothills at the southern tip of the Mother Lode, Hornitos was a town steeped in Western lore—a place where the grand tragicomedy of life had played out in isolated miner's cabins, whiskey-drenched saloons, chintz-filled brothels, and dark tunnels a thousand feet below the surface of the earth.

Its very origins were forged in violence. In 1850, a white "Law and Order Committee" in neighboring Quartzburg drove out, at rifle point, a group of Mexican miners, gamblers, and dancehall girls. The white vigilantes claimed to be clearing out vice but most likely coveted the Mexicans' mining claims. These outcasts, who landed in what would become Hornitos, would have the last laugh: Hornitos was even richer in gold than Quartzburg and would go on to become one of the most prolific mining districts in all of California.[1]

The name Hornitos—Spanish for "little ovens"—is of murkier provenance. Some say it refers to the above-ground tombs that the Mexicans used to bury their dead, which looked like adobe ovens. Others say it refers to the actual adobe ovens the Mexicans used for cooking. The definitive answer has been lost to the dustbin of history. But "little oven" is also an accurate description of summer in

Hornitos, when the temperature blasts past 100 degrees and the relentless sun bakes the vegetation into brown straw.

After news of Hornitos's gold strike spilled into the world, a stampede of men of every nationality and caliber arrived at this real-life El Dorado. Bandits, including the legendary—and likely fictitious—Joaquin Murrieta, were said to value the town's secluded location, not to mention the secret tunnel under the fandango hall, which gave them a head start whenever the sheriff's posse thundered into town.[2]

Buried treasure, fast women, an abundance of cheap booze—Hornitos was an adventurous young man's garden of delight. Miners stored their gold in small leather bags called pokes and paid for goods and services in gold dust, meted out one pinch at a time. Nuggets were sold to the local Wells Fargo agent, who shipped them to San Francisco on stagecoaches protected by riflemen riding shotgun. In its heyday, there was enough wealth in Hornitos to support a line of boutiques selling everything from French pastries to gold nugget jewelry to ambrotype photographs. At the San Nicholas Saloon, just below the Wells Fargo office, the "best of liquors, wines, ale, porter and all beverages desirable to the thirsty and wayworn" were offered "at all hours and in any style."[3]

In a brick-and-fieldstone building across from the central plaza, Domingo Ghirardelli sold groceries and worked on the chocolate confections that would someday make him famous.

But danger and misfortune continued to hang over Hornitos. Shocking stories of revenge killings and cold-blooded murder that took place in the small town were published in newspapers throughout California. Men who were friendly drinking buddies by day became truculent as night fell, until it was easier to reach for a rifle than a riposte. Accused criminals were shackled to an iron ring in the town's one-cell jail—which was fortified by two-foot-thick stone walls and built on bedrock to prevent anyone from trying to dig their way out—until they could be brought to justice.[4]

By the time Elsie and George arrived in the fall of 1915, however, Hornitos had begun its long slump toward ghost town status and fewer than 150 people remained, according to census records. After independent prospectors scooped up the "easy pickings" from the gravel streams and surface-level quartz veins, hard-rock mining operations had moved in to drill down to the deeper ore deposits. When those were tapped out, the town began to shut down. Ghirardelli's humble store, abandoned many years earlier, was slowly imploding into a pile of rubble. The bawdy houses were permanently shuttered, the fandango nights a feeble memory.[5]

But Hornitos's vicious legacy remained embedded in the town's very architecture: although the blood that reportedly stained every threshold had been hidden beneath successive coats of whitewash, bullet holes were still visible in door and window frames. Piles of charcoaled boards were all that was left of a Chinese neighborhood that had been torched by a racist mob decades earlier; a tall, double-sided iron door was all that remained of an opium den.[6]

Fortune hunters like Robert and Phil still occasionally blew into town, lured by the intoxicating thought of buried treasure. As the California pioneer and writer Dame Shirley wrote, "Gold mining is Nature's great lottery scheme." Robert and Phil hoped to win that lottery, but they had failed to disclose to Elsie just how deserted Hornitos was.[7]

When I came to Hornitos, the plaza had long been empty. The flagstones were caving in over the secret get-away tunnel that led from the Fandango Hall to old Ramon Martinez's saloon . . . and thence to a thousand coyote trails. In the crumbling adobe of the old walls, blue lapin was in bloom . . . [and] wild doves nested. And the old pans and picks rusted in the gorges where, half a century before, the owners had thrown them down.[8]

The housing "situation" was also rougher than she'd expected. Their lodgings, as such, consisted of an abandoned shack. It had no electricity, running water, or indoor toilet.

We proceeded to make a home for ourselves. We washed in the scummy water of the creek—drank the same water after boiling it. Cooked on anything that would go over a mesquite knot and under a frying pan.[9]

In the dry air, George began to behave like an ordinary child. With deep gratification, Elsie watched him play without stopping to gasp for air, without that petrified look in his eyes. *For the first time he was breathing free—glowing with the radiance of desert health.*[10]

If she could just keep him in Hornitos until he finished puberty, when his lungs would be more fully developed, she believed she could infuse him with enough health to last the rest of his life.[11]

Robert's claim, the Duncan Mine, comprised forty-four parched acres at the confluence of a seasonal creek and a ravine about a mile and a half south of Hornitos. The diggings, situated along a quartz vein, consisted of a series of open pits and shafts. In the late 1890s, the Duncan Mine produced 246 ounces of gold—worth about $440,500 at the time of this writing—but the site had been deserted for twenty years before Robert and Phil arrived. The two men spent their days crushing rock and searching for glints of gold, driven by the conviction that they'd find another rich pocket of ore.[12]

What little money Christie sent went far in Hornitos, where they moved into a cheap rented house and their biggest expenses were the tins of ham and bags of flour and beans purchased at Gagliardo's General Merchandise.[13]

For the second time in her life, Elsie embraced domesticity—this time knowing her labor was supporting the independent life she was creating. She hauled water from the creek, cooked over a campfire, and checked George's progress on his sixth-grade primers. (George was likely a student at Hornitos School, the only school in town—housed in a small white building with a wooden porch and picket fence, though school records were tossed or destroyed long ago.) It was coarse living—the opposite of her pampered life in Brattleboro. But there was freedom in this paring down, in dispensing with the stuffy Victorian protocols that regulated everything from cutlery to conversation. There was beauty in falling asleep to a symphony of crickets or the wind swishing through the trees. Their days were quiet and slow, ruled by the simple rhythms of the earth.[14]

Look back at your own life. When were you the happiest? Was it the night of that big banquet on which you had counted so much?

The trouble is that we start out with the wrong idea of pleasure. Whereas on the most ordinary occasion, for no reason whatever, joy wells in you like a tide. The leap of pleasure from the simplest things—a hearty handshake, a spray of flowers on a garden wall, the merry caper of a little dog, the tingle of the wind across your face—the crackle of a fire on a rainy night.[15]

Their bohemian idyll didn't last, however. Despite weeks of arduous work, Robert and Phil did not strike gold again. They resorted to milling the dumps of waste rock excavated by previous miners, but this was just worthless shale and schist. Their visions of easy prosperity quickly receding, they gave up working on the site altogether in January 1916.[16]

Phil, who needed medical attention related to the burn injuries he suffered in Chile, decided to return to the Bay Area. Robert stayed on, as did Elsie and George.

By this time, Elsie and Robert's friendship had blossomed into a passionate affair, though Elsie would deny it for the rest of her life—even after Christie discovered evidence of the relationship.

The pair must have felt protected in their newfound anonymity in Hornitos, with its transient population of miners.

They'd effectively erased their pasts and social status and were living among common folks who weren't liable to ask pesky questions to which there were no easy answers. For although upper- and middle-class society considered cohabitation sinful, it was more acceptable among the working class.[17]

When Christie learned his wife was living in Hornitos "alone" with Robert, he was furious. Elsie denied she and Robert were the only adults in the small bungalow, insisting—rather improbably—that other men boarded with them.

Christie cut off her allowance, trying to force her back to Brattleboro. But Elsie had seen her son's seemingly miraculous improvement in Hornitos and was determined to stay. *I had come to the desert to save the boy's life.*[18]

Without financial support from Christie, Elsie's situation grew increasingly dire.

Picture yourself, strapped, with a sick child depending on you in a wilderness without offices, industries of any sort or even homes needing service. Facing a prospect like that, try and pick yourself a career! What assets had I? None—outside monumental nerve. So I figured that—there being no precedents for gals in my fix—I'd make one.[19]

Her desperation drove her to apply for a job at the last hard-rock mine still operating in Mariposa County—the Ruth Pierce Mine, four miles north of Hornitos.

The operation, with only ten full-time employees, was just a shell of what it once was, but you could still hear the constant and thunderous clanging of the mine's ten stamps—thousand-pound weights that dropped eight

inches one hundred times per minute to break rocks, separating gold from quartz—for miles in any direction.[20]

Robert, who likely started working at the Ruth Pierce
Mine after the Duncan Mine failed, tried to talk her out of
it. Women had ancillary roles in mining communities—as
wives, cooks, schoolteachers, boardinghouse owners, and the
like—but they left most of the perilous digging to men. Not
only was mining back-breaking work, it was also perilous. It
was easy to die in a mine. You could fall down a shaft. Drown
in a claustrophobic tunnel if the sump pump malfunctioned
and groundwater flooded in. Get buried alive if the timbers
holding up the drifts failed. Burn to death if methane pooled
underground and your carbide lamp sparked an explosion.[21]

Elsie was well aware of the risks. Mining deaths were
regularly covered in newspapers. A hard-rock mining disaster at the Speculator Mine in Butte, Montana, would make
headlines when a three-ton electrical cable, part of an underground sprinkler system, slipped 2,500 feet down a shaft,
stripping away the lead covering and exposing the oiled par-
affin that was used as an insulator. When a foreman lifted
his lamp to inspect the damage, the open flame ignited the
cable, which acted as a giant wick and turned the shaft into
a chimney, burning timbers and consuming oxygen. Of the
168 miners who died that day, the majority suffocated. A few
of them managed to survive a few days in the tunnels, where
they scratched out notes to their loved ones and waited for a
rescue that never came.[22]

Hornitos had had its own share of fatalities. A few
years before Elsie and George arrived, an eighteen-year-old

mucker, the son of the mine blacksmith, lost his balance
and fell down a hundred-foot shaft to his death. His father
had helped hoist his son's mangled body to the surface.[23]

Elsie's new male acquaintances took Robert's side, at-
tempting to talk "sense" into her.

*A woman—a lady—mining? It was inconceivable.
Gallantly—and with exquisite tact—they offered to ante up for
my keep and just let me loaf around. But I couldn't see it. I not
only needed, but I wanted, to be in the show.*[24]

Before she worked up the gumption to knock on the
superintendent's door and ask for a job, she fashioned a
miner's getup of sorts, sewing a long, loose skirt from tent
canvas and borrowing a man's flannel shirt, hobnailed mining boots, and sombrero. She hoped that if she looked the
part, she'd get the part. Knocking on the superintendent's
door took guts. She spared him no detail about her situation, telling him about her son's precarious health, about
her estranged husband's seeming indifference. She was
blunt: she needed money. And she promised to work as hard
as any man on his payroll.

*I admitted I wasn't any Powerful Katrinka. But if some of
those gangling males could man a pick handle, why couldn't I?
He let me have my way.*[25]

And so Elsie became a miner.

She often took George, now twelve, with her to work.
She knew a mine was no place for a child. But she considered the possibility of George having an asthma attack, at
school or alone in their cabin, four miles away, to be an even
greater—and more likely—danger.

The Ruth Pierce Mine consisted of a central six-hundred-foot-deep shaft that had six drifts, or tunnels, branching out from it as it followed a four-foot-wide quartz vein deep into the earth. Elsie became a "roust-about," taking a series of menial jobs, sometimes laboring in the cool tunnels, other times above ground.[26]

I sat on the dump—often with sonny helping—under a 114-degree sun and picked over the ore after it had emptied from the skip . . . looking for the tell-tale streak, feeling for the tell-tale jag that might lead to a pocket.

Mucking, panning, timbering—during the first summer it was all one blurred delirium. Of one thing only was I constantly and acutely conscious—that heat.

Heat—God, what heat!

Days that ate like acid. Days when the flesh shriveled and shrank from the scorched bone . . . when the brain withered to a dry kernel within the skull . . . when, on a mashed finger, the blood powdered to dust before the vein could empty.

I took any job that came along—glad to get it. I was still a lanky outfit. But I couldn't let that matter—any more than a man could let it matter. It's amazing what you can do, if you can't do anything else.

I mucked—which means shoveling mud and broken stone into a wheelbarrow . . . carting it off . . . clearing the tunnel or shaft so the men can work on the face of the rock.

I helped timber—bracing beams against the slimy, slipping menace of the hanging-wall until the men could nail them fast . . . feeling the ooze rise steadily up about my knees . . . feeling the weight and horror of the bulging darkness settle down upon my skull.

I "gophered" through old diggings . . . crawling, belly flat, through eighteen-inch fissures . . . under rotting timbers that whined and cracked.

Hour after hour the sun clanged across the hard, hot anvil of the earth. Hour after hour we crawled . . . gray specks . . . in an infinity of blazing light. No thoughts. No emotions. No sense of outer world or inner plan. Only that blistering heat. Only that blasting light . . .

Then the God-given relief of night. At first I could only sprawl headlong where I dropped. Too tired to eat or clean myself or even undress. Too beaten to think. Beauty above? Adventure below? They did not exist. Only coolness existed . . . blessed coolness . . . blessed darkness—

I had crossed the wall—left woman's world behind me. Now I was with men . . . always with men . . . only men. I heard no other voices . . . knew no other problems.

When they raced up the shaft—away from the shot—I ran with them. When they piled down into the shaft again—fumbled, gasping, through the half-cleared air to peer for the miracle of gold across the face of the rock, I piled and peered with them.

Sometimes we didn't get up quick enough, or came back too soon. Then, when a shot went wrong, I held them in my arms . . . gagging, cursing, howling huddles of pain . . . while some calloused fist yanked slivers of steel and rock from mangled eyes and flesh. Or—when the emergency was graver—sat on their struggling chests, holding the ether cone by main force, until they went limp beneath me, while someone rode hell-bent for the nearest doctor, ten miles away.

Scared? I was so scared that my toe nails would have curled if there'd been room! But when your only chance of living is to keep going . . . and it's a cinch you'll die like a smashed toad if you stop . . . why you just naturally cut out the hiccoughs and wiggle right along.[27]

Her family would find it hard to believe that Elsie worked as a common mucker in the Ruth Pierce Mine. Yet despite the very real possibility of death or injury, Elsie prospered. After she proved herself to be a hardworking and capable colleague, the other miners accepted her into their fold.

Not only did she make enough money to sustain herself and George, she came to understand the power of her own grit.

Sorry for me? I'm tempted to let you get away with the idea. Being—in spite of everything—feminine, there's nothing I love to feel as much as the patter of pitying tears. But the simple truth is that I had the time of my life . . . and so would almost any other woman under the same circumstances.

What happened to me in the desert? Comradeship happened to me. And if there is a finer thing on earth, I do not know it.[28]

Not since she swiped watermelons with the neighborhood boys back in Benicia did she feel so fully herself—not at Northfield, not inside Lindenhurst, certainly not within the confines of the house she shared with Christie on Myrtle Street. In Hornitos, she could let out a wild laugh over a meal. She could flop on the ground after a day of hard work or join her fellow miners around a campfire to belt out "Silver Threads Among the Gold" or "Love's Old Sweet

Song." In Hornitos, Elsie experienced a near total erasure of formality and class. It was a way of being in the world that she found equally liberating and intoxicating. Beneath the labels imposed by society, there were commonalities linking all people, a shared humanity.

I made camp with a murderer one night. He was a mining surveyor. He was staking claims. After chow we sat by the fire and talked. He told me about the murders. There were five of them. He told me about his dog, and the best time to plant sweet peas, and a fishing trip he once took with his dad. And then about his Little Girl. He showed me her picture—she was lovely.

After that, I lay awake for a while. I could hear the murderer snoring over behind the mesquite bush. He snored just like other men. I looked up at the stars. They blinked back at me—and they didn't blink a bit brighter at me than they did at the murderer. We both looked alike to the stars.[29]

Hornitos was real life, and she inhaled every rough, dirty, undignified bit of it.

HORNITOS . . . over the years my heart turns back to you! And again I hear the killdeers calling from the dry creek bottom— and smell the acrid fragrance of your baked, white soil—and taste the sweat-salt on my cracking lips . . . and see my boy come running down the hill against the high, bright light.[30]

❧

IN AUGUST 1916, Christie wrote to Elsie asking for a divorce. He'd already met another woman, someone of his class, whom he wanted to marry: Dr. Grace Burnett, a highly regarded (read: not embarrassing to the Crowells) doctor, the first female physician in Brattleboro.[31]

Elsie knew this day would come; Christie had every right to move on as well. And yet it was still shocking to read his words, which signaled a definitive end to the possibility of a reconciliation. She'd never fully pondered the ultimate consequence of her insistence on staying in California. *So solemn was marriage, so shameful divorce, that the thought of separation had never as yet crossed my mind.*[32]

In 1916, only 1 percent of marriages ended in divorce. Many Americans believed divorced men and women were morally suspect and that divorced mothers, in particular, were to blame for undermining family values. That last jab was one reason that women often continued to refer to themselves as a "Mrs.," or marked their civil status as "widowed," rather than admitting that their marriage had ended.[33]

Californians wouldn't be able to pursue no-fault divorce, the country's first such law, until 1970. In 1916, couples had to prove one of the statutory "fault" grounds—usually adultery, abandonment, cruelty, or neglect, and for a divorce to be granted, a judge had to find the defendant guilty of the charges.

Elsie was only vaguely aware of the complexities of ending her marriage. But now that divorce loomed irrepressibly on her horizon, it behooved her to move quickly and make the first legal move. Because the only thing worse than filing for divorce was being named as the defendant in a divorce suit—especially for a woman. In the court of

public opinion, the spouse who filed for divorce—the plaintiff—was seen as the innocent, aggrieved party, and the defendant was assumed guilty as charged. Likewise, being the
plaintiff increased the woman's chances of gaining custody
of children and receiving alimony.[34]

In early December, Elsie hitched a ride to the county
seat in Mariposa, where she consulted with an attorney
named R. B. Stolder—a man with a caterpillar mustache
bristling over his lip—whose office was directly across from
the superior court building. On Stolder's advice, Elsie fired
the opening shot: she filed for divorce, accusing Christie
of desertion and demanding custody of George and $100 a
month in alimony. The lawsuit filing was mailed to Christie
in Vermont and duly published in the *Mariposa Gazette*.[35]

Christie had a choice. Since he, too, wanted a divorce,
he could simply not respond to the lawsuit, and, assuming
Elsie proved her grounds, their marriage would end with
Christie being found guilty and accepting the brunt of social scorn. Or else he could drum up his own allegations for
divorce and try to make Elsie suffer the fallout, including
possibly losing custody of George.

Christie decided to respond with aggression. He
counter-sued Elsie for divorce, alleging willful desertion—
and adultery.[36]

The language of his complaint was unsparing: The
"petitioner avers that the said Elsinore R. Crowell, did, to
wit, on the 1st day of September 1913, and on diverse other
days and times during the said year of 1913 to the present
time, commit the crime of adultery [in California] with one

Robert Wallace, and others to your petitioner at present unknown."[37]

Christie was clearly trying to ruin her reputation. He also alleged that, because she had "deserted and abandoned" him, he was under "no legal obligation whatsoever to provide anything" for her support.

The adultery allegation did not surprise Elsie, but it left her boiling. She believed he'd accused her of it out of spite. It was possible, though, that Christie was merely trying to protect his own standing: as a conservative Baptist, he believed the Bible only permitted divorce in cases of adultery.

Some day it will seem incredible that any woman should have faced such shame, such deliberate torture, as I was now to face.

Adultery was a crime. In colonial New England, adulterous couples had been banished, whipped, and even hanged. In the early decades of the twentieth century, adultery convictions in Vermont still carried harsh sentences: the state's "chastity and morality" statutes decreed that adulterers could be imprisoned for up to five years, fined $1,000, or both. (The law wouldn't be repealed until 1981.) During Elsie's last few years in Brattleboro, Vermont averaged thirty-three adultery prosecutions a year, with the guilty parties often serving prison terms. In two cases from February 1916, for example, the *Brattleboro Reformer* reported that three "fornicators" were sentenced to one- or two-year terms.[38]

The male judges and all-male juries of the day were more punitive toward women who had affairs than men. In a 1911 case from West Wardsboro, Vermont, for example, the jury acquitted a man who shot and killed his wife's lover after surprising them in bed, finding the husband had acted in "self-defense." Meanwhile, the wife was locked up.[39]

Elsie denied she'd had sex with Robert, which seems hard to believe, given Robert's overtly sexual past and Elsie's desire for passion. Nonetheless, in her cross-complaint, Elsie stated that Christie had accused her of adultery *maliciously and for the sole purpose of causing her great mental suffering and unpleasant notoriety.*[40]

In a one-two punch, Christie also sued for custody of George, claiming that Elsie was "keeping said child under such conditions and in such circumstances because of her relations with one Robert Wallace as are detrimental to the best interests of said child." To strengthen his argument, he somehow finagled a copy of Robert's private psychiatric records. Robert's "Physician's Certificate," appended to the lawsuit, consisted of the opinions of the two doctors who examined Robert over a five-day period in 1911 at the Brattleboro Retreat and determined that he suffered from "chronic alcoholism," "mental deterioration," and "grandiloquent ideas for acquiring wealth."[41]

Because divorce was so rare, it was considered newsworthy by local papers, which recounted each motion filed and appearance made in a scandalous, Page Six–style fashion. The *Crowell v. Crowell* saga would play out in newspapers on both sides of the country for over a year, in a slow-moving, long-distance, and acrimonious game of legal ping-pong.

How was I feeling about that man in the east—about the cruel unfairness of it all? A man can put a thing like that behind him—walk away. But a woman can't. A woman keeps chewing things over. So while I was doing all these man things, how was I feeling as a woman? I was feeling mean. As far as my personal desires went, there was just one thing I wanted to do: commit one of the most complete murders in human history.

But there was the boy.[42]

By rejecting a conventional life, Elsie had inadvertently jeopardized the one thing that mattered most to her: her relationship with her son. Her audacity had resulted in George's improved health, true, but now she faced a new risk: having her son taken away from her.

Chapter 9

TYPEWRITER

ELSIE LIKELY LEARNED TO TYPE ON THIS TYPEWRITER,
discovered by the authors during a research trip to Hornitos. It was in
a back room of the long-shuttered post office, alongside other artifacts
and detritus, covered in thick, undisturbed dust.

Photo courtesy of the authors.

T HE TINY HORNITOS POST OFFICE SAT CATTY-corner to the tumbled-down remains of Ghirar-delli's former store and wasn't in much better shape. The white stucco overlaying the loose fieldstone walls had mostly worn away, giving it a shabby, half-ghosted appearance. Built only a few feet off of Main Street, dust clouds billowed through the open French doors whenever a Model T rumbled past.[1]

In 1917, as the dry season slowly starched the lush vegetation into brittle sprigs, Elsie could often be found inside the post office's hushed confines, where the dim interior provided a welcomed respite from the merciless sun.

At first, she stopped by to conduct business—to mail or collect personal or divorce-related correspondence. But as the months wore on, she walked through the doors with no agenda other than to visit with the postmistress—the prim Black woman in wire-framed spectacles who stood behind the counter.

In Luola Rodgers, Elsie would find a true friend, a cheerleader, and, after spending her days surrounded by men, some much needed female companionship. Luola— thirty-eight years old to Elsie's thirty-four—had led an existence that was in many ways as unique as Elsie's. Her father, Moses Rodgers, was born a slave in Missouri and brought to Hornitos as a teenager in the late 1840s when his owner came to mine for gold, but he was liberated when California entered the Union as a free state in 1850. Moses then began a spectacular rise to regional fame and fortune by using his mining acumen to run the Washington and Mount Gaines Mines. In its heyday, the Washington Mine employed eighty-five workers who fed ore into a thirty-stamp mill, which rendered $2.2 million worth of gold by 1900 (about $64 million today).[2]

Moses married a Black woman from Stockton, Sarah Quivers, and the couple had five daughters, the third of whom was Luola. Because Hornitos didn't have a high school, at some point the family relocated to Sarah's native Stockton, a city of fourteen thousand some ninety miles away, so that their girls could continue their educations. Luola, however, decided to remain in Hornitos. She moved in with the Olcese family, first working for them as a housekeeper, and later helping Mr. Olcese, the town postmaster, sort mail. Decades later, she unofficially stepped into the position herself.[3]

Like Elsie, Luola was well acquainted with grief. Both of her parents were dead, and the year before Elsie arrived in Hornitos, Luola's sister Vivian, the first Black woman to graduate from UC Berkeley, had died, at thirty, of typhoid fever—the same disease that killed Elsie's brother Paul.[4]

In Hornitos, both women moved at the fringes of the town's social structure. Both were single, middle-aged, and living unconventional lives. Luola stood out for her dark skin. Elsie for her ad hoc miner's getup and her domestic arrangement. By now, most Hornitians knew that Elsie was shacking up with a man who wasn't her husband and working as a grunt at the Ruth Pierce Mine. The old-timers had watched waves of gold-seekers come and go over the decades, but Elsie seemed to be the first "lady miner" that anyone could remember.

Between postal customers, the two women traded confidences across the arched counter window, discussing the circumstances that had landed them in the fading town and kept them there.

Luola preferred the quiet pace of Hornitos. After living with the Olcese family, she moved in with a childhood friend, Jennie Gagliardo, who managed her family's general store and was also single. Luola had a great fondness for children and filled her dress pockets with gumballs and jellybeans to hand out whenever a child stopped by the post office. If she saw children walk past struggling with a heavy load of groceries, she'd rush out from behind the counter to help carry the parcels. In her spare time, she taught teenage girls to sew on an ancient treadle machine kept in the post office's back storeroom or worked on intricately embroidered linens—one of which was shown at the 1915 World's Fair, the same exposition Elsie, Christie, and George had attended. But at a time when *The Birth of a Nation*—a film extolling the "glories" of the Ku Klux Klan—was the highest-grossing film in America, one can only imagine the painful "otherness" Luola may have felt living as a person of color in Hornitos.[5]

As the two women grew more comfortable around each other, Elsie worked up the courage to tell Luola her dearest dream: she wanted to become a full-time, professional writer. She recalled the comfort and validation she derived from reading books borrowed from the Brattleboro library and the deep satisfaction she felt as she cobbled a story together for *John Martin's Letters*. She wanted to return to creative work, and not just aimed at children: she wanted to reach adult readers as well.

It was, after all, the heyday of American magazines. Dozens of popular magazines launched between 1885 and 1905, including *McClure's*, *Cosmopolitan*, and *Popular Mechanics*, fueled by the creation of brand-name products. Until the late 1800s, stores carried household items in bulk—barrels of generic rice, flour, coffee, etc.—and consumers brought their own containers to be filled with goods and weighed by the merchant. The advent of packaged goods, sold under distinct company or brand names, exploded the commercial landscape. Procter & Gamble's Ivory—the "99 44/100% Pure" soap—debuted in 1879 with the catchy logo "It Floats." P&G took out elaborately illustrated ads in national magazines to introduce Ivory to Americans and the marketing investment paid off in spades; instead of asking merchants for generic "white soap," customers requested Ivory by name. Other manufacturers followed suit, and soon magazines were filled with eye-catching ads for Campbell's Soup, Victor "Talking Machines" (early records), Quaker Oats, and Lipton Tea, among dozens of other branded products.[6]

Magazines quickly found they could make more money selling advertisements than by selling subscriptions. Publishers had stumbled onto a winning economic formula: sell magazines for less than the cost of publishing them to boost circulation numbers, then use the large circulation numbers to attract fat-cat advertisers. After US magazines decreased their prices to as little as ten cents a month, their total circulation tripled between 1890 and 1905.[7]

With the proliferation of magazines came an increased demand for writers to supply editorial content—everything from in-depth reportage to poetry and short stories. The November 1914 issue of *McClure's*, for example, consisted of a whopping 208 pages and included a lengthy feature on how American households had used the telephone since its invention, thirty-eight years earlier. (*McClure's* reported that phones were "abolishing" loneliness in rural areas because solitary housewives could now connect with friends and family nationwide and that farmers were increasingly conducting business over the phone instead of in person.) Another article from the same issue delved into the lucrative international trade of art forgery. But most of the issue's pages were dedicated to fiction, in the form of seven short stories that ranged from a romance to a murder mystery. Magazine work had launched the careers of many fledgling writers who'd become household names, including Ida Tarbell, Willa Cather, O. Henry, Rudyard Kipling, and Zane Grey.[8]

Elsie aspired to join their ranks. But she had a logistical problem that seemed insurmountable in a tiny, isolated town like Hornitos: she'd recently learned that magazine submissions had to be typed. While *John Martin's Letters* had published her children's stories in her tidy cursive, busy editors at publications of the stature of *McClure's* and *Cosmopolitan* didn't have time to decipher a writer's chicken scratch.

Elsie complained to Luola that she didn't own a typewriter and was too poor to buy one. Luola's face brightened. She turned and disappeared into the dark storeroom at the back of the post office and came back lugging an ancient Smith Premier No. 2 typewriter in a metal carrying case, complete with exercise charts for learning the "touch system" of typing.

"Go to it," she urged Elsie, setting the heavy machine on the counter.[9]

It was a small thing, the loan of an outdated typewriter. But it represented so much more: at a time when Elsie felt uncertain about so many things in her life, Luola had faith in her ambition. This was the encouragement she needed to give her dream her best shot.

Elsie hauled the clunky machine back to her bungalow and heaved it onto an old packing box to use as a table. She dragged over a large kerosene can to use as a chair and cut a length of butcher paper to wind into the carriage.

The Smith Premier didn't have a shift key to change the case of the letters. Instead it was built with two separate keyboards, referred to as fingerboards in the accompanying pamphlet, the top one for uppercase, the bottom one for lowercase. It was an upstrike or "blind" typewriter—the keys struck the bottom of the platen, so the writer couldn't see the line she was typing unless she pulled the carriage forward to peek at it.[10]

Following the chart, Elsie spread her calloused fingertips over the keys, index fingers on the F and J, little fingers on the A and semicolon. The goal was to type by touch alone so that your inability to see what you were typing wouldn't matter. She tied a towel around her head to cover her eyes, per the instructions, and began doing drills, firmly striking the keys and thumbing the ovular space bar.

After she mastered the finger positioning, she worked on high-frequency words: "my, by, try, turn." Then, a series of sentences, some of them oddly didactic: "The chains of habit are generally too small to be felt till they are too strong to be broken. Few of the things that come to the man who waits are the things he has been looking for."

Each evening—after working nine hours in the mine and walking four miles back to town to cook Robert and George a hasty dinner, clean up, and go over George's lessons—she sat before the machine and typed by candlelight, the quiet evening broken by the *clack-clack-clack* of keys slapping the platen and the triumphant *ding!* when she reached the edge of the paper and had to drag the carriage back to its starting position.

I "rassled" with words, stopped to cook a rabbit—wrote again—stopped to kill a rattlesnake—wrote again—stopped to mend overalls or work out a Boy Scout knot—went on again, while the stars flared and faded . . . and the morning light flushed, then flamed—

I grin to-day when I read requests from ambitious youngsters asking how they shall begin writing . . . or whines from temperamental oldsters who complain that their genius is being frustrated because they can't "have the proper conditions for writing." Proper conditions? I wonder what they are? I never have known them. How did I start writing? After everything else was done.[11]

In a few weeks, her skills were advanced enough to transcribe a short story she'd written by hand. It was a tale she'd concocted during her long hike to and from work—dodging rattlesnakes hidden in the high grass in summer and enduring icy lashes of rain in the winter—as she passed the cattle ranches lining either side of the road to the mine.

Many of the plotlines were pulled from her own experiences. In a short story titled "The Little Maverick," the young female protagonist, "Ricky," was born into a Hornitos ranching family and is *mannish in dress, in talk, in ambition and enterprise*—a woman who claimed *all masculine rights and then some*.

On Western cattle ranches, a "maverick" is an unbranded calf that is born on the range and doesn't follow its mother, a term that also described Ricky, who defined herself in opposition to her *sedate* and *composed* New Hampshire mother.

When Ricky's mother tries to feminize her unconventional daughter by sending her to *Miss Smyth's Seminary* in San Francisco to be *roped, branded and halter-broken*, Ricky refuses to conform and becomes a corrupting influence on the other female students. After returning to Hornitos, she talks her way into a successful business partnership with a handsome young rancher, then buys a long-deserted gold mine. She soon discovers, however, that the men she hires to work in her mine have a "fundamental contemptuous distrust" of their female boss. This friction between Ricky and her male employees reaches a dangerous climax one night when she descends into the mine and a disgruntled employee turns off the sump pump, allowing the shaft to fill with groundwater. Ricky nearly drowns before the brawny rancher appears to rescue her. The story is a convoluted tale of female liberation and workplace politics with a dash of cowboy romance thrown in. But as she pulled the last sheet of "The Little Maverick" from the Smith Premier, she felt hopeful.

Modesty never having been my besetting sin, I decided to sell my First Story to the Atlantic Monthly.[12]

The *Atlantic Monthly*, launched in 1857, was then the country's most prestigious literary magazine, publishing the likes of Robert Frost, Ralph Waldo Emerson, and Harriet Beecher Stowe. Elsie proudly carried her story to the post office, where she folded the pages into an envelope and carefully wrote the *Atlantic*'s Boston address on the front before sealing it. Luola weighed the letter on her Triner Scale, and as she doled out the postage in 1¢ and 2¢ Washington stamps, she must have felt a vicarious thrill at Elsie's bold stab at something beyond their remote, contracted lives.[13]

And then there was nothing to do but wait.

And wait.

Weeks later, a reply finally arrived. Luola handed the envelope to Elsie and watched as Elsie's excitement turned to crushing disappointment: the *Atlantic* had rejected her story and returned the manuscript. She walked back to her cabin with her tail feathers clipped.

The rejection letter did contain a tip, however: the editor suggested she contact a New York agent named Lewis Allen Browne, who helped writers place magazine pieces. The agency Browne worked for, Wildman Magazine and News Service, took a small commission of each article it sold. Elsie sent "The Little Maverick" to Browne and he

responded. Thus began a lively, cross-country correspondence—Browne from his gleaming Manhattan office, Elsie
in her dusty middle-of-nowhere shack—in which Browne
gave Elsie a crash course in the fundamentals of good writing for an adult audience.[14]

Much of Browne's advice was ripped from the pages of
a guide called *Writing to Sell*, which Wildman Magazine and
News Service marketed to would-be writers. It contained
classic tips on how to grab a reader's attention, plot a story,
and arrive at a satisfying conclusion—precisely the type of
instruction that Elsie needed.

"Writers who succeed," the book declared, "must know
and feel their characters, understand the stories, fiction or
otherwise, that they paint. In this study of experience they
learn the lesson of appeal . . . you must cultivate a habit
of analysis, of observation of every kind of human nature
with which you come in contact."[15]

Browne reworked her story, "The Little Maverick,"
and sent it to *Black Cat* magazine, a highly regarded literary publication headquartered in Salem, Massachusetts.
Devoted entirely to fiction, *Black Cat* billed itself as "the
cleverest short story magazine in America."[16]

With a circulation of fifty thousand, *Black Cat*'s editorial page advised that the magazine "pays nothing for the
name or reputation of a writer" and "pays not according
to length," but "to strength." This democratic approach
helped many authors establish themselves as literary lights.
Among them was Jack London, who was struggling to pay
the rent when its publisher, Herman Umbstaetter, printed

his first story, "A Thousand Deaths." Published in May 1899, the piece was about a mad scientist who repeatedly kills and resurrects his son. London would later credit Umbstaetter with saving "my literary life, if not my literal life. . . . The marvellous, the unthinkable thing Mr. Umbstaetter did was to judge a story on its merits and to pay for it on its merits. Also, and only a hungry writer can appreciate this, he paid immediately upon acceptance."[17]

The *Black Cat* editors were captivated by Elsie's tale of a lariat-swinging, freethinking female entrepreneur and published "The Little Maverick" in its July 1918 issue as the lead story.[18]

This success reassured Elsie that she wasn't wasting her time elaborating plots in her head as she lay awake in the predawn light or roamed the bald hills surrounding Hornitos. She took to heart Browne's suggestions that she develop an eye for human motivation and desire, the elements that fired the engine of any story. In Hornitos, she had an opportunity to study a wide range of humanity in the form of the solitary male miners who were drawn to her doorstep by the scent of baking bread and a longing for home. Although she'd at first been wary of these men—who looked like a menacing band of roughnecks as they trooped through the dust with sunburned faces and heavy boots—over time she'd become a sort of den mother to many of them, and had come to appreciate them as individuals, each with his own aspirations and, often, a troubled backstory.

She began to see them as rich literary characters. Tough-tender men started to people her fiction, interacting with her own brash alter-ego female protagonists. The central tension of her early stories features misunderstandings between characters from different socioeconomic classes, or women fighting patriarchal double standards. Elsie's heroines behaved as Elsie did in her own life: as freely—and as lustily—as men.

In "Buck Calhoun's Woman," published in the pulp *Breezy Stories*, a miner and a prostitute fall in love and move in together. *They were having the time of their lives*, Elsie wrote in the story. *And they weren't married. And they didn't give a darn.* The couple live a sweet romance until a group of god-squadders from the local *Women's Uplift Society* begins to hound them. Elsie wrote the story while she herself was "living in sin" with Robert, at a time when most Americans viewed cohabitation as immoral and some towns considered it a jailable offense.[19]

In "Shall the Woman Tell?," published in *McClure's*, a conservative rancher falls for a free-spirited socialite. On their wedding night, the bride must decide whether to tell her husband that she's not a virgin. She rages at a society that allowed men to have "reckless experiments" in their youth, but not women: *Weren't her body and mind and soul her own property to be used as she chose? Why should any man demand from any woman a reckoning of her past?*[20]

She depicts Californians (stand-ins for herself) as nonconformists who embody progressive ideals and New Englanders (stand-ins for the Crowells) as dour puritans who cling to rigid dogmas. In story after story, she frames characters from Vermont, and specifically from Brattleboro, as the antagonists, full of "restraint and intolerance," "with ice in their blood," people who are incapable of warmth, empathy, or passion.

In Brattleboro, her writing was purely a creative endeavor, a distraction from her loveless marriage, an amusement for her chronically ill child, a break from the stultifying monotony of housewifery. In Hornitos, though, her writing acquired a new urgency: she wondered if she was skilled enough to make a living as a writer.

I couldn't stay in the mines forever. Some day we'd have to leave. What then? Comparatively easy to live in the hills where rent and grocery bills hardly existed—and a pair of overalls was a complete wardrobe. But when we went back to the city? What could I do in a city?[21]

As her divorce case dragged on at the Mariposa Superior Court, she often thought of the pampered life she'd left behind. Her father-in-law had recently died, and the black wreath of mourning must have hung once again on the front door of Lindenhurst, where Mrs. Crowell and Christie remained, *mousing about their mammoth mansion*. In the space of a few years, she'd gone from belonging to the New England aristocracy—a world of petticoated servants and fish forks—to squatting in a demimonde of unwashed men and meals scooped from a common pot. She preferred the warmth of the common pot over the regimentation of the fish fork, however, and suspected that other women would, too.[22]

Ninety-nine out of one hundred women would give their eye teeth to live, at least once in their lives, exactly as I did . . . without benefit of housekeeping, and in the exclusive and highly

diverting association of cowboys, gamblers, miners, hobos, bar-
keeps and various incognito gents who traveled fast and light
and answered no questions. And if you don't believe that most of
the Model Wives and Mothers of your acquaintance would leap
at the chance of swapping their jobs for such adventure—just
ask 'em![23]

In the fall of 1917, however, she received a crushing legal blow: Christie's divorce case had sailed through the
Vermont court, and a mere three months after he filed it,
a judge ruled in his favor. The Windham County Superior
Court found Elsie guilty of "willful desertion" and "adultery" and had granted Christie a divorce. Elsie's case in California was subsequently dismissed. Although their divorce
was a logical outcome of an icy marriage, the stakes had
now risen dramatically: the same court that ruled her an
adulteress must now decide which parent should be granted
custody of thirteen-year-old George.

❧

ELSIE'S ODDS DIDN'T look good. At the time, courts generally awarded children under seven to the mother, in what
was known as the "tender years" doctrine, and children
older than seven to the father—especially if they were boys.
Class also factored into the decision. Christie was financially
secure while Elsie's income was erratic, and in an era before
mandated child support, courts usually favored the more
solvent parent.[24]

Distraught at the possibility of losing her son, Elsie sat
down at the Smith Premier to formulate the most difficult

and urgent piece of writing she'd ever composed: an argument laying out the reasons why she should retain custody of George. During the divorce saga, Elsie's lawyer advised her not to reply to Christie's lawsuit; doing so would have automatically placed her under the jurisdiction of the Vermont court, where Christie held an advantage. But now that Christie had won the divorce battle anyway, she refused to censor herself any longer.

Her side of the story would finally be revealed in Brattleboro, her voice heard. She brought all of her narrative skills to the table, depicting herself as the wronged protagonist and the Crowells as the villainous antagonists. The story's central stake was her son's very survival. She typed out more than two thousand heated words, then marched the pages down to the post office and asked Luola to send them to the *Brattleboro Reformer*.

On Monday, November 19, 1917, a few days before Thanksgiving, the *Reformer* published her statement in its entirety.

To the People of Brattleboro—

I ask you to hear me, not for my sake, but for my boy's. For his sake I left my home and am living in exile; for his sake I waived contest in your court when, knowing how that absence could be misconstrued, Mr. Christie Crowell publicly charged me with the most shameful sin and divorced me on that charge; for his sake, I now lay pride aside and come before you, a woman cruelly persecuted, asking no kindness for herself but only a hearing for a little child. For, though by sacrifice I may save his body, his honor lies in

the hands of the world; as you judge the mother, so will you treat
the son. For his honor, hear the defense I could not make in court.

She proceeded to take direct aim at the Crowell family.

I came among you a western girl, a stranger to your ways of
life and thought. I know I blundered often and misunderstood. I
was unwelcome in the family where I went. Christians, they yet
set aside the bidding of Christ that a man should leave mother and
father and cleave to his wife. I do not blame them now. They were
not capable of greater vision.

The years were sad. In time, I found joy in writing and illus-
trating and always my little son and I had our life apart. To him,
I was not a westerner unwelcome, but his mother.[25]

She revealed that Christie himself had helped her obtain
guardianship of Robert, supported their plans to go to California together, and suggested Robert stay with Elsie at her
mother's new home in Berkeley. He'd even invested $1,500
($40,000 today) in Robert's mining venture and sent him
boxes of cigars when he struck gold.

It was Christie who deserted her, she wrote. After
George's asthma worsened and they were *forced to live in the*
mountains, she pressed Christie to join them, but he continued to rebuff her.

I was first threatened with poverty if I would not give up
custody of the boy. I refused. I was willing that he should at times
visit his father in the East if possible, and at any time see him
here. But I wished to retain custody. Then they threatened me
with a charge of desertion and adultery if I did not agree. I said
that nothing, not even death, would make me abandon my boy to

those whom I know by bitter experience to be cold and merciless to the weak.

In her closing paragraph, she made a final plea.

I ask you to judge, not from pity for me, but so that if in the days to come, this child, who is dearer than life to me, should ever meet you who were once my people, he may not feel shame in your eyes.

When the *Reformer* hit Brattleboro newsstands, the stately windows of Lindenhurst must have rattled with mortification. The mighty Crowells—always careful tenders of their status as church and civic leaders—were once again the target of salacious gossip. Not since Herbert killed himself were they so vulnerable to sideways glances; Mary Crowell must have been relieved that George Sr. wasn't alive to witness this degradation. They had sent Christie to California to recover his spiritual equanimity after losing saintly Louisa. But he'd fallen for a brazen California hussy who'd thrust herself into their midst with bitter consequences. One can only imagine the sharp friction that lay between mother and son that Thanksgiving as they fumed in separate quarters of their rambling mansion.[26]

In Hornitos, the winter rains came, pounding the dust into mud and flooding the seasonal creeks with water. Elsie surely tried her best to transform her humble home into a cheery dwelling for Christmas, stringing popcorn and cranberry garlands on a scrappy pine tree. When she folded George into her embrace, she tried to hide her growing fears at what the coming months might bring.

Chapter 10

SAN FRANCISCO

A PHOTO OF GEORGE
Alexander Crowell as
a young man. While
his health improved
in Hornitos, it was
uncertain if he'd be
permitted to stay with
Elsie in California.

*Photo published in
Hearst's* International-
Cosmopolitan, *June 1934.*

I N JANUARY 1918, ELSIE FORMALLY PETITIONED the Mariposa Superior Court for custody of George and braced herself for a new round of fighting with Christie.[1]

A wretched business—it left both of us scarred. I was branded. But the boy was never penalized. He never knew what his father did to me. To the contrary, I taught him to respect and love his father—told him that ill health, alone, prevented him from standing by us. Magnanimous? Not at all. Merely, as I see it, mature. It was our quarrel—not the boy's. He suffered enough, God knows, without my adding the burden of my bitterness. I have no use for those vindictive females who force helpless children to share their personal vendettas.[2]

The weeks passed and her petition went uncontested. Perhaps Christie was still mortified by his ex-wife's scandalous exposé in the *Reformer*. Perhaps he was worried about a new editorial lashing. After locking horns over George for so long, it didn't seem possible that Christie would just back away. Yet that's precisely what he did.

One late-winter morning, Elsie set out for Mariposa once more, this time in a jubilant mood. Over the past few years, she'd spent many bitter hours in the white clapboard building that housed the superior court. The giant clock tower perched on the roof was a constant reminder of just how slowly her case progressed in California compared to Christie's in Vermont. The hearings, presided over by wall-eyed Judge J. J. Trabucco, were held in the stuffy upstairs courtroom—barely thawed by an anemic woodstove in winter, sweltering hot in summer.[3]

The weather on this day, however, was perfect. The rain-drenched foothills were covered with tender green grass and bright pops of wildflowers. Everything seemed to take on the sheen of her joy: her son would not be wrenched away from her. She was almost too stunned to believe it. After having her hackles up for so long, it was hard to relax into that knowledge.

In the downstairs clerk's office at the courthouse, she read the affidavit—"I do solemnly swear that I will faithfully perform, according to the law, the duties of guardian of the person and estate of George Alexander Crowell, a minor"—and carefully placed her full name, "Elsinore Robinson Crowell," on the too-short signature line.[4]

The *Mariposa Gazette* duly reported the news—which was reprinted, more prominently, in the *Brattleboro Reformer* under the headline "Mrs. Crowell Gets Custody of Child."

Years of anger dropped away—hostility toward Christie and fury directed at herself for her own missteps. None of it mattered now. She had George.

We have all nursed a grouch. Felt abused. We may be Shining Examples in every other respect but when it comes to Hate we all tote a chip on our shoulder. Which, when you come to think about it, is just about the silliest and most futile form of human activity.

You could have refused to let it get under your skin.

You could have deliberately barred your mind against it.

THE BEST WAY TO REPENT—is to forget it and plant new gardens.[5]

That spring and summer, Elsie's articles began to sell at a faster clip. She was feeling more confident as a writer, able to convert the exoticism of her life in Hornitos into everything from fiction to travelogues to essays.

But that fall, her life was again thrown into chaos. World War I—which had largely played out unnoticed by her in Hornitos, aside from reading newspaper articles—had drawn to a close, and with it, the war manufacturing boom. Factories laid off workers. The US economy slumped. Without warning, Ruth Pierce Mine, having already slowed production, shuttered.

Money was too chancy to be risked on holes in the ground.[6]

The implosion of her remote haven had been a long time coming. As the output of Ruth Pierce fell by nearly 75 percent in two years, Elsie had watched the men she'd come to view as family shuffle out of her life forever, peeling off in search of new jobs.[7]

Robert, ever the dreamer, had bought a stake in a gold mine eighty miles north of Hornitos and planned to move there, certain that *this* time he'd finally hit the jackpot.[8]

Elsie decided to try her luck in San Francisco. George was fourteen, a high schooler in a town with no high schools. She wanted him to have the experiences of a normal teenager, to begin ninth grade at a school bustling with other kids. It was time to move on.

She lugged the Smith Premier back to the post office, where she bid Luola a fond farewell. It must have been difficult, on that last day in Hornitos, for the two women to say goodbye; their sisterhood had been nurtured by hopes and dreams, by confidences small and large shared over the modest expanse of a postal counter. While Elsie once again faced an unknown future, Luola took comfort in the small, evaporating town that she cherished and would never leave. (Luola remained in Hornitos for the rest of her life, living with her good friend Jennie Gagliardo in what some neighbors believed was a romantic relationship; after both women died, in 1955 and 1960, respectively, the townspeople erected a monument to both of them across from the plaza.)[9]

On the afternoon of their departure, Elsie and George carried their scant possessions toward a stagecoach that would transport them to the nearby train station.

The desert was through with us. We owned only the clothes we stood in. We had to go back. It was evening. Like a bright mirage, the low hills, the wide desert floated unreal and golden on the wide, green sky. For a long moment the sunset flared and flickered and then was gone. A killdeer called—was still. A small wind lifted—passed. The sky went gray, then violet—then blue-black. Was that a star above the worn old trail? I did not know. I felt for that which never failed me, son's hand. We turned—smiled at each other—went away from there.[10]

But what of Robert Wallace?

In her memoir, Elsie drops all mentions of him soon after they arrive in Hornitos. We can only conjecture about the reasons for this. During the divorce proceedings, she danced around the subject of their cohabitation, first denying, then confirming it. Perhaps the deep shame of publicly being labeled an adulteress created an ongoing tension in their relationship. Maybe Robert's alcoholism, delusional get-rich schemes, and mental health struggles proved too much for her, despite his intoxicating masculinity and charm. Or perhaps Elsie and Robert's relationship had simply run its course.

A woman has no more business to make a man's love "her whole existence" than she has to center all her happiness on a plate of French pastry.[11]

Robert never reconciled with his wife or children, according to his daughter Janet, who, in a written reflection, stated she had fond memories of him. "Father was delightful as far as we were concerned, always kind and witty," she remembered. Without equivocation or sentimentality, she added, "I never saw him again after I was ten."

Public records reveal scant details of his post-Hornitos life. In 1918, he was working his stake in the Montana Mine, deep in California's Calaveras County. The 1920 census shows him residing in an apartment in San Diego. The 1930 census has him living as a boarder in Carthage, Texas—known as the "Gas Capital of the United States"— where he apparently moved to try to make money during the Texas oil boom. He was still living there in 1939, when he died of a heart attack, alone in a hotel, at age sixty-nine. None of his get-rich-quick schemes panned out. His

estranged family shipped his remains back to Massachusetts to be buried in the Wallace family plot at the Springfield Cemetery, despite his total absence from their lives
for almost three decades.[12]

❧

ELSIE ARRIVED IN San Francisco in the fall of 1918, right
before the Armistice, completely unaware of how the war
had transformed American society. The city's population,
already large at the turn of the century, had exploded during
the war years as droves of workers arrived to take jobs in
munitions plants and shipyards. Facing a housing crisis, San
Francisco had disinterred 150,000 bodies from old city grave-
yards and moved them to farmland in the neighboring town
of Colma. Along Market Street, the city's main drag, trollies
and Model Ts played chicken with mobs of pedestrians who,
in an era before crosswalks, meandered across the street
willy-nilly amid the blare of horns. After the empty stillness
of Hornitos, Elsie found the volume, size, and crowds of
San Francisco overwhelming.[13]

When I left San Francisco in 1915, it had still borne the mark
of those pioneer days in which I had been born. Now everything
was changed. Here was a new City, which stared at me with
amazed and amused eyes as I strode up Market Street in mining
boots and mackinaw. Browned, lean, with a face so calloused and
corrugated by heat that it might have been a contour map of the
Sierra itself. Tall, yet slouching, with that long sagging stride I
had learned behind a wheelbarrow. Outwardly I was poker-faced,

*having learned that art in many a Black Jack game. Inwardly I
was bewildered, terrified. Everything was different. Skyline. Traf-
fic. Tempo.*

*But, most of all, the women were changed. These astounding
mobs of females . . . so swift, so sleek, so sophisticated and com-
petent . . . what had happened to them . . . to everything? The
answer was plain enough—the Machine Age and the World War
had happened. But to us, drudging dully in the wilderness, the
Machine Age had simply been increasing advertisements of auto-
mobiles—the World War a distant thunder, an occasional newspaper column of unbelievable horrors, unreal as a nightmare. The
War had never become a living issue to me. Of its effect on life
in general, and on women in particular, I had not the slightest
conception.*[14]

In 1918, American women were no longer mincing Victorian blossoms; they were becoming a force to be reckoned
with. They had stepped into jobs vacated by soldiers—not
just factory jobs, but all types of traditionally male positions, from bus drivers to police officers to store clerks—and
once they had a taste of economic freedom, many refused
to go back to unpaid domestic labor.[15]

Fashion reflected the modern woman's changing circumstances. Gone were the tight dresses and rib-cracking
corsets. In were loose-fitting frocks with natural waists that
allowed you to move with ease. Victorian rules that tied
hem length to age were ignored; women refused to wear
their skirts dragging on the ground as a sign of modesty
but preferred them cut above the ankle, which allowed longer, faster strides. As women strove to be taken seriously,

they put aside yesteryear's girly pastels and flowery calicos in favor of traditionally masculine colors—muted grays, navies, and browns. Likewise, they boxed up their "picture hats," with their adornments of dead parakeets and wobbling sprays of silk flowers, for discreet, small-brimmed hats or the plain lace headband that would soon become the preferred headgear of flappers everywhere. Hairstyles, too, were radically changed as women lobbed off their long tresses in favor of the short, stylish bobs that were once only worn by prostitutes.[16]

If I had landed on Mars the changed world could not have seemed greater. Here were women who, four years before, would have timidly asked their fathers, husbands or big brothers, if they could step out to the corner movie with Nellie. Now they were living in bachelor girl apartments . . . experimenting in "affairs" . . . going wherever they pleased, with whoever they pleased, at any hour . . . and paying their own way.

Here was a strange new sex! Hard, where once it had been shrinking soft. Raucously realistic, where once it had been sentimental. Shrill where once it had been reserved and retreating. A strange new sex—or was it merely the same old sex strutting its own stuff at last? Had women always been like this, under the skin? I suspect they had.[17]

With $50 in her pocket, Elsie began searching for a place to live. She chose not to move back in with her family in the East Bay; they had their own financial burdens and she didn't want to add to them. She found a small, cheap, basement-level apartment at 400 Duboce Avenue, where cable cars clattered past at all hours of the day. But Duboce Park, a verdant, three-block oasis bound by dollhouse Victorians, was a five-minute walk in one direction and Market Street was one block in the other.[18]

But these small steps forward were marred by the one thing she most feared would happen: George began to have breathing problems again. She'd held out hope that he'd "outgrown" his asthma in the foothills. But his symptoms returned almost as soon as they reached San Francisco— the chest tightness, the opened-mouth gulping in of air as the carbon dioxide levels rose in his blood, the frightened, pleading look in his eyes. It was agonizing for a mother to watch.

The boy went to bed, gasping, to stay for months—his hard-won mountain vigor wiped out in forty-eight hours by city fog and grime.[19]

Now that he was almost fifteen, Elsie allowed George to smoke "asthma cigarettes" made from the same dried jimson weed that she burned as a kind of medicinal incense in his room when he was younger. The plant's tropane alkaloids worked as a sedative to stop bronchial spasms, but the effect was fleeting. (Modern inhalers wouldn't be invented until 1956.)[20]

And another danger loomed: once again she'd arrived in a city that was under quarantine. At Northfield, the scourge had been scarlet fever; now it was the great influenza epidemic. After rumbling around the East Coast in the spring and summer of 1918, the virus reached San Francisco that fall. On October 9, the city recorded 169 cases; a week later the number jumped to more than 2,000. The city shut down—businesses closed, churches held outdoor services. Mask use in public became mandatory and police officers fined "mask slackers" $5 for "disturbing the peace."[21]

In an era when scientists were just discovering the link between bacteria and disease, most people still believed respiratory illnesses were caused by dirty air, or miasmas—a belief that was reflected in a popular children's rhyme of the time:

I had a little bird, its name was Enza. I opened the window, and in-flu-enza.

Asthmatics, their airways already restricted, were at an even higher risk for severe illness and death. Whenever George started to wheeze, Elsie rushed to his side, wondering if it was "just" asthma or if he'd been infected with the killer flu.

The boy was failing—Oh, God! Don't let it happen! Let me keep him! Help me find a way. I'll do anything, anything! Only let me keep him! Don't take my boy—DON'T TAKE MY BOY![22]

Her panic was compounded by the fact that she could not find work. She was forced to leave George alone for hours at a time to *pound pavements, looking for any job that would keep us alive. The poor have to eat. And we were poor.*[23]

Skimming the classifieds under FEMALE HELP WANTED in the *San Francisco Chronicle*, she was dismayed to find ad after ad under the headline "Attractive Positions for Young Women" or "WANTED—Neat young woman." Dozens more made it clear that Elsie, at thirty-five, need not apply. With workplace age discrimination legal until 1967, ads seeking "Girl for cooking" or "Bright young girl for light duties" appeared in the paper week after week.[24]

What could I possibly do that would bring us even a starvation wage? Cook? Sew? Scrub floors? I could and was willing to do any of these, but the city swarmed with younger women who seized every chance.

Take an office position? These, too, were overcrowded. And, outside of my ability to type, I had no knowledge of office work. I could hardly add a column of figures and I would have murdered the average male boss, out of sheer boredom, within a week.[25]

Writing freelance magazine articles was no longer an option. Even if she did write a piece on spec and managed to place it, it would be many months before she got paid and she needed money immediately. Like Jack London, she had learned that not every publication paid as quickly as *Black Cat.*

One day, paging through a newspaper, she was struck by advertisements for everything from pimple-removing "arsenic complexion wafers" to fishing tackles that promised relaxing weekends to harried men. Studying the text, she felt a bolt of hope. Perhaps her optimism was unfounded, but she was stirred by a new possibility, one that hadn't occurred to her until that moment.

I had never written a regular ad. But I thought I knew what people wanted when they read one. Not just the price and description of a commodity but an opening door into that world of beauty and adventure which life had denied them.

I knew that was what they wanted because that was what I wanted myself. I knew how a homely girl felt when she read about a Tissue Cream. I was homely myself. I knew how a tired man felt when he read about Fishing Tackles. I, too, was chained in city walls with a heart that yearned and yammered for the wide horizons. Maybe, if I could put some of that feeling into an ad—[26]

Finally, here were two jobs she qualified for—advertising illustrator and copywriter. She decided to give both prospects a try.

Under the dim light of a fly-spotted globe, on paper tacked to the bread board, I lettered and illustrated some ads and tried them out on Sonny—and the next morning went out to peddle them.[27]

There were three competing newspapers in San Francisco in 1918: the *Call and Post*, the *Examiner*, and the *Chronicle*, all situated along Market Street. Elsie gathered samples of her drawings and published writing, made sure George had several "asthma cigarettes" within reach, and left the apartment to join the throngs of working women on the city's sidewalks, hoping to soon become a member of their rank.

I entered my first newspaper door. I did not know that most ads are written in commercial agencies, not in newspaper buildings. Also, I was so dumb that I applied at the editor's sanctum instead of the advertising department. But it made little difference—I was turned down anyway. It's surprising that they even let me past the door. I looked—and doubtless acted—like something out of Buffalo Bill's Wild West Show. No wonder they did not even let me start to say my piece![28]

Defeated, she slumped back home.

The holidays were approaching and the windows of all the big downtown department stores brimmed with toys. She walked into a few with her advertising mock-ups and talked a couple of managers into hiring her to illustrate a few promotions—but it was never enough work to cover her expenses.[29]

I had to do something. I had to do something! Our money was dwindling.

Day after day, day after day, I scraped together a breakfast for my son. Straightened his bed. Piled old magazines at his hand—with the medicine always near. Kissed him—held him close—turned to look back once more at his smiling face—then went out to start the search all over again.

Pounding pavements—how I wished for the first time in my life that San Francisco had flat streets. Those miles of up-hill cobbles and cement . . . with the cold mud oozing up through the paper that patched my shoes . . . and the colder terror seeping into my soul.[30]

After a month of barely scraping by, she felt utterly crushed. Hunger made it hard to sleep, to think, to keep pressing on. Walking by restaurants was agonizing; the scent of fried steak and onions, of coffee and banana fritters, made her stomach clench. She went without food so George could eat. On Thanksgiving, she served hot dogs.

Self-doubt assailed her. Once again she asked herself if she had made a series of huge mistakes. If she had ruined her life—and possibly her son's—by chasing wild dreams instead of putting up with a soul-crushing marriage in exchange for financial security, as so many other women did. She wondered if she had become just as delusional as Robert.

She missed confiding in other adults. She missed Robert, and the intimate pillow talk they'd shared. She missed Luola, and their heart-to-hearts over the mail counter. She couldn't express herself fully to her son—for him she had to appear strong, even as she trembled inside.

When George turned fifteen on December 4, she could barely scrape a plate of food together for him. She recalled the lavish birthday parties she'd thrown for him at Lindenhurst. When he was a toddler, she'd organized a summer birthday bash for thirty children on the mansion's lawn, overseeing a display of cut dahlias and the construction of an arch of evergreen boughs at the entrance. The servants stood at the ready as the children tumbled over the manicured grass and frolicked in a sand pile; each received a ball or a doll as a party favor. George, the diminutive center of attention, had glowed with happiness that day, and his radiance had briefly become her own.[31]

It all seemed like an improbable dream when she looked back on it. Now, that boy of bright promise lay in bed, his face drained of color as he struggled for air. In a few weeks it would be Christmas. At Lindenhurst they'd surely have their traditional Christmas feast of roast duck and plum pudding, served at the long dining room table where she'd also had a place for almost a decade.

Her anguish overwhelmed her one December night. Out of sorts and unable to continue her cheerful façade for George, she faltered.

I had been turned away from the last door. Gone home. Puttered around. Said, honestly I wasn't hungry—go on, darling, eat it all. Then, pretended, with much mysterious smiling, that I had something exciting to do outside. Would he mind if I went out— for just a little while?

Always I shall see him as he smiled back—his poor thin shoulders bolstered high by the ragged pillows, working so desperately for his tortured breath, but his dear eyes bright and brave. Of course he wouldn't mind! Did he guess—behind all that brightness—what the errand really was? God grant he didn't!

And so I went out. But twice I turned back, to kiss him again, to pretend there were great things doing, putting the memory of his face away, deeper and deeper into my heart. Then at last I managed to get going—And I walked straight and hard, down Market Street, my long hair falling over my shoulders like a wild woman's, my eyes staring blank and dead.[32]

She kept walking, dark thoughts swarming, a hardness creeping over her. Christmas lights twinkled in windows, and groups of merrymakers parted to let her through.

I walked without seeing the lights, or hearing the crowds or even, for once, smelling the food . . . straight ahead, not turning, block after block . . . past the glittering shops and the blazing theaters, on and on, till the buildings grew smaller and shabbier . . . and the lights were dimmer and fewer . . . and the sound and smell of the sea came up to meet me.

Then I was on the waterfront . . . the Embarcadero we call it . . . where the big docks stretch out into the bay. The Ferry Building lay in a great core of light. I turned to the left and walked north, past one dock after another until I came to a place that was very dark and still, with only the sound of the water, fumbling and slobbering beneath my feet.

For a long time I stood listening—not thinking—just leaning against one of the piles, running my hands aimlessly over the rotting wood.

I was past feeling. There had been too much. There had been too much misery and despair, too much terror and hunger, and wild, useless rage. Perhaps it was my own fault. Perhaps it wasn't. But, whether it was or wasn't, this was certain—there had been too much. And now I had come to the end.

I wasn't sad anymore. Not mad anymore. I was simply through.

Something seemed asking me what I was going to do . . . and something in me was answering back—

I knew that there were only two things I could do.

No, that was wrong. There was only one thing I could do.

For, of course, I could not kill myself.

I wanted to kill myself. It would be easy to step off into that darkness—and go down and down into that soft, mumbling water.

But I couldn't do it. For there was my boy.

As she had walked down side streets toward the bay, solitary men had turned to watch her pass, calling and beckoning to her—assuming she was a prostitute. Respectable women did not walk through San Francisco alone at night,

especially not around the Tenderloin or Union Square. The
Red Light Abatement Act of 1917 had closed the city's brothels and driven prostitutes into the streets, where, lacking the
protective presence of other women, they were often subject to violence.[33]

But sex work continued to be a far more lucrative trade
for women than other nonskilled jobs. The minimum wage
in California in 1918 was 21 cents an hour or $8.40 week, for
forty hours of work. A pair of leather boots sold at Sears,
Roebuck and Co. cost $11. If a woman spent more than a
third of her monthly wages on shoes, how could she pay for
rent, food, clothing, medical bills, and transportation—not
to mention any extra expenses incurred by dependent children? Streetwalkers charging an average of $1 a trick could
easily best the $1.68 a day that unskilled laborers took home
each day, which is why so many women resorted to selling
their bodies.[34]

"Pay girls a living wage and vice and evil will take care
of itself," one prostitute lectured a crusading anti-vice
preacher when the city shuttered its bawdy houses.[35]

Elsie was familiar with the mechanics of the trade.
She recalled that searing glimpse of ecstasy between a sailor
and his consort in Benicia. At Northfield, she'd written the
story about the Chinese girl, Pun Yee, who fell in love with
a young fishmonger, only to be sold into sexual slavery to
an older barber. Elsie was no longer a naïve schoolgirl or
a virginal bride. She knew sex could be reduced to a simple, physical transaction—quick, usually painless. She had

already been labeled a harlot by Christie and the state of Vermont; what would it take to actually become one?

So now that all the other jobs had failed . . . and since there was the boy, and since somehow I must live for him and save him . . . there was really only one thing I could do—

But even standing there alone in all that darkness—not mattering any more to anybody—not mattering, even, any more to myself—I could not name that thing which I knew I would have to do.

I could not, would not, name it, but I knew what it was.

And how could I help but know, with the weak, watery eyes leaping, and the wet, floppy lips leering, and the foul hands fumbling every time my big, strong body swung past?

What difference did it make to them whether I could type or file or write according to rule? What difference, even, if my clothes were ragged and my face worn and old beyond my years? For perhaps they could live again, even yet—poor burnt out husks that they were—if they had a great, gay, strong, reckless woman like me to comfort and warm them back to manliness!

I stood there as still, as cold, as the damp, dead steel of the chain that lay coiled at my feet.

I was past tears. I was past words. I was up against it at last.

To-morrow we would eat.[36]

Chapter 11

OAKLAND

THE *OAKLAND TRIBUNE* CIRCA 1920. THE "GREAT PRESSES," located in the basement, were visible to pedestrians through street-level windows.

Photo courtesy of the Oakland Public Library, Oakland History Center.

ELSIE RETURNED, VERY LATE, TO HER APART-
ment. She let herself in quietly and went to her
son's bed; he was blessedly peaceful as he slept.
He had such an absolute, childlike, and enduring faith in her
ability to save them.

She recalled those long-ago days in Brattleboro, when
she worked on stories at the kitchen table while beans sim-
mered on the stovetop and George, a mere toddler, napped
upstairs. How strange to finally recognize the simple contentment of those quiet afternoons. Her pencil raced over
the page, ideas flowing faster than her fingers could move.
When George woke from his nap, she'd pull him onto her
lap and show him her work. His delight kept her despair
at bay.

Her imagination had entertained her son, yes, but it
had worked an even deeper magic on her: art had saved
her, pulled her back from the edge of despondency. In the
parallel worlds that she created, she had power—she ma-
nipulated characters' fates and fortunes and decided which
deeper morals were at play.

She gazed down at his sleeping face, which was beginning to take on the handsome angularity of a man's, and
grew determined to rally once again, for his sake. For *both*

their sakes. She would not yet be reduced to selling her body; she would give the creative powers of her brain another go.

The fog passed. And the night was over. I came home to my boy—and that "one more chance." Writing still seemed my only out.[1]

The next day she bought drawing paper and ink and enough food to last for two days, and hunkered down at the kitchen table. She had an idea for a story about a group of animal friends that harkened back to the whimsical tales she'd written and illustrated for *John Martin's Letters*. The formula had been successful then, why not now?

Her timing was fortuitous: children's literature was having a moment. Following World War I, there was a national focus on early childhood education and welfare, and publishers responded by establishing editorial departments specializing in children's books. In libraries across the country, children's reading rooms were introduced, and in 1922, the American Library Association launched the first children's book award in the world, the prestigious Newbery Medal. The rise of juvenile publishing had a secondary effect: it finally gave women entrée into the male-dominated publishing world—not in low-paying clerical positions but in children's book divisions as copy editors, proofreaders, and even "editresses" who acquired and shaped manuscripts. Women were seen as more suitable to handle children's literature—regardless of whether they were mothers themselves—by the simple fact of their sex.[2]

The next morning, Elsie walked to the three San Francisco papers, her illustrated children's story in hand. While the publishing industry was just starting to focus on juvenile literature, newspapers had long included children's pages. One of the first such sections in the country debuted in the *National Tribune*, based in Washington, DC, on August 1, 1880, and included a morality tale about a girl who lied to her mother about eating too many sugary treats and then dreamed that a "troop of hideous little gnomes" shot her mouth full of darts.[3]

Each of the editorial departments of the *San Francisco Call and Post*, the *Examiner*, and the *Chronicle* turned her away. There was only one major paper in the Bay Area she hadn't tried: the *Tribune*, across the bay in Oakland. *Oakland was a huge "home town." Yet its largest paper had no juvenile department.*[4]

She rode the ferry from the Embarcadero, across the velvet blue waters of the bay to the Oakland pier. Oakland was half the size of San Francisco, with a population of 215,000 people—many of whom had arrived as refugees after the 1906 earthquake and fire destroyed their homes. The *Tribune*'s gleaming new building wasn't hard to find; its massive clock tower could be seen from blocks away, with a huge clock facing in each direction. Spanning the top of the clocks was a four-sided sign that ran half the length of the building and spelled out "TRIBUNE," again, in each direction.[5]

Elsie pushed through the glass doors, consulted a directory, and walked past the marble counters of the advertising department to a wall of elevators. Editorial was on the fourth floor. The newsroom was huge—a space spanning nearly the full length of the building—and filled with men in suit jackets shouting into phones, banging on typewriters, and smoking cigarettes. Two pneumatic tube systems stretched across the ceiling, each curving dramatically toward the floor, allowing messages to be whooshed between departments. Several reporters turned to watch the tall woman in the outmoded dress enter their sanctum and stroll toward the desk of the well-respected managing editor, Leo Levy. "Mr. Levy," as his reporters deferentially called him, was a soft-spoken man, given to terse, sometimes acidic, comments. He'd risen through the paper's ranks for nine years and would go on to lead it for another forty.[6]

Levy looked up at Elsie, a bemused expression on his face. She handed him her pages.

A queer creature I must have seemed to him, standing there in my rags—with the room going around me in a gray blur. But his gaze sharpened as he began looking through the drawings and stories.

"Kid columns," he assured me, "are a flop."

I began, mechanically, to gather my material together again.

"I've tried it before and failed."

His voice, receding, further and further, still persisted.

"But perhaps—" the room steadied—became enormously still. "—there's something to this stuff."

"So, if you're interested, I'll give it a chance. A column, weekly—animal stories, illustrated—at twelve dollars per week."

It took a moment for her to steady her thoughts and form words to speak.

"I'm interested," Elsie said, making sure her voice matched Levy's even tone.

"Then you might bring the first column to-morrow."

"That would be all right."

She managed to keep her composure until she left the building.

Then, somehow, I was on the elevator, going down—I was sitting on a stool before a short-order counter, wolfing down three hamburger sandwiches, one after another—with people looking curiously at me, nudging—

I was starting for the ferry—turning suddenly—ducking down a back alley—vomiting—vomiting—

And presently I was running down the hall, into the apartment, shouting, calling, throwing myself across his bed—my arms full of flowers and food—kissing him, crying—laughing, laughing!!

I had my first newspaper job. I would not have to go on the streets. And my boy and I could eat! [7]

❧

A TEASER FOR her first column ran in the *Oakland Tribune* on December 19, 1918, under the headline "Kiddies, Look Here!" She was introduced as both Elsinore Crowell and "Aunt Elsie"—a woman who could talk to animals and "share all their secrets."

I don't believe in hammering in morals, she'd later state. *I just believe in telling children's stories which will make them happy.*

Her column, "Trestle Glen Secrets," named after a wooded area near Lake Merritt in downtown Oakland, hit the paper on Sunday, December 22. It ran adjacent to L. Frank Baum's far more prominent column, "The Wonderful Stories of Oz," a series based on his popular second book, *The Marvelous Land of Oz*. Using the same intimate, animated voice of the stories she published in *John Martin's Letters*, she wrote and illustrated a tender-hearted tale of a group of animal friends—Jimmy Squirrel, Mattie Mud Hen, Billy Owl—who come to the rescue of two orphaned mice siblings on Christmas Day.[8]

The story was a hit and fan mail poured into the *Oakland Tribune*'s mail department from kids across the city.

Based on the enthusiastic response, and coinciding with Baum's death, Levy expanded Elsie's column. On May 11, 1919, she was given a weekly, one-page feature called *Aunt Elsie's Magazine for the Kiddies of the Oakland Tribune*. In 1920, he shortened the title to *Aunt Elsie's Magazine* and expanded her feature to two pages. And in 1922, Levy assigned Elsie an entire section—a whopping eight pages—for her juvenile stories.[9]

She wrote separate sections for children based on their ages, including thrillers that played out over several installments for older readers and cartoons and crafts for younger kids. One week's handicraft included directions for how to make a camp stove from an empty can of tomato juice; another included cutouts to design an elegant paper wardrobe for a clothespin doll.

Elsie encouraged her young readers to write to her at the "Tribune House" and promised to write them back. *Tell me about the happys—and tell me about the sads*, she wrote in her "Jewel Box" column for girls. *Because I had sads too, little girl. If you don't want me to print the sad letter in the paper, send me a stamped envelope with your address on it and I will write you a letter all your very own that will make you know that my arm is around you and that I love you very much.*[10]

Now with a stable paycheck, one of the first purchases she made was a cheap tweed suit. Too cheap, it soon ripped in the derriere—as George gleefully pointed out one afternoon when she returned home. No matter. She ripped out one of the pockets and fashioned it into a patch before joyfully returning to the throngs of professional women striding down Market Street.

Her success kept growing. Her columns were passed from child to child, and Aunt Elsie clubs, sponsored by the *Tribune*, formed across Northern California with thousands of members. At one point, there were chartered Aunt Elsie clubs in sixty-five towns—ranging from Redding, 200 miles to the north of Oakland, to Monterey, 120 miles to the south, to Nevada City, 140 miles to the east—covering a territory far larger than the *Tribune's* distribution.[11]

Children received membership cards that entitled bearers to "ALL THE GOOD TIMES AND PRIVILEGES" of the club and proudly wore membership pins featuring an enamel red heart against a white background with the words "Aunt Elsie Club Member" around it. Club members organized parades for which they built ornate floats and wore costumes indicating their favorite section of the magazine— the "Witches' Cave" (for girls) or "Pirates' Den" (for boys).

They competed in drawing and short story writing contests for the chance to have their work published in the paper.[12]

The *Tribune* began to host Aunt Elsie parties in an assembly hall on the top floor of the Tribune Building and stage variety shows at local venues. These events were so popular that the Oakland Police Department dispatched officers for crowd control.

"One, two, three, four blocks of kiddies! Count 'em! Stretching clear around the American Theater block, everyone grinning, waiting in the sunshine for the show to begin," ran a feature about one such event in the *Oakland Tribune* on April 9, 1922. The price of admission was "a cheerful smile," and entertainment included song-and-dance revues by the Tribune Juveniles performance troupe, screenings of (silent) movies—and, of course, heavily applauded appearances by the lady of the hour herself.[13]

Aunt Elsie's tremendous success even triggered a blatant rip-off: On July 2, the *San Francisco Chronicle* launched "The Chronicle's Kiddies' Corner" featuring "Aunt Dolly." Children were invited to write letters to Aunt Dolly, join the Chronicle Kiddies' Club, and submit their own stories for possible inclusion in the paper. The column's introductory message contained familiar hype: "Aunt Dolly will arrange theater parties for her Chronicle Kiddies' Club—when they'll see new films and plays and leading playhouses—absolutely free."[14]

As Elsie's fame shot up among the school-age set, parents began to read the comforting words she offered their children, and before long, they also began to write to Elsie, seeking advice for their own quandaries.

Bored, bewildered, often embittered by the chaotic times, Mother and Dad wanted to talk things over with somebody in the know. . . . The unconventional style of the Aunt Elsie work put them at ease. So Mother and Dad began writing in, asking what, why and whither.[15]

The *Tribune*, seeing an opportunity to expand its circulation, assigned Elsie a homemaking column called "Curtains, Collars, and Cutlets: Cheer-Up Column." The section ran with her own name as the byline, "Elsie Robinson." Before long, the title was shortened to "Cheer-Up" and the scope expanded to attract male readers. She'd often add her own illustrations, signing them "ERC" or "ER."[16]

In 1920, she began writing a second adult column, "Cry on Geraldine's Shoulder"—with Elsie as "Geraldine"—which focused on relationship problems.[17]

Is your one wife too many? she asked in an announcement for the new column. *Is your husband or your complexion growing dull? Let us then discuss the value of soft soap on complexions—and husbands. . . . We shall sit together on the edge of the world. You have wanted a friend. I'M IT.*

When Elsie landed in the news business, she did so by building on the fame and success of women writers who preceded her. This included stunt reporter Nellie Bly, who in the late 1880s wrote accounts of her voluntary confinement in one of New York's most notorious insane asylums and her effort to beat the globe-trotting record of Phileas Fogg, the fictional hero of author Jules Verne's book, *Around the*

World in 80 Days (she did it in seventy-two). Around 1900, newspaper editors began to hire female reporters to write human interest stories, believing women wrote more "emotional" copy than men—noting such details as, say, the tears in a widow's eyes or her trembling hand. Subsequently derided as "sob sisters," the highly sentimental writing style of these reporters went out of vogue by the 1910s—yet these journalists paved the way for future generations of newswomen like Elsie.[18]

Elsie knew, however, that she had to work even harder than her male counterparts to make it, and she rarely turned down Levy's requests for more copy.

For those first two years I did not know Sunday from week day, holiday from working day. I worked every night until 2 A.M. Then I slept, on a couch beside my table, until 6:30. For two hours I cooked, cleaned house, helped son off to school if he was able to go. By 9 A.M. I was at it again.[19]

Although she tired under the strain, she kept her head down and did whatever task Levy assigned her, elated to have such steady and satisfying work. Decades later, when her readers suggested a mother's only job should be raising her children, she pushed back.

Of your mother, "Do you think she would have been a wiser guide if she had taken a more active part in the outside world? Could you have confided in her more easily—trusted her judgment more certainly if her own career had been wider and more colorful? Or would you keep her just as she was, never changing a hair of that dear, devoted head?"[20]

ELSIE'S THIRD ADULT column appeared in January 1921 and marked her transition from local phenomenon to national figure. Called "Listen, World!," the column was syndicated in newspapers across the country by the George Matthew Adams News Service and would make Elsie Robinson a household name. The appointment would also make her one of the first syndicated columnists in the United States to draw her own accompanying editorial cartoons.

Announcing the new column to readers of the *Quad-City Times* in Davenport, Iowa, the editors ran a photo of Elsie (slight grin, friendly face) and noted that "Listen, World!" would run daily on the second page. The editors of the *Modesto Morning Herald* in California chose a different photo of Elsie (chin out, wide smile) sitting on a garden wall. In promoting her new column, the *Herald* editors gushed, "It is brilliant. It is refreshing. It is original and ingenious."[21]

The sheer volume of her writing and illustrating work was remarkable. At one time, she was turning out four bylines—her eight-page *Aunt Elsie's Magazine*, which appeared on Sundays; her "Cheer-Up" and "Cry on Geraldine's Shoulder" columns, which received a half-page daily and two pages on Sundays; and her nationally syndicated, six-day-a-week "Listen, World!" column.

During that time I worked for twelve dollars—eighteen dollars—twenty-five dollars a week. At the age of thirty-eight, I celebrated by getting my first manicure and buying a pair of silk stockings. When I reached thirty dollars I had so much money I didn't know what to do with it. I could, of course, have received more. But I was too green to realize that I was grossly underpaid. And, naturally, no one bothered to wise me up.

For this sum I did everything myself without an assistant or secretary. Wrote serial stories, poems, handicraft directions. Drew twenty or more illustrations, including big cartoons every week. Answered scores of letters daily. I did not perform this amount of labor because I was bent on making a record. I was simply too ignorant about newspaper work to realize that it was a record . . . that I might have had help.

I was working like a gang of tractors—literally turning out acres of copy—and bitterly grateful for the chance.

And how was I living all this time? I was living as we had always lived—in the same apartment, facing the same tragedy.

The boy failed steadily in the stuffy rooms, the city fog. When son was well enough to go to school he went. Otherwise, he lay propped in the bed and I worked beside him, alternating writing and drawing with cooking, cleaning and nursing.

At first there was no money for adequate medical attention. But for one man, the end would have come very quickly.[22]

That one man was a recent med school graduate named Abelson Epsteen. Epsteen, a bespectacled competitive chess player who'd specialized in urology, refused to charge Elsie for his services. He helped George simply out of compassion and as a fellow asthma sufferer.[23]

He came—any hour of the day or night—to give what relief he could, though often he was gasping for breath himself. And always he brought so much more than medicine . . . a laugh, new hope! The boy's face lifted smiling, at the sound of his step.[24]

But even Dr. Epsteen's intervention wasn't enough. George, now sixteen, was languishing and falling behind in school.

It came time to do the hardest thing I have ever done in my life—save one. I had to send my boy back to the mountains, so he could breathe.

We had always known it would have to come some day— just as soon as there was enough money. Yet we had never dared face what it would mean. Always, we had clung to each other— been part of each other in some beautiful, pitiful, indissoluble way. Now, out of the very love I had for him, I had to send him away—

I could not go with him even for a day. The work must go on—it was his only chance. We tried to pretend that it would be just for a little while. We tried to joke—go through the old teasing patter—But everything seemed to have stopped.

Then he was leaning out of the car that was to take him away—laughing down at me. And I was reaching up—putting both my hands on either side of his thin, white face, trying terribly to laugh with him, but with the sounds falling back, like lead, into my dry throat—

And then he was gone . . .

I went back to that shabby place where we had lived in such poverty, yet known such a paradise of love. I pulled down the blinds and locked the door but I did not work. I lay face down on the bed where he had lain . . . feeling such anguish as I had never known before.[25]

She arranged for George to stay with a family in Mariposa, old friends from their Hornitos days. Back in the temperate climate, his health quickly improved. He enrolled at Mariposa High School, where he took up hunting, attended dances, and—following in his mother's literary footsteps—helped launch and edit the school newspaper. Elsie bought him a cherry red Model T so he could drive back and forth to San Francisco to visit her.[26]

A new phase had emerged in Elsie's life. After long years of hardship and hunger, of pushing away regret and fear as she pursued what had once seemed like an impossible fantasy, she had found success. George, although he was three hours away, was safe and enjoying a normal life, even taking girls on outings in his flashy red car. Elsie felt profoundly satisfied: life was good. And it was about to get even better.

Chapter 12

LISTEN, WORLD!

FROM THE START OF HER NATIONALLY SYNDICATED "LISTEN, WORLD!"
column in 1921, Elsie pushed women to demand respect and think more
broadly about self-fulfillment. She drew this editorial cartoon to accompany her column on December 31, 1923.

Original publication, George Matthew Adams News Service.

ACROSS THE BAY, THE MANAGING EDITOR OF the *Call and Post*—one of the three San Francisco newspapers that had turned her away when she sought advertising work—had been closely tracking the spectacular rise of Elsie Robinson.

Fremont Older didn't shy away from hiring female writers, believing they expressed themselves better on the page than most men. A lifelong newspaperman, Older was born in Wisconsin, where, as a young boy, he'd worked as a "printer's devil"—mixing tubs of ink and fetching type—before moving to the West Coast at age sixteen. In San Francisco, he moved up the newspaper food chain to become a reporter and eventually the managing editor of the *Call*, a publication owned by multimillionaire newspaper magnate William Randolph Hearst.[1]

A tall man with deep-set brown eyes, a handlebar mustache, and a love of good cigars, Older was a fearless muckraker who pursued corrupt politicians with glee. His dogged pursuit of truth and justice made him the target of death threats and once he was kidnapped at gunpoint—an episode that did not silence him but that he described, in dramatic detail, in his own memoir.

Older boosted his circulation numbers by publishing racy first-person accounts of people who lived on the fringes of polite society, including ex-cons and gamblers. He called these "confessions" and hoped that readers would "recognize themselves" in the plight of a stranger and thereby gain greater empathy for their fellow humans. His most famous serial was that of a prostitute who went by the name of Alice Smith, an "average" girl who was forced by poverty to "join the ranks of the forlorn."[2]

He recognized Elsie's facility of language in her nationally syndicated "Listen, World!" column and the refreshingly frank columns she wrote for the *Tribune*. She didn't coddle or talk down to readers but challenged them with well-reasoned arguments and provocative jabs at conventional wisdom. In Elsie, Older saw a fellow truth-teller and rabble-rouser.

In 1923, Older persuaded Elsie to join his stable of writers, offering her $95 a week (her highest salary yet) and entry into the bigger and more prestigious market of San Francisco.[3] (The *Call and Post* had 94,000 readers compared to the *Tribune*'s 52,000, a circulation increase of more than 80 percent.) At the *Call*, Elsie started a column for the lovelorn called "Tell It to Elsie," an offspring of her unsigned "Cry on Geraldine's Shoulder" at the *Tribune*.[4]

What's striking is how she chose to introduce herself to readers at the paper. She criticized popular female columnists who wrote under pseudonyms—the big names of the era included "Beatrice Fairfax" (Marie Manning), "Dorothy Dix" (Elizabeth Meriwether Gilmer), and "Nancy Brown" (Annie Brown Leslie)—even though she'd recently written as "Geraldine" herself. She wanted to portray herself as a real, everyday woman in whom readers could confide, not a "persona" hiding behind a fake name.

I am Elsie Robinson, she declared in an article promoting her forthcoming column on Wednesday, September 5. *That means nothing to you yet. As a mere name, Elsie Robinson is valueless. . . . However, it is a real tag on a real person. Most newspaper names which head departments like this aren't real tags, Pal. They're made-up trade marks. For two years, I wrote for the folks of the East Bay under just such a trade mark. It was called "Geraldine." Someone else is writing under that trade mark now. But I grew tired of it. I wanted to come to you straight—as me, myself. With the name my father gave me— ELSIE ROBINSON.*[5]

Five days later, on Monday, September 10, in a tone that was both provocative and humorous, Elsie welcomed readers to day one of her column.

Here begins the Big Experiment! What are we going to do? Write letters. Publish letters. . . . You may not like my answer. I may not like yours. . . . But we'll fight it out here where all the world may listen.

This is YOUR column. To it you may bring any problem or discuss any question, provided you do so in decent language and with friendly intent. You may give your name and address and they will be published or not, just as you desire. Or you may write under an assumed name. Letters roasting me will be published promptly.[6]

While Elsie wooed San Francisco readers, George started classes at the California Polytechnic State University,

four hours south of San Francisco. He threw himself headlong into campus life, majoring in mechanical engineering,
working on the school paper, *The Polygram*, and joining
the drama club, where he scored the lead in a play called
A Tailor-Made Man. Despite a hectic schedule and active social life—he joined a fraternity, entertained his friends by
playing music on his Graphophone, signed up for mandatory military training, competed in rifle competitions (and
was considered one of the "best shots" in his class)—he still
made the honor roll.[7]

Elsie upgraded his red Model T to a sporty, two-seater
roadster, which, *The Polygram* contended, made "George
real popular with the ladies." He wooed a girl named Ethel,
a dark-eyed brunette with a modern shingled bob to whom
he penned tender love notes and poems.

Months after Elsie started at the *Call*, her "Listen,
World!" column attracted the attention of Arthur Brisbane,
editor of Hearst's most profitable newspaper, the *Evening
Journal* in New York, whose circulation was fast approaching a million readers. Brisbane was such an integral part of
Hearst's inner circle that other folks in the business called
him Hearst's "alter ego."[8]

Brisbane wrote Elsie a brief note to say he'd stumbled
across her column while traveling through the South, where
he'd picked up a newspaper that syndicated it. *Would I mind
telling him a little bit about myself?* he coyly wrote. *And would
I pardon him asking—since he had "a sort of interest in writing?"* (Not only did Brisbane run the *Journal*, he was also

one of the country's most prolific and influential newspaper writers.)[9]

Brisbane's pleasantries marked the beginning of his relentless campaign to bring Elsie into the Hearst universe. He was well aware of what she represented: a ticket to more readers, always the bottom line in the newspaper business, and by far the most important metric of success to "The Chief," William Randolph Hearst. Brisbane had quickly absorbed his boss's ethos in 1897 when Hearst lured him away from Joseph Pulitzer's the *World*, and he'd been in the news business long enough to know that Elsie, with her whip-smart prose and talent to distill her complex ideas into provocative editorial cartoons, was a unicorn.[10]

In 1924, Brisbane invited her to Manhattan so they could meet. At the time, Hearst's empire was reaching its zenith. It was reported that one in four Americans read a Hearst paper and millions more read articles published by the Hearst-owned King Features Syndicate. He also owned International News Service and a slew of national magazines, including *Cosmopolitan* and *Good Housekeeping*—the latter a successor to George E. Crowell's journal, *The Household*.[11]

Elsie read and reread the letter and then phoned George, her excitement amplifying her voice. Her work had been noticed by an editor in New York City, she told her son, one of the most important men in the entire news business, a man who reported directly to Hearst himself. Then her mind snagged on something rather insignificant: she realized she didn't have a proper winter coat to visit Manhattan.

Fur collars were all the rage and her long wool coat had a plain collar. George came to the rescue, mailing her the pelt of a coyote he'd shot in the foothills. She gamely threw the fur around her shoulders, bought a hat, and boarded a train headed east, this time not as an apprehensive teenage bride, but as a forty-year-old woman basking in her own, self-realized success.

Brisbane put her up in the most luxurious hotel in New York City: the Plaza. Overlooking Central Park, it had all the opulence of a French chateau, including rare marble imported from around the world. Its interior was lit by 1,650 crystal chandeliers and the predominant color was gold— in the form of gilded mirrors and gold-encrusted dinner plates, teacups, and saucers. Clearly, Brisbane aimed to impress her.[12]

There was a suite waiting. I sat on the edge of the bed and looked out on the empire of the mighty and waited for that success feeling to begin. But it didn't. For the life of me I couldn't feel any different than I had when I sat on the edge of that mining dump in Hornitos and picked over ore in a 114-degree sun. Only more scared. And I bet if the truth were told that's all there is to this fame business anyway.

Then I went down to see Mr. Brisbane. Or, to be accurate, I went down and up and around and under and across and inbetween to see Mr. Brisbane. Mr. Brisbane at that time was ensconced in the old Journal building on William Street. It was umpty ump miles—and several cycles in evolution—from the Plaza to those jumbled up rookeries under the Brooklyn Bridge.

But, having arrived there, you had only started your search for Mr. Brisbane.

First, you went up the freight elevator. Then you began an interminable scrambling down halls, along dark runways, over bales of mysterious merchandise, around packing boxes, beneath shadowy avalanches of refuse . . . all this through an increasing dimness and dustiness. Presently, time and space having long since vanished—you found yourself in a peculiar aperture where papers—of all ages, conditions and dimensions cluttered, clung to and clotted every available inch of floor, wall and ceiling.

And, an instant after, forgot everything as you faced the steady gaze of a pair of blue-gray eyes.[13]

A middle-aged man in wire-rim glasses sat before her, his thin salt-and-pepper hair neatly combed over his crown. Arthur Brisbane, who'd risen from the reporting ranks to become an editor and syndicated columnist, was a tireless worker. Unlike many of his brethren in the newsroom, he didn't smoke or drink. His messy desk—awash in news-papers, photographs, and a beat-up New York City tele-phone directory—was a testament to the furious pace of the news and Brisbane's relentless drive to retain the *Evening Journal's* competitive edge.[14]

He had defied expectation . . . a quiet, serene person in the rumpled suit.

For a long moment Mr. Brisbane sat quite still and looked at me.

"Miss Robinson, I presume?"[15]

She had entered the room in a flustered state because she'd snagged her stocking on a packing box, ripping it. She left the room elated, and in a state of disbelief: Brisbane had offered her a contract at $20,000 a year—about $335,000 in today's dollars—to syndicate "Listen, World!" The highest-paid newsman in America would make Elsie the highest-paid newswoman in the Hearst organization.[16]

I signed the contract. Then I went back to the Plaza.

I sat on the bed. I sat on a chair. I walked to the window and looked out at New York. There wasn't enough room anywhere.

So I lay face down on the floor . . . stretched my arms as far as they could go . . . dug my nails into the carpet and laughed and cried and shouted and prayed and promised God impossible feats, in a madness of gratitude.

Then I suddenly fell asleep. I had not known I was so tired.[17]

Chapter 13

ST. LUKE'S

THIS PHOTO OF ELSIE AND GEORGE WAS LIKELY TAKEN AT CAL POLY, where military training was mandatory. Elsie is wearing a hat veil, a popular accessory at the time.

Image published in Hearst's International-Cosmopolitan, *August 1934.*

THERE WAS MONEY NOW. MONEY, PERHAPS, TO control George's asthma once and for all. Money for specialists, for the newest treatment—an injection that swiftly alleviated bronchial spasms—money for anything that would help her son breathe easier. *Now, at last, he could have his chance!* A deep sense of optimism and well-being flowed through her as her train raced across the heartland toward California.[1]

George drove up from Cal Poly in his roadster to meet her at the station. She stepped from the train onto the platform and there he was—her tall, handsome son—with a jubilant smile on his face.

I was running, running—with my arms open to him and his arms open to me—and we were whooping, hugging each other, dancing like laughing loons!

I remember a few months in which our laughter never seemed to stop . . . in which it swelled until the stars were not tall enough nor the horizons wide enough to bound our new joy. . . . I remember a doctor telling us that we might, at last, dare hope for a complete recovery. . . .

I remember a handful of shining adventures . . . the day we walked down store aisles and bought all the silly little things we had always wanted to buy. The day he told me about The Girl

and we planned for her future and his. The night he showed me
his fraternity pin.

Joy! Joy! We crossed our fingers! We knocked on wood! We
said it couldn't be possible. We kidded—trying to hide our wild
gratitude. I crept to his room at night—after he slept—and lis-
tened to that unbelievable, easy breath—[2]

In the fall of 1924, however, George, back at school, was
again laid low by asthma. The Central Coast's cool, humid
climate, combined with a high pollen count, sent him into
prolonged fits of coughing. Nights were the worst; lying
down exacerbated his sense of suffocation, so he sat up, but
was then unable to sleep and too exhausted to attend lec-
tures the next day. After weeks of struggling to breathe, he
was forced to drop out of Cal Poly.[3]

That December, just two days after George turned
twenty, Elsie bought a magnificent home at 235 Edgewood
Avenue, in San Francisco's Sunset Heights neighborhood.
The new house was full of light: it had sunrooms, a sleeping porch, a breakfast nook, and windows on three sides
that offered unobstructed views of the bay.[4] It offered
George serenity as he regained his strength with Elsie, who
worked from home, always nearby to minister to his needs.
Surely they celebrated an opulent Christmas together, even
if George was still convalescing while they unpacked.

Nearly a year later, in November 1925, George was
feeling well enough that Elsie helped him transfer to Sacramento Junior College, in the state's more temperate interior. He quickly made the most of this second chance at

college life. He became assistant leader of the "yell team" (the 1920s version of a cheer team) and led chants through a megaphone to whip up enthusiasm during the Cardinal and Gold's basketball and football games.[5]

There was only one niggling—and new—health concern that developed early in January 1926, a few weeks after his twenty-first birthday. It seemed minor. George had a small lump on his foot that bothered him when he ran. He wasn't sure what had caused it—perhaps a fall from a horse. *Such a little thing—after all the terrible tall mountains of agony he had climbed.*[6]

He scheduled an outpatient procedure in Sacramento to have the lump removed. The doctor said the minor surgery would take an hour at most.

But something went wrong. The procedure itself went smoothly. But after George was discharged from the hospital, his health inexplicably took a turn for the worse. Suddenly he was wracked by fever, chills, a persistent cough, and chest pains.

He returned to San Francisco to recover at his mother's home. Elsie tucked him into bed, as she'd done so many times over the past twenty-one years, and kept vigil at his side.

Although she didn't share the particulars of her troubles with her readers, her anguish is palpable in her January 13 column.

I'm afraid. . . . Fear runs through all my life. I cannot mark its course with a definite line, but its grim shadow tinges my brightest moments and noblest dreams. . . . I have only found one way

to manage fear. . . . Go on! No matter how terrible your inward
agony, go on! Don't wait until the darkness lifts. Grab each small
task, whether it appeals or not! Keep doing something! Go through
the gestures of normal life! Eat, talk and smile as though all things
were well. Then gradually your inner body will conform to your
firm fighting front. Your thoughts will cease their maddened ham-
mering at your skull. You will not banish fear, but you'll have con-
quered it and made it run to heel.[7]

That winter, the influenza virus was particularly
deadly—and it appeared that George had been infected.
The flu's seasonal creep across the country would kill 41,000
Americans. The flu vaccine had yet to be invented and there
was no way to determine whom the virus would strike next.
George could have been exposed to it in a crowded lecture
hall or leading cheers in a packed gymnasium, or even at
the hospital where he had his surgery. However he became
infected, the virus took its usual course and settled in his
lungs, where it further constricted airways that likely had
been scarred and narrowed by lifelong asthma.[8]

When George showed no signs of improvement, despite her constant tender care, a distraught Elsie consulted with Dr. Epsteen, who urged her to bring George to
St. Luke's, a new hospital in San Francisco with state-of-the-
art equipment and plenty of beds. Dr. Epsteen met them
there and examined George himself, pressing a stethoscope
to his chest. He worried that George's flu had turned into a
bacterial bronchopneumonia, which could lead to a buildup
of pus in the area between his lungs and chest wall, known
as the pleural cavity. An infection in the pleural space could

in turn develop into a dangerous condition called empyema, which had three stages: first fluid filled the pleural cavity, then it thickened, and finally, it prevented the lungs from fully inflating—depriving the patient of life-giving oxygen.[9]

In 1926, empyema was frequently a death sentence. Penicillin, the first widely used antibiotic that could have treated George's bacterial infection, wouldn't be discovered until two years later.

The hours ticked by at the hospital as Elsie watched George fight for air, his frail chest straining under the hospital sheets.

Saturday, January 23, broke clear and mild in San Francisco. Along Market Street, the big news story—hawked by newsboys up and down the sidewalks—was that Prohibition agents had busted up an illegal gin mill near Union Square. The most popular song in America was a snappy foxtrot number called "Don't Wake Me Up Let Me Dream" by the Howard Lanin Orchestra. And at St. Luke's hospital, a distraught Elsie hovered over her dying son as he drifted in and out of consciousness.[10]

His dreadful rasping filled the room. His lips and fingertips turned blue as cyanosis set in. And his skin felt so, so cold, no matter how many blankets she bundled around him.

At around noon, George Alexander Crowell—after twenty-one years, one month, and eighteen days of life—took his last ragged breath and slipped away. He had been hospitalized for nineteen days.

Details? What do they matter—now? There are no details when the thing you have loved best goes on. Only a wailing, witless darkness.

Grief—we expect that. Heart-breaking sorrow—flesh rending pain . . . loneliness beyond all measure of imagining—But we never anticipate that most poignant of agonies which death inflicts upon the bereaved—the sense of utter bankruptcy.[11]

The cause of death, as Dr. Epsteen had feared, was empyema.[12]

Elsie paid $100 for a metal casket with a gray silk interior and $1 for a black tie, which the undertaker fastened around George's neck in a schoolboy knot.[13]

After a small, private funeral featuring an organist, his body was cremated.

Chapter 14

SONORA

ELSIE HARDLY TOOK A BREAK AFTER GEORGE'S DEATH.
This editorial cartoon ran alongside her column on May 22, 1926.

Original publication, King Features Syndicate.

THROUGHOUT THE HARROWING LAST MONTH of George's life, Elsie had missed only three columns. Two days after George died, "Listen, World!" carried a breezy piece about women who are too attached to their mothers. In the weeks and months that followed his death, she doled out her lively perspective to the masses, fulfilling her job as a public sage who was seemingly untouched by life's upheavals herself.[1]

I can walk into my office and close the door. And when I close the door, I can deliberately leave myself outside. I can leave my personal hopes and worries, my humiliations and tragedies outside that door, just as surely as I can leave my bedroom slippers and bath-robe in my room at home. I wouldn't wear those personal garments in my living room. . . . I wouldn't dream of wearing them to my place of work. To do so would be the height of bad taste. So I close the door, and I lock out the self that is Elsie Robinson, her private life, her private tears and fears. And another self sits down at the typewriter—a larger, impersonal self who is part of all the tears and laughter, the hopes and fears of the world.[2]

She threw herself into her work, churning out two columns that she both wrote and illustrated (her nationally syndicated "Listen, World!" feature for Hearst and her "Tell It to Elsie" for the *Call*)—as well as a reported article each Saturday. Months after George's death, she wrote a piece on resilience, and the accompanying cartoon showed a man with a bindle walking on a winding path; "KEEP MOV-ING!" she wrote beneath the figure.[3]

Years later, she'd write a lengthy poem, "A Monument to Love," about living without her only child, abbreviated here:

Where are you, darling?
Was it yesterday you died—
Or have long ages passed
Since you went from my side.
And left me here, alone?

How strange life is!
We who have buried
Half our hearts
Must live two lives
In one.
One part of me
Lives here—
Works, plays, loves, laughs,
As if it knew
No other life but this:
Yet, all the while
Unseen by those who watch
My secret self
Goes groping on your trail—
Goes calling . . . calling . . .
Do you ever hear?

Easy enough to raise
A monument to grief—

But how shall one
Build monuments to joy?
Erect a shaft
To pride and gratitude?

A slab of stone?
No—stone's too cold
And dead—
Your body died,
And, with it, half my heart,
But not one throb
Of our warm love has cooled—
It burns as brightly
As before you passed—
Why mark a living love
With piles of cold, dead stone?

Then what can I do
To show the world, and you
That love goes on—triumphant,
That love always pays?
DEAR—I CAN LIVE!
OF MY OWN LIFE
I'LL BUILD YOUR MONUMENT!

Yes, love can work
That shining miracle—
AND MY STRONG LIFE
SHALL BE YOUR MONUMENT![14]

But Elsie's workaholism could not outpace her grief. On a business trip to New York in the summer of 1928, she was hospitalized for a nervous breakdown. At the time, she'd told her editor at the *Call and Post*—her now good friend Fremont Older—that she'd had surgery for gallstones, but in a letter she wrote him on April 10, 1929, she came clean.[5]

There is nothing chronically wrong with me, but I have seriously strained myself by overwork for many years. You have always thought that I did my work very easily and with great rapidity. In a way that was true, but I also did it at a cost which no one suspected. I have worked every night for the last ten years. I have sacrificed all my social life to maintain my tremendous production. I did this gladly for my boy's sake. Now he is gone. After his death, I began to feel the result of the long strain, but at first I would not acknowledge it, even to myself.

When I was in New York last summer I broke badly. There were days when I could hardly remember my own name. They told me that I would inevitably "crack" unless I dropped a great part of my work.

I can no longer work at the pace, nor under the conditions, which were once possible.

This decision is not a hasty one with me. I have not spoken of this because I did not want to mix personal problems with business, and also because I have been proud of my record as a big producer and genuinely desirous of maintaining that record.

And in a foreshadowing of the kind of bold stance she'd take eleven years later in her contract dispute with "The Chief," Elsie's letter to Older included several demands that would enable her to keep writing "Tell It to Elsie" for him, in addition to writing "Listen, World!" for Hearst.

First, she needed more help managing reader correspondence from her "Tell It to Elsie" and "Listen, World!" columns. She received thousands of letters each week—from readers asking for her advice, or complaining about her advice—and she and her one secretary could no longer read, sort, and respond to the deluge on their own.[6]

Second, she wanted to work remotely. A month earlier, she had purchased a second home, a modest cabin in Sonora, a small town in the Sierra Nevada foothills. She wanted to stay up there for a while, away from the constant interruptions and phone calls of her office in the city.[7]

Her most pressing desire, however, was to finally carve out time to start a series based on her own life—a memoir project that Older had encouraged and that she finally felt she had the fortitude to begin.

The *San Francisco Call and Post* editor, who'd hired Elsie away from the *Oakland Tribune* and watched her rocket to national fame and then continue meeting her crushing workload even after George's death, agreed to her terms.

A few weeks later, she stepped into her car and drove away from her home on Edgewood Avenue—away from those empty rooms that still pulsed with memories of George—and returned to the low hills of the Sierra Nevada, where she and her son had lived their best adventures.

Like Hornitos, Sonora was founded by Mexican gold miners, who had named it after their hometown of Sonora, Mexico. The town shared Hornitos's history of gold-related violence, but by 1929 it had mellowed into civility, with an opera house at one end of the main drag and an elegant Victorian inn at the other.[8]

Elsie's cabin, located at the end of a winding dirt road, was a rustic affair constructed of split pine logs. The main room had a fieldstone fireplace and built-in shelves for her books. There was a small kitchen and bedroom. The place's rough-hewn modesty was yet another reminder of Hornitos—of the evenings she spent reviewing lessons with George, of nights trying to capture the turbulence and sweetness of their vagabond life on the page.[9]

She had a portable typewriter now. It was so much lighter and sleeker than the dual-keyboarded Smith Premier monstrosity she'd used back then. The cabin was sited next to a creek and overlooked a sunny meadow of native grasses and flowers—spires of purple lupine, lacy white yarrow. She pulled her writing desk over to the doorway to see it all better and to hear the burbling creek and the cheery, flute-like calls of meadowlarks. A clean breeze wafted through the open door and skimmed over her pince-nez glasses and graying blonde hair. The serenity of nature soothed her, just as it did growing up in the embrace of her mother's garden.

I've found healing for almost everything in the beauty of the world.[10]

It was only at this remote place, and on her own terms, that she was finally able to quiet herself long enough to focus on her own heart. After years of writing about other people's problems, she now found it odd to put words to her own tragedies. She wound a blank sheet of paper into the typewriter. As she raised her hands to the keyboard, she was seized by a mixture of resolve and defiance, a kind of audacity that propelled her to finally speak her entire truth.

This is my own story and I'm going to tell it in my own way. If I want to swear, I'm going to swear. If I want to sing, dance, weep, fight, make faces, relate shockingly intimate and obviously indiscreet facts; thumb my nose at the status quo—I'm going to do just that.[11]

She went on to narrate her life's drama—from Benicia to Brattleboro and Hornitos to Hearst—in gritty detail, using the same frank, immediate voice that won over millions of newspaper fans.

She found comfort in searching for connections and meaning in the tangled knot of her experiences. After years of doling out advice to melancholic readers, she realized that her own woes were but *common bread*.

Remembering her life with George often made her smile with fondness or laugh aloud. Other times, it felt like she had inherited her son's incapacity to breathe.

The memory of touching the clothes he had worn . . . clothes which still bore the odor of his flesh . . . of groping back and forth, back and forth, through rooms which still held the echo of his laughter—

There's an ache in my heart that never will heal. No cry was ever more bitter than mine in that black moment.[12]

She turned to narrative storytelling as a grief-stricken forty-six-year-old columnist for the same reason she turned to it as a lonely twenty-six-year-old wife: *To save my life.* When she grew tired of the ruthless accounting, she stepped into her radiant meadow, where the sight of a cypress tree against the soaring turquoise sky was enough to fill her with rapture.

She typed her story in chronological chunks, often working all day and into the night, until her thoughts blurred and moths swarmed the lamplight.

One week went by. Two. One month. Day after day, the chapters of that serial story went down to Fremont Older. Day after day, he sent back warm encouragement.[13]

The final pages had her stumped. She'd always had a knack for wrapping up her advice columns with a bit of encouragement or an exhortation, depending on the nature of the reader's dilemma or the larger point she was trying to make.

But other people's problems were abstract. This was *her* life she was writing about. How do you conclude your life story when your life is not yet over?

She knew the landing—the final words, the concluding wisdom—was always the hardest part. Clever wouldn't work here; clever didn't stick. To resonate, to be remembered, the ending must be profound.

She wrestled with tone. With the order of the sentences. Went for quiet walks through her meadow to reflect. One day, toward evening, she had a flash of insight. She rushed back to her desk and reached for the keyboard.

It is twilight as I finish this writing. I am sitting in the doorway of my cabin. Below me, the land falls away into a wide bowl, then rises again into the vast heave of the Sierra. Now the shadows are filling the bowl with their blue tide. Through it I can see only a vague bulk of rock and tree, tilled land, walled garden. Far off, against those clear, bright vistas which open into night, the great peaks flash . . . then fade. . . .

Low in the east, the first star burns—And it seems to me that my whole life has been like that. A glimpse of substance, through a sea of shadow. A brief, bright flash of peaks . . . a star . . . then night.

Was any adventurer ever really born "brave"? Was there ever an adventure that was not bought at the price of fear and agony? Are not the bravest also the terrified? I know it was so with me.[14]

She reread the lines she had typed. They were good. She lifted her head to look out at the falling night and a deep peace welled within her.

The only person who fails in life, she thought, is the person who doesn't dare live it.[15]

⚜

EPILOGUE

PHOTO OF ELSIE AT WORK, A FRAMED PICTURE OF George over her shoulder.

Image published in Nebraska State Journal, *April 23, 1942. Photographer unknown.*

WITH GREAT FANFARE, *COSMOPOLITAN* magazine serialized Elsie's memoir over seven issues, from February to August of 1934. Readers were privy to her "scintillating" life experiences and promised more vicarious adventures at the end of each installment: "Next month Elsie Robinson tells how she defied the conventions of Puritan New England—for her child's sake" and "Next month Elsie Robinson's further adventures as a miner—one woman among many men."[1]

That fall, Farrar & Rinehart published the series as a book, titled *I Wanted Out!*

Elsie's story landed at the height of the Great Depression, a time when many Americans were reeling from economic hardship and looking for hope—and her tale of persevering despite tremendous obstacles gave it to them. *Kirkus Reviews* hailed *I Wanted Out!* as a "story of struggle against insuperable odds. A story of inner conflict, of unpreparedness for life, of an unquenchable determination." The *New York Times* raved, "Mrs. Robinson's account of the years of bitter struggle and undaunted courage that followed are deeply touching and demand of the reader sympathy and admiration for their heroism." The *Washington Post* called her "brutally frank" memoir "an exhilarating potion."[2]

Elsie continued to improve and expand her Sonora property, planting orchards and vineyards, buying horses, pigs, and chickens. She employed a ten-person staff, including a cook, a maid, and gardeners—and three male secretaries who dealt with reader correspondence. Why male secretaries? she was often asked. She answered this question in a glowing profile—"Elsie Robinson—Study in Contrasts"—published in the *St. Louis Post-Dispatch*.[3]

The ranch is eight miles from the nearest town and the quiet up there is profound. Women can't stand it. I've tried women secretaries, but I find that before long up there on the ranch they begin to develop ulcerated teeth or husbands threatening divorce. The men are different. When the stillness begins to get on their nerves, they can go into the nearest town and get drunk. That breaks the tension and they come back to the ranch ready for work.[4]

Over the decades she used her national platform to express her increasingly progressive and political views.

She supported labor unions and scoffed at Prohibition.

She denounced the death penalty as an inhumane, *stone age* punishment.

After the Nazis rose to power, she advocated repeatedly in defense of Jews and urged Americans to *take our stand in support of Jewish refugees.*[5]

She called out racism and condemned violence against people of color. She excoriated the Daughters of the American Revolution for refusing to let baritone Paul Robeson perform in their concert hall in Washington, DC. *And on what, may I ask, do you base your supremacy? You didn't choose*

*your ancestors—unless biology is entirely cockeyed. You happened
to be born white, and that is no great feat. You could have put
aside ignorance and prejudice and contemptible snootiness and
have given your lives for unity. But you weren't big enough. You
weren't brave enough.*[6]

And in 1930, when a white mob stormed a Texas courthouse where a Black man stood trial for raping a white
woman, set fire to the building, and killed and mutilated
the accused man, she called the culprits *shoddy weaklings.
The easiest way for that kind of white man to achieve herodom
is to kill or torture some black or yellow man under some noble
pretext.*[7]

William Randolph Hearst sent Elsie to cover breaking
and major news and often edited her stories himself. Her
stories included the kidnapping of the infant son of avia-
tors Charles and Anne Lindbergh; the Bonus March, when
a haggard band of forty thousand jobless World War I vets
and their supporters marched to Washington, DC, to demand a promised cash bonus and were brutally suppressed
by police and US military troops; and the cantankerous 1940
Democratic Convention in Chicago when President Frank-
lin Delano Roosevelt was nominated to an unprecedented
third term.[8]

*The entire selection and nomination of the present candidates
was utterly unAmerican and undemocratic. It was dictated from
start to finish and rammed down the delegates' throats whether
they liked it or not . . . and Stalin himself could not have perpe-
trated a more ruthless piece of political log-rolling.*

Meanwhile, Elsie kept expanding her personal brand. She added radio to her repertoire, writing for a hugely popular NBC program called *I Want a Divorce*, which dramatized stories of fictional couples whose marriages were on the rocks but who ultimately managed to work things out. Launched in October 1937—a time of soaring divorce rates among Americans—the show was profiled in major metropolitan newspapers and sponsored by S&W Fine Foods, distributors of S&W Mellow'd Coffee, and quickly won 54 percent of listening audiences on the West Coast stations where it aired.[9]

As she broadened her reach into radio, Elsie devoted ever more energy to growing her "Listen, World!" audience and deftly making sure she was credited for it. She launched a new column called "Young America," which asked readers under thirty to sound off on topics ranging from atomic energy to whether women should drink alcohol or split a bill on a date. As with the Aunt Elsie clubs that formed in response to her work at the *Oakland Tribune*, college students and young professionals created Young America clubs that used her columns as in-person discussion prompts. These new readers *are the greatest asset the Hearst organization has*, she wrote The Chief.[10]

In conjunction with the popularity of "Young America," Hearst sent her on a cross-country campus speaking tour that culminated in a June 13 luncheon feting her at the stately Warwick Hotel in New York City. The celebration was hosted by Joseph V. Connolly, head of King Features

Syndicate, and must have made Elsie burst with both pride and resentment in equal measure; a few weeks earlier she'd been denied a long overdue raise.[11]

Alongside her triumphant career, Elsie continued to wrestle with grief, including the death of her mother in 1933 at the age of eighty-seven. She sometimes published poems in her column space as she reached for a more elevated mode of expression, and these would be collected in a book called *Listen World!*, published by Chapman & Grimes in 1934. Many of her poems deal, obliquely, with the death of George, whose loss she referred to as *an agony which must endure until I die.*[12]

In a prose poem called "Go On—Make the Gestures!," she seems to be offering readers her own recipe for resilience:

You do not have to "face a new day." You have only to face one moment at a time . . . make one gesture at a time. Small, mechanical gestures. Put your foot on the floor. Walk into the bathroom. Brush your teeth. Wash your face. Comb your hair. Start the coffee percolator. Put on your dress. Powder your nose. Start the toast. Pour out the milk. Smile. Say good morning to the family. Make some light, pleasant remark. Put a quiet, friendly hand on a worried shoulder. Sit down—And so, on and on through the day. No matter how you feel—sad or mad or bewildered—that is all you need to do to live life bravely and beautifully and, in the end, abundantly. Just make the gestures.[13]

In another poem, "Don't Try to Forget," she writes, *You had a great tragedy? Death took the one you loved best, broke your heart? THEN BE GLAD THAT YOU COULD LOVE GREATLY ENOUGH TO HAVE A BROKEN HEART. Be proud because your life once held such glory. And, in your ploughed soul, plant richer harvests of love.*[14]

Her message, always, boiled down to perseverance. How despite pain, we must go on. Despite loss, we must persist. Despite grief, we must learn to love again.

One subject, however, would continue dominating Elsie's work: the status of women. Both in her journalism and in her fiction, she continually examined the place of women in marriage, in the workplace, and in the world. Ray Long, head of the Hearst magazine division and editor in chief of *Cosmopolitan* from 1918 to 1931, credited Elsie with writing the kinds of short stories for his magazine that "discuss life from angles that may shock other women. But stories that every woman will *know* to be true, though some may refuse to admit it."[15]

At a time when most Americans believed women possessed a "maternal instinct," Elsie disagreed.

We are beginning to realize that it is as absurd to trust "mother instinct" in caring for children, as it would be to trust "aviator instinct" in flying a powerful plane.[16]

She took on the sacred cow of motherhood itself, telling women that having a baby was no guarantee of happiness and that fulfillment must also stem from pursuing their own passions.

No mother can do her full duty to her children who does not do full duty to herself.[17]

Neither, she wrote, was romantic love the key to joy in a woman's life.

Love is not "woman's whole existence" unless she's a fool.[18]

She urged women to find gratification outside of the home, as their husbands did, by participating in public life and holding careers.

Elsie's writing would be debated from Wichita to Manhattan, clipped by Henry Ford, quoted by Ann Landers, cherished by Lisa See's grandmother in the author's best-selling memoir, *On Gold Mountain*—even entered into the Congressional Record when a congressman from Arkansas read a poem she wrote about the resilience of youth to his fellow politicians.[19]

She'd also make history because of her editorial cartoons. "Women have always found political or editorial cartooning the most difficult illustration specialty to break into," writes Martha H. Kennedy, past curator of popular and applied graphic art at the Library of Congress in her seminal book, *Drawn to Purpose: American Women Illustrators and Cartoonists*. Once those inroads were made, women brought attention to often-overlooked topics, including women's rights, the kind of work, Kennedy argues, "that one cannot imagine any male cartoonist doing."[20]

Elsie was a trailblazer not only because her illustrations were nationally syndicated and covered new topics; she was also unique in that her editorial cartoons accompanied her own columns instead of illustrating the sentiments of other writers.

"I am not aware of any person who was nationally syndicated with a column and accompanying editorial cartoon prior to 1921," said Jenny Robb, curator at the Billy Ireland Cartoon Library & Museum at the Ohio State University.

Dave Astor, archivist at the National Society of Newspaper Columnists and a reporter who covered newspaper syndication for *Editor & Publisher* for twenty-five years, concurred that Elsie was an outlier in this way. "I can't remember a single person who wrote and illustrated their own column—male or female."[21]

As an outspoken, high-profile woman who was unafraid to kick the hornet's nest of pervasive American sexism, she was a frequent target of crude barbs lobbed by male detractors, including one writer who dismissed her as a "breast beater" with no right "telling others how to think, act, and live." She should stick to her lane, he argued, and write about the "innocuous subjects of marriage and young love." Even the name of her column—"Listen, World!"—was attacked for being "offensive" and "presumptuous." And although she refused to call herself a feminist, a term many Americans equated at the time with "man-hater"—she was indeed a feminist in her thoughts, words, and actions.[22]

The "place" of American women would continue to be hotly debated for decades as religion, tradition, and the media continued to deify the image of the sweet, submissive, June Cleaver housewife—and conversely, the stern, lordly, Ward Cleaver family patriarch. It was only in 1963, when journalist Betty Friedan burst onto the scene with *The Feminine Mystique*, that Americans started paying attention to "the problem that has no name" among depressed homemakers—the exact same problem that Elsie experienced as a young wife in the early 1900s and wrote about during her entire journalistic career.

❦

A FEW MONTHS after George died, Elsie impulsively wed her San Francisco neighbor in an action she later called a *cruel mistake*; the marriage was annulled after two years. In 1933—the same year that Christie's third wife divorced him on the grounds of "intolerable severity"—Elsie married for a third time, to Benton Fremont, a construction engineer from Sonora and the grandson of the famous Western explorer General John Charles Fremont, known as "The Pathfinder."[23]

Benton was forty-five, Elsie was fifty. *He is helping me live*, she wrote in her memoir. Benton had custody of his seven-year-old son from a previous marriage and Elsie raised him as her own child, even building him a swimming pool at her Sonora property so that he and his friends could cool off during the scalding foothill summers.[24]

After marrying Elsie, however, Benton seems to have used her tremendous wealth for his personal gain. In 1936, he launched a congressional campaign against a popular Democratic incumbent from California's second district, perhaps hoping to follow in the footsteps of his grandfather John Charles Fremont, who was one of the first two US senators representing California, and later the governor of Arizona. But Benton Fremont's political aspirations came to a thudding halt after he lost the congressional race by a three-to-one margin.[25]

And there was a larger money pit that Benton was sinking funds into: a seventy-year legal battle between the

Fremont family and the US government. During the Civil War, the US Army had seized a 13.5-acre property that the Fremonts owned in San Francisco to construct a coastal battery against a potential Confederate invasion. After the war ended, the property—which stood on what's known today as Fort Mason, in the city's Marina District—was neither returned to nor purchased from the Fremont family. For decades, General Fremont repeatedly petitioned Congress for compensation and Congress repeatedly voted to settle with the family. But the measure was always shot down by Southern politicians who held a long-simmering grudge against Fremont, who'd been an outspoken abolitionist. After General Fremont died in 1890, his son Major Francis Preston Fremont led the legal battle before handing it off to his son—Elsie's husband Benton. For more than three decades, until his death, Benton waged a one-man war against the government—funded by Elsie's paychecks—seeking remuneration for what he regarded as his birthright, land that was valued at $2.4 million upon his death in 1960 (and $35 million in today's dollars).[26]

Throughout the years, Elsie continued to work for long hours, with few breaks. Her physical and mental health suffered because of it. On May 30, 1936, during the period that Benton was campaigning for Congress, and ten years after George's death, Elsie was hospitalized after overdosing on sleeping medicine. She was alone in her San Francisco home at the time but able to dial an operator to ask for help before lapsing into unconsciousness. Benton told the United Press news agency that Elsie was "suffering a nervous breakdown brought on by overwork," as well as insomnia, and had taken too much of the sedative by mistake. In an interview published on June 9, 1940, she quipped, *Forget it. It was an awful breach of etiquette. Newspaper people aren't supposed to ever get sick.*[27]

But in early 1942, she suffered a worse health emergency, one at first referred to as a "sudden illness" in newspaper accounts. For over two months, her column didn't run. Get-well cards and telegrams flooded her office from concerned readers, like this one from a woman in Chicago: "I hope this letter may help a little to repay for all you have given me. I have been reading your column for 14 years and have clipped a number of them and put them in scrapbooks for my children when they are older. I hope you are well on the road to recovery and I will remember you in my prayers."[28]

On April 24, an article in Pennsylvania's *Wilkes-Barre Record* shed light on Elsie's absence, stating that "she was hospitalized in February with serious injuries, the result of an accidental fall," and was convalescing at her Sonora home. Her column resumed on Monday, April 27, with a poem titled "When Dusk Comes Down," which dealt with trying to find peace amid fears of war. (The US had entered World War II a few months earlier.)

Details of her fall—which was severe enough to break both of her hips and disable her for the rest of her life—remain a mystery. She would never refer to it in her writing.[29]

In a column written soon after her return, she acknowledged the distress of parents whose sons had been shipped overseas to fight in the new war. *Not easy business facing these hundreds of tear-stained, fear-warped letters. Desperate mothers seeing their boys sent away. Stricken fathers seeing all the pride and plans of their life wiped out. I, too, have known a house grown still. My boy also will never come back.*[30]

Her sedentary lifestyle certainly didn't contribute to good health. Plagued by high blood pressure, she developed hypertensive heart disease.

One of the last "Listen, World!" columns to run before her death appeared on Wednesday, September 5, 1956. In it, she wrote about letting go of anger.

You can't pick your universe, nor elect your own boss for it, but you can pick your own viewpoint. Love is positive, and hate is negative. Love gets you somewhere. Hate holds you back.[31]

Three days later, on September 8, a Saturday, shortly after two p.m., Elsie died at her home in San Francisco. She was seventy-three. The medical examiner listed her cause of death as "pulmonary edema secondary to hypertensive cardiovascular disease." Pulmonary edema is caused by excess fluid in the lungs—in a tragic mirroring, Elsie died struggling to breathe, just as her beloved son George had, thirty years earlier.[32]

Her body was cremated and buried next to her father and brother Paul in Benicia—in the same hilltop cemetery where, as a teenager, she'd made a midnight plea to God to "give her the works."[33]

An Associated Press obituary ran in newspapers across the country. It began, "Elsie Robinson, famed columnist whose writings gave hope and encouragement to millions of persons, died at her home here." *Time* magazine reported that her syndicated column "Listen, World!" had started "twanging heartstrings" as soon as it was launched, and the *New York Times*, while praising Elsie's work as an illustrator, duly noted what brought her "fame, and fortune" was her "widely distributed, 'Listen, World.'"[34]

Most of that fortune had evaporated by the time of her death; her bank account only contained $1,500. It's not clear how much of her money Benton squandered on his family's hundred-year lawsuit, although one of Elsie's former secretaries would tell an interviewer that "Benton freely spent Elsie's money and incurred several large debts." Benton himself would die a pauper four years later, in 1960, without having received a single penny in compensation from the US government. Today, Fort Mason is a designated landmark, and the former military barracks that were built on the Fremont land house two dozen nonprofit and arts organizations.[35]

Elsie sold her Sonora property to the Girl Scouts in 1953, which in turn sold it to the Stanislaus County Department of Education in 1974. Today the county uses it for its Foothill Horizons Outdoor School, a program that offers nature-based classes and activities to middle-schoolers.[36]

Elsie had written so much advance copy for "Listen, World!" that her column would continue to appear in newspapers across the country for a full two months after her death.[37]

Beyond the thirty-five-year run of "Listen, World!," Elsie's first columns would continue even longer, written by alternates who adopted her phrasal ticks and tone, extending her work by decades.

"Cry on Geraldine's Shoulder" would run until 1961, for a total of forty-one years.[38]

The Aunt Elsie brand would live on for a whopping fifty-one years. The last "Aunt Elsie" column in the *Oakland Tribune*, published on November 27, 1970, still mimicked her slangy style, referring to kids as "pals," asking about their Christmas plans, and printing their poems and drawings.

A few former Aunt Elsie club members, now well into their golden years, still retain their club pins and the letters they received from Aunt Elsie. Howard Gardiner, ninety-four, reminisced about writing stories for the column when he was seven and sometimes getting them printed in the *Tribune*. "I never forgot that I was published," he said, the pride still evident in his voice during a phone interview. Other former club members went on to become professional writers and authors, crediting Aunt Elsie with giving them their first boost of publishing confidence.[39]

✦

ELSIE ROBINSON WANTED *the works*—a larger, more meaningful existence—and pursued this objective throughout her seven decades. Ultimately she triumphed, living a life far grander than the one she was born into or the one that was prescribed to her as a woman. All the while, she encouraged others to live as intensely as she had and to seek out the healing balm of writing that she credited with saving her life innumerable times.

GO AHEAD—WRITE A COLUMN!

No, I'm not fooling. You've been complaining, haven't you? Saying you were sick of life . . . wishing you could "get away from everything." But notta chance! Other people have all the luck. They can go wandering when the restless mood strikes them. But not you! You've got to stick to the same old rut—doing the same dreary old household or office chores—day after day, year after year. And, holy mackerel, how sick you are of it!

So what? So why don't you do something about it? You can't do anything?

Oh, yes you can. No matter how poor you are or how burdened, how ignorant or obscure, there is one thing you can do which will fill your days with new excitement and your heart with new eagerness—and blast your boredom to smithereens.

YOU CAN WRITE A COLUMN!

But only columnists write a column! Wrong again! Anyone can write a column. It doesn't require special education, nor special preparation or position, to write a column. Anyone, anywhere can write a column out of the common makings of their daily life. All that is needed is—

A willingness to turn from yourself, forget yourself entirely—

And think of the Other Fellow—

Seeing him as he really is, and his problems as they really are—

Will a publisher accept your column? Probably not. But that isn't the point. If you "turn columnist" you'll find something far more precious than cash—YOU'LL FIND ESCAPE AND HEALING FOR A BOUND AND BITTERED SOUL.[40]

Elsie found that escape and healing. She also found validation. From her early days as Aunt Elsie and throughout her career writing "Listen, World!," Elsie's readers let her know that her thoughts, ideas, and opinions were worthy and that she mattered. Through her writing, Elsie was finally heard. She was seen.

Perhaps, there were also parts of Elsie that relished being a columnist because the act of offering guidance and affection to millions of readers helped her survive the boundless grief of losing George.

Everything you are feeling, somebody else has felt, somebody is feeling right at this moment. You are not alone.

Once I too felt as you are feeling now. I too felt that nobody else had suffered as I was suffering; nobody else had ever been so bewildered, so discouraged, so empty.

And then I took this job. And each day, across my desk, flowed the record of hundreds of other lives. Always those invisible millions had walked with me, wept with me, despaired with me!

No matter what happens to me now, I know that I am not alone. I know that all the rest of the world walks with me.

That knowledge is my richest possession.[41]

REMEMBERING ELSIE

FOR ALL OF ELSIE'S FAME AND SUCCESS, THERE emerges an inevitable question: Why has she been forgotten? There are three primary reasons: sexism, carelessness, and a lack of foresight.

When it comes to learning history in American public schools, a recent study by the National Women's History Museum found that only 24 percent of all the historical figures studied from kindergarten through twelfth grade are women.[1]

"To learn new histories, we have to discover new histories," explained Martha S. Jones, Johns Hopkins University history professor and author of *Vanguard: How Black Women Broke Barriers, Won the Vote, and Insisted on Equality for All.* "To teach new histories, we must also write new histories."[2]

Alexander Cuenca, chair of the College and University Faculty Assembly of the National Council for the Social

Studies, argues that the sidelining of women in social studies classrooms is due to the fact that curriculum standards in public schools are "doggedly masculine." The overarching focus on military, political, and economic history marginalizes the areas where women have been the most active and powerful, including civil rights, labor rights, immigration, arts, and journalism.[3]

This discoverability problem underscores the second factor contributing to Elsie's invisibility: carelessness.

In 1962, Marguerite J. Reese, staffer at the publishing house that printed *I Wanted Out!*, made a mistake in filling out the routine copyright renewal forms for Elsie's memoir. She stated that Elsie had requested the transaction, but the US Copyright Office canceled the request when a clerk discovered that Elsie was already dead. Nobody at Holt, Rinehart and Winston (by this time Farrar & Rinehart had folded into a new configuration) followed up to make the necessary adjustments to the application, and the book fell into the public domain. Abandoned, *I Wanted Out!* was never nurtured as part of the publisher's backlist of titles. Neither was an attempt made to renew the copyright for Elsie's book of poetry, *Listen World!*[4]

And last, the fact that Elsie's writing was never curated into a single collection shows an unfortunate lack of planning by her newspaper and magazine employers. Most of her work is accessible only in hard copy, on specialized databases, or on microfilm, discoverable only by those who know where to look. Instead, details of her career and correspondence are buried within the archival papers of the men who employed her—William Randolph Hearst, Fremont Older, and Arthur Brisbane.

None of this is to say that Elsie gets a free pass. Elsie outlived her parents, all four of her siblings, and her only child, George. Her widower, Benton Fremont, was too distracted by his legal battles to consider his late wife's legacy, apparently. Why she didn't tend to her legacy herself is a mystery. Elsie could have made arrangements to hand over her papers to a library or historical society. But she didn't.

Surely there is a lesson here for all of us about taking control of how we'll be remembered by future generations, if only within our own families.

❧

To read more about Elsie and see more of her artwork and editorial cartoons, please visit www.elsierobinson.com.

PHOTOS,
EDITORIAL CARTOONS,
AND MORE

AT THE HEIGHT OF HER CAREER, ELSIE WAS HEARST'S HIGHEST-paid female columnist. She published at a breakneck pace: a columnist and reporter for forty years, she wrote approximately nine thousand stories. Elsie also wrote short fiction for leading magazines, including *Cosmopolitan*.

Photo courtesy of the San Francisco News-Call Bulletin *newspaper photograph archive, Bancroft Library, University of California, Berkeley.*

AFTER ELSIE MARRIED CHRISTIE CROWELL IN 1903, THE COUPLE moved into the Crowell family mansion, Lindenhurst. The thirty-seven-room estate, which the *Brattleboro Reformer* called "one of the largest and most pretentious dwellings in Southeastern Vermont," was torn down in 1936. Today, the property is a community park; the original foundation is still visible in the woods behind it.

Photo courtesy of Brattleboro Historical Society, Brattleboro, Vermont.

ELSIE BEGAN HER CAREER as a children's writer and illustrator while living in Brattleboro. In 1911, she wrote and illustrated stories for *John Martin's Letters*, a subscription service that delivered stories to children by mail. A young wife and mother at the time, Elsie wrote under the pen name "Comfy Lady."

John Martin's Letters, *Courtesy of Library of Congress.*

FOLLOWING THE success of the first books she illustrated in 1913, *Behind the Garden Wall* and *Within the Deep Dark Woods*, Elsie landed a deal to illustrate two more books for early readers. Both were published in 1914 and each featured more than a hundred pages of Elsie's original

artwork. In *First Reader*, Elsie illustrated a story about a boy in a wheelchair who lives a full and empowered life—a positive depiction of disability that was groundbreaking for its time.

Illustration originally published in First Reader, *Doub & Company, 1914.*

ELSIE WAS HIRED BY THE *Oakland Tribune* to write and illustrate children's stories in 1918. Within a few months, her feature became so popular that the paper expanded her work to eight pages. *Aunt Elsie's Magazine* encouraged children to submit stories, poems, and drawings, and Elsie published many of them to their giddy pride and delight. The newspaper kept the Aunt Elsie brand going for decades. The last known mention of Aunt Elsie in the paper was November 27, 1970—fifty years after Elsie left the paper and fifteen years after her death.

Launch of Robinson's Aunt Elsie's Magazine, *May 11, 1919.*

Dozens of Aunt Elsie clubs were established throughout California, and the *Tribune* created membership cards and pins for her young and passionate fans. Clubs held parades with members dressing up in tribute to their favorite section of *Aunt Elsie's Magazine*—the "Witches' Cave" (for girls) and "Pirates' Den" (for boys). The *Tribune* also hosted variety shows at local theaters. As many as three thousand children would attend the live shows, with lines snaking for blocks and police on hand to handle the crowds.

Parade float photo courtesy of Special Collections, University Library, University of California Santa Cruz. Photo of pin courtesy of Allison Gilbert.

ELSIE BEGAN WRITING AND illustrating "Listen, World!" in 1921. During an era of rapidly changing mores, Elsie challenged gender inequality, racism, elitism, and anti-Semitism. This editorial cartoon was published on September 2, 1924. In the accompanying opinion piece, she wrote, "Marriage is no longer the only job open to women."

Original publication,
King Features Syndicate.

ALTHOUGH ELSIE BRISTLED at the word "feminist," she was a lifelong champion of women's rights and an indefatigable advocate for equality, as reflected in this March 8, 1926, editorial cartoon. Advocates for gender equality at the time frequently used inaccurate comparisons to slavery. In the accompanying article, she wrote, "The place to find the actual standing of the old fashioned home is not in the poetry books, but in the law books of a nation."

Original publication,
King Features Syndicate.

IN HER LANDMARK BOOK, *Ladies of the Press*, author Ishbel Ross described Elsie and her writing this way: "She is whole-hearted, original, intense. She deals in short words, short paragraphs, a punch in every line." Ross also wrote that her "Listen, World!" column "burst like a thunderclap" on Hearst readers. On October 21, 1926, Elsie examined the place of religion in schools.

Original publication,
King Features Syndicate.

ELSIE'S ILLUSTRATIONS CONTINUE TO BE provocative. During his time in college, Elsie's son, George, was deeply moved by widely publicized cases involving capital punishment. He expressed interest in becoming a lawyer and fighting against it. Elsie shared his concern and wrote several columns opposing capital punishment. This illustration ran alongside one such piece on September 10, 1925. Three convicts had just been hanged for killing a police officer. Now these young men "are a rotting crop," she wrote. "Ploughed under by the cruel blade of hate and ignorance."

Original publication,
King Features Syndicate.

HR13   TO ALL MORNING PAPERS AND EVENING PAPERS WHERE NO MORNINGS:

THE ARTICLE BY ELSIE ROBINSON ON VETERAN KILLED IN WASHINGTON IS
RELEASED FOR PUBLICATION IN ALL MORNINGS AND EVENINGS WHERE NO MORNINGS
ON TUESDAY, AUGUST SECOND.   CHANGE DATE LINE TO QUOTE WASHINGTON, D.
C., AUGUST 2 UNQUOTE.

CHIEF INSTRUCTS THAT IF NOTHING OCCURS TO INTERFERE, THIS ARTICLE
SHOULD BE USED ON FIRST PAGE, SET IN TWO COLUMN MEASURE, USUAL TYPO-
GRAPHY, ETC. OF SUCH ARTICLES AND FIRST PAGE EDITORIALS, NEXT TO THE
NEWS OF WASHINGTON DEVELOPMENTS IN THIS MATTER.

J. WILLICOMBE SAN SIMEON CAL. 7/31/32.

ELSIE ALSO COVERED BREAKING NEWS, AND HER REPORTED ARTICLES
were given prominent placement in Hearst newspapers across the country. Here, she was dispatched to cover the Bonus March in Washington,
DC, in 1932, a protest by forty thousand World War I veterans and their
supporters over delayed military service payments. In this directive,
"Chief" (William Randolph Hearst) instructs editors nationwide to give
Elsie's article front-page placement.

*Courtesy of William Randolph Hearst papers, Bancroft Library, University of
California, Berkeley.*

POEMS

PAIN

(Poems That Touch the Heart, *Doubleday, 1956*)

Why must I be hurt?
Suffering and despair,
Cowardice and cruelty,
Envy and injustice,
All of these hurt.
Grief and terror,
Loneliness and betrayal
And the agony of loss or death—
All these things hurt.
Why? Why must life hurt?
Why must those who love generously,
Live honorably, feel deeply
All that is good—and beautiful
Be so hurt,
While selfish creatures

Go unscathed?
That is why—
Because they can feel.
Hurt is the price to pay for feeling.
Pain is no accident,
Nor punishment, nor mockery
By some savage god.
Pain is part of growth.
The more we grow
The more we feel—
The more we feel—the more we suffer,
For if we are able to feel beauty,
We must also feel the lack of it—
Those who glimpse heaven
Are bound to sight hell.
To have felt deeply is worth
Anything it cost.
To have felt Love and Honor,
Courage and Ecstasy
Is worth—any price.
And so—since hurt is the price
Of Larger living, I will not
Hate pain, nor try to escape it.
Instead I will try to meet it
Bravely, bear it proudly:
Not as a cross, or a misfortune, but an
Opportunity, a privilege, a challenge—to the God that
gropes within me.

I BUILD HAPPINESS

(Listen World!, *Chapman & Grimes, 1934*)

You are not happy—you say? You wonder if you ever will be happy again? I do not know. I can only tell you something I have discovered about happiness. Perhaps that will help.

I have learned to build my happiness—collecting it bit by bit.

Once I did not need to do this. Once happiness came without effort or plan . . . as naturally as the sunrise, the song of the bird, the sweep of the glittering tide.

I had youth. I had curiosity and conceit. Best of all, I had love. Someone to work for—

Then suddenly all that was swept away. Life became a brooding desolation.

Nothing moved in that desolation. Nothing spoke. Nothing shone. Everything was over. My happiness was gone.

And at first I did not care.

But life does not let us stay that way. Life demands that we shall go on living—go on desiring—

And so I began to wish that happiness would come back to me. But I wished as a paralyzed man might wish for movement.

The paralyzed man thinks of motion coming back to him in a sudden miracle. I thought of happiness coming back to me in that way.

I felt that I, myself, could do nothing about it. It would just have to happen—without my volition. And I waited for it to happen—

I waited for happiness to come sweeping back again like a glittering tide . . . like the song of a bird . . . like sunrise.

But it did not come.

Weeks, months, years I waited—but happiness did not happen. And my life was going stagnant—it was becoming a malignant thing because I was not happy.

Then dimly I began to perceive that I was wrong. Happiness would not, could not, ever come back that way. For that sort of involuntary happiness was part of something that had gone forever.

EVEN IF A TRAGEDY HAD NOT BEFALLEN ME, I WOULD HAVE LOST THAT SORT OF HAPPINESS.

For it was part of youth—part of the exuberance and ignorance of youth—part of youth's irresponsibility. And it could not possibly continue when life became older and wiser and more responsible.

That did not mean, however, that happiness was over. It simply meant that one had to be grown-up about happiness as about everything else.

I was no longer a care-free child in any other department of my life. I had learned to earn my own living—to make my own decisions—to take care of my business, my property, my body. Now I would have to learn to take care of my happiness.

Things were not given to adults, freely, without thought. Neither could happiness come freely, without thought, to a really grown-up person.

Happiness must be planned for, fought for, achieved.

And so I learned to build happiness.

I NO LONGER WAITED FOR HAPPINESS TO HAPPEN. I MADE IT HAPPEN.

I realized I had to be happy.

I decided to be happy.

I decided to find happiness—

And I began looking for it.

I began looking for it in every common incident of my life.

I took joy wherever I found it—in trifling experiences, in fleeting moods, in brief glimpses.

It wasn't easy at first. It was dreadfully hard. It was like going through a complicated, tiresome, senseless drill. My heart was heavy as lead—my imagination refused to budge. I longed to retreat into the easy refuge of grief and despair. But I persisted—

And gradually something began to stir in me . . . warm in me . . .

And I saw that my life held happiness again . . .

Not the radiance and ecstasy I had once known . . . but a deliberate delight which could find food for joy in the most barren places—and which no grief or loss could ever shake again.

So I came to build happiness. You can, too, if you will.

ACKNOWLEDGMENTS

This biography relied on the outsized patience and generosity of dozens of librarians and archivists who helped us navigate their institutions through the Covid-19 pandemic. Stretching across the country—from California to Vermont—these individuals paved the way for us to withstand building closures and staffing shortages. It is only because of their goodwill and expertise that we were able to research and write this book during such a challenging time.

In Benicia, California, our greatest thanks to Beverly Phelan at the Benicia Historical Museum and Caroline Davis and Fran Martinez-Coyne at the Benicia Public Library. Special thanks to Jim Lessenger of Community Congregational Church, who provided invaluable details about the property where Elsie's childhood home once stood. It is with deep sadness that we extend our gratitude to Benicia historian Donnell Rubay, who died before this book was published. Donnell was so passionate about preserving Elsie's legacy that she produced a live event at the Benicia Capitol State Historic Park in 2017 that reenacted seminal moments in Elsie's life. At the time of the performance, which we attended, Donnell was quoted in the *Benicia Herald* as saying that Elsie was too important to be forgotten. "I wanted to remedy that," she told a reporter. Donnell, we hope this book carries your mission forward.

In Brattleboro, Vermont, we are fortunate to have worked with the Brattleboro Historical Society, in particular John Carnahan, Carol Farrington, Sharon Hodge, and Lee Ha, and we benefited enormously from Jeanne Walsh and Starr Latronica at Brooks Memorial Library. Only in Brattleboro would a librarian, out of the kindness of her heart, pay a visit to the local courthouse on our behalf to retrieve documents related to Elsie and Christie's divorce. At First Baptist Church, we learned important details from Helen Ruth Belanger and Sylvia Seitz, and it is because of Ed Morse (Brattleboro Lodge #102) and Walter Hunt (Grand Lodge of Massachusetts) that we got to know critical information pertaining to Christie Crowell's and Robert Wallace's involvement with the Freemasons. Special thanks to Ed for a private tour of the Brattleboro Lodge back in 2013. We are also so very grateful that Jane Fletcher, Brattleboro's assistant town clerk, was able to locate George Crowell's original elementary school records. And in one more "only in Brattleboro moment," we remain exceptionally thankful that Maureen Macdonald opened her home to us at what was once 13 Myrtle Street. (House numbers have since changed.) What an absolute joy to spend time inside Elsie's onetime home.

Thanks, also, to the many individuals who helped us access and understand Robert Wallace's patient records, including Pat Murray, Wallace's great-granddaughter, and Katherine Novak at the American Psychological Association. And for their expertise researching Wallace's childhood and family, our thanks to Anna

Mickelsen at Springfield City Library, Jeff Kontoff, a wonderfully able volunteer researcher at Springfield Museums Genealogy Library and Archives, and Maggie Humberston at Lyman and Merrie Wood Museum of Springfield History.

Every school should have an archivist as capable and kind-hearted as Peter Weis at Northfield Mount Hermon. Our initial outreach to Peter was in 2011, and over the years there was never a question he couldn't answer or a document he couldn't find. Thank you, Peter, for opening the window into what Northfield Seminary was like for Elsie.

Elsie wrote extensively about working in a Hornitos gold mine but never disclosed which one. Before we embarked on our research trip, we needed to know exactly where to go. To that end, in 2016, we compiled a list of clues based on Elsie's descriptions (types of rocks, depth of shafts) and shared them with John Clinkenbeard (supervising engineering geologist, retired, California Geological Survey) and his colleagues, Fred Gius (supervising engineering geologist) and Brenda Callen (senior engineering geologist). It is only because of their expertise (and Brenda's tenacity!) that we know that the only mine where Elsie could have worked was Ruth Pierce. Thank you so much, John, Fred, and Brenda, for everything. Armed with this information, we were then able to work with Jason Sarmiento at the UC Davis Library, the institution that houses the Ruth Pierce archives. Jason helped us by setting up a remarkable Zoom: using a camera mounted above a pristine table and wearing protective gloves to mitigate any potential damage, he slowly and methodically unfolded dozens of original and fragile documents for our remote review.

Our Hornitos research was aided immeasurably by Miranda Fengel at the Mariposa Museum and History Center, and Tom Phillips, who was somehow able to answer every question we had about the region and its gold mining past. We'd also like to thank Janet Chase-Williams, Mariposa County Librarian, for her encyclopedic knowledge. Miranda and Janet made the kinds of suggestions and introductions that changed the course of our reporting. Among those individuals, we owe special thanks to Leroy Radanovich, Trent Williams, Joyce Barrett, Mary Ann Visher, Shaun Quinn, and the Ortizes—Delores, her husband Carlos (Poncho), their daughter Keri, and Poncho's brother Richard (Richie).

We had no idea that the access we were given to the old and abandoned Hornitos post office would be so valuable. It is here that we discovered the typewriter shown in the photos that begin Chapter 9. Matching the precise vintage and description of the typewriter Luola Rodgers loaned Elsie, we found it in a back room during a research trip in 2021. The building has not been used since 1956, one year following Rodgers's death. Our deepest gratitude to Eric Erickson, current owner of the property that was once Ruth Pierce, for giving us an unhurried tour of his land. There was no better way to get a feel for what Elsie endured than to see the rugged and sweeping landscape in person. We are forever grateful, too, for those warm and welcoming chocolate chip cookies.

To plot Elsie's train itinerary between California and Massachusetts, we worked closely with Bill Howes, former director of the Pullman Company and author of several books on American railroad history. Bill, we could not have deciphered 1901 train schedules without you! Utmost thanks to Larry Tye, author of *Rising from the Rails: Pullman Porters and the Making of the Black Middle Class*, for connecting us. In the same detective vein, forensic handwriting expert Ruth Breyer helped us confirm that Elsie was indeed the writer behind Comfy Lady. Elsie mentioned her work for *John Martin's Letters*, never the exact stories she wrote. We painstakingly compared sections of Elsie's handwritten Northfield application to dozens of handwritten stories that appeared in *John Martin's Letters* between 1909 and 1911. Ruth, that process of discovery was one of the great highlights of writing this book.

We treasure the information provided by Jay and Paul Schweitzer (Gramercy Typewriter Co.), Paul Robert (Virtual Typewriter Museum), Alan Seaver (Machines of Loving Grace), Richard Polt (Classic Typewriter Page), Linda Gross (Hagley Museum and Library), and Wendy Metros and Lauren Brady (The Henry Ford) who helped us understand the mechanics of the typewriter we believe Elsie used in Hornitos to kick-start her career.

To help us write about Elsie's home in Sonora, we first thank Jessica Hewitt, director of the Foothill Horizons Outdoor School, for her enthusiasm and partnership. With much of the terrain unchanged and with a few original buildings still standing, Jessica graciously took the time to shoot videos for us (capturing the views and natural sounds) so we could get a clearer picture of Elsie's surroundings and write about them. She also gathered an abundance of old photographs that enabled us to see inside rooms long since demolished. We couldn't have connected with Jessica without Julie Betschart and Cindy Neves from the Stanislaus County Department of Education, and we thank them both for their assistance. The Girl Scouts of Northern California Heritage Committee, including Ann Watrous and Cheryl Brown, was also exceedingly helpful, passing along information from scrapbooks, including a detailed narrative accounting of the property and a priceless hand-drawn map of its roads and buildings from the time the Girl Scouts purchased the land from

Elsie. We couldn't have traced the property paper trail, showing the transfer of ownership of Elsie's land over time, without the expertise of David Marquez of the Yosemite Title Company, and Connie Celaya, recording manager, and Rachel Jones, assistant assessor-recorder, in Tuolumne County.

An array of highly skilled archivists and researchers guided our work in various institutions, including Bancroft Library (Theresa Salazar, Lorna Kirwan, Susan McElrath, and Michael Maire Lange); San Francisco Public Library (Wendy Kramer, James Mabe, Katherine Etshokin, and Tom Carey); Oakland Public Library (Christine Ianieri and Dorothy Lazard, both retired, and Emily Foster); Bay Area News Group (Veronica Martinez and Nate Jackson); Alameda County Historical Society (Ed Clausen and Dennis Evanosky); Special Collections Research Center, Syracuse University Library (Nicolette Dobrowolski); Health Sciences Library, California Pacific Medical Center (Florence Cepeda); McHenry Library, Special Collections and Archives, University of California, Santa Cruz (Luisa Haddad and Rachel Jaffe); California Historical Society (Frances Kaplan); California Polytechnic State University (Matt Lazier, Laura Sorvetti, and Jessica Holada); Library of Congress (Abby Yochelson); California State Library (Elena Smith and Emily Blodget); University of Southern California Libraries Special Collections (Suzanne Noruschat); de Grummond Children's Literature Collection, McCain Library and Archives, University of Southern Mississippi (Amanda McRaney and Brooke Cruthirds). And for tracking down and scanning Elsie's first pieces of published writing we are wholly indebted to Library Special Collections, Charles E. Young Research Library, UCLA (Molly Haigh) and Cathy Martyniak, who, until recently, oversaw UCLA's Southern Regional Library Facility. We also want to thank New York

Public Library (Julie Golia, Elizabeth Rutigliano, and Nailah Holmes) and the wonderful humans at Irvington Public Library in Westchester, New York (in particular Rosemarie Gatzek and Keshet Roman), for accommodating, quite literally, hundreds of requests for books not held within their walls.

To place Elsie into historical context, we are grateful to have spoken with experts and historians in multiple fields, such as women's studies, journalism, and illustration. We are so appreciative of the following individuals for sharing their knowledge with us: at the Billy Ireland Cartoon Library and Museum at the Ohio State University (Jenny Robb, Lucy Casell, Ann Lennon, and Caitlin McGurk); the Association of American Editorial Cartoonists (Jen Sorensen); National Society of Newspaper Columnists (Suzette Martinez Standring and Dave Astor); the National Women's History Museum (Holly Hotchner, Lori Ann Terjesen, Jennifer Herrera, and Liz Eberlein); Arthur L. Carter Journalism Institute at New York University (Mitchell Stephens and Brooke Kroeger, professor emerita); Sarah Lawrence College (Priscilla Murolo); St. John's University (Lara Vapnek); and Cornell University (Mary Beth Norton).

Our understanding of early twentieth-century divorce and guardianship law was informed by dozens of conversations and emails with Joanna Grossman, Ellen K. Solender Endowed Chair in Women and the Law at SMU Dedman School of Law. Joanna, thank you for your patience as we tried to keep up with you. For helping us get smarter on asthma and its earliest treatments, we are so very grateful that Dr. Michael Stephen, pulmonologist and author of *Breath Taking: The Power, Fragility, and Future of Our Extraordinary Lungs*, would so readily share his wisdom with us and review our earliest drafts for accuracy. And to Arlene Shaner, Historical Collections Librarian at the New York Academy of Medicine, we owe singular thanks for never turning us away when we had "just one more question."

Writing a biography takes a village, and our village was built more efficiently because these indefatigable researchers helped us: David Smith, D. Joshua Taylor, Mary Bakija, Margaret Sullivan, Deborah Falik, Christina Cerio, and Amy Frazen. We were heartbroken to learn that Linda Lorda, the first genealogist to join Team Elsie in 2011, passed away during the time it took to complete *Listen, World!* She loved her work and was deeply committed to it. This is how she ended one email to Allison: "I am leaving this morning and will be traveling much of the day. I will have cell phone and internet access throughout my trip and will be able to continue some online research." Linda was an author's researcher. She was accurate and fast. And she never tired of the hunt. We wish Linda could have seen the fruit of all her labor.

From 1924 to 1956, Elsie worked for Hearst Corporation, and we are grateful for the help and support of C. J. Kettler, Tea Fougner, and Scott Olsen at King Features Syndicate. At *Cosmopolitan*, the support of Nicole Burrell and Laurie Feigenbaum allowed us to print the photographs of Elsie and George that appeared across several issues in 1934. We also want to thank Susan Nagib for her technical expertise cleaning up the images of Elsie's editorial cartoons that we captured on microfilm.

Seal Press quickly became Elsie's perfect literary home. Laura Mazer, how grateful we are that you understood Elsie's significance from the very start, and that Emma Berry, you so ably and passionately carried that enthusiasm forward. We must also acknowledge Abigail Mohr's guidance and the indefatigable efforts of the publicity and marketing team, including Liz Wetzel, Jessica Breen, Jenny Lee, Meghan Brophy, and Kara Ojebuoboh. Special kudos to Kimberly Glyder for designing the exquisite book cover!

Ultimately Elsie's story wouldn't be in your hands without the devotion and support of Lara Heimert, publisher of Basic Books. Lara, we are profoundly grateful for your extraordinary support of this biography.

It has been exceptionally meaningful to have met so many men and women, ranging in age from their late seventies to 101 years old, who were once Aunt Elsie club members. They proudly shared with us their pins, membership cards, and congratulatory letters they received from "Aunt Elsie" after a story or drawing they submitted was published. Newspaper clippings were saved, in near perfect condition, over a lifetime. Special thanks to Howard Gardiner, Hannah Glanzberg, Diana Sychr, Ron Genini, Charles Holland, and Evie Lederer, for giving us so much of your time.

And last, what an honor it has been to get to know Elsie's family over the course of writing this book. Robin Lovering, Beth Tauczik, and Carl Taussig, we are humbled that you trusted and shared your memories with us.

JULIA

I'm thankful to my family, who put up with me working weekends and evenings—and even missing a camping trip—to get this book done. I hope they're proud of the result. I'd also like to acknowledge my agent, Kim Witherspoon, for her peerless knowledge of the publishing industry and ongoing support.

ALLISON

Every author should be lucky enough to find an agent as whip-smart and supportive as Richard Morris at Janklow & Nesbit. Richard and I were introduced nearly twenty years ago, and I've been the beneficiary of his fairy dust ever since. His belief in this project never wavered, not even when I hit significant research and writing roadblocks and couldn't figure out how to get around them. Instead of convincing me to abandon the project, Richard pushed me harder and offered advice. But even more important than his commitment to the work was his unflinching belief in me. His encouragement was the kindling I needed to keep going, to continue wrestling with Elsie's story, and the result, I am ecstatic and relieved to say, is in your hands.

In 2011, when Richard and I decided that *Listen, World!* was the next book I was going to tackle, I joined several biography-specific writing communities, and the friendships I made have nurtured me in many important ways. At Biographers International Organization, members have the opportunity to join small writing groups based on genre (African American Studies, Hollywood, Women's Literature, and more), and the gathering I continue to be part of has sustained me. Eve Kahn, Amy Reading, Diane Prenatt, Elizabeth Harris, Mary Ann Caws, Sallie Bingham, Harriet Reisen, Christine Cipriani, Sara Catterall, Penelope Rowlands, Elaine Showalter, Shelley Mickle, and our fearless leader, Carla Kaplan, your wisdom informed my writing, and your camaraderie bolstered my confidence.

I am proud to be a member of the Women Writing Women's Lives Biography Seminar, a mighty group of journalists, academics, and independent scholars engaged in writing biographies and memoirs from a variety of feminist perspectives. I've learned from every one of my Seminar Sisters, in particular Dona Munker, and thank them all for welcoming me into their esteemed fold.

My brother Jay Coen Gilbert learned about Elsie the same day I did, in 1996. We were both in our twenties, our mother had recently died, and we had returned to our childhood home to begin packing up her belongings. I was clearing out her books when I found a piece of paper folded up inside one of them: it was a poem titled "Pain" and it was attributed to someone named Elsie Robinson. The poem floored me. Every tough-love word and phrase seemed written just for me. These were the words that I needed—to comfort me, to make me realize that I was fortunate to have had a mother worth missing. But who was Elsie Robinson? I showed the poem to Jay, hoping that he'd recognize her name. It is because Jay didn't know her name either that my mission began, to research a woman whose writing had meant so much to our mom that she had typed the poem on a piece of onion skin paper and saved it, by our estimate, for nearly forty years. Jay, writing this book has made me feel closer to Mom, and to you. I love you so much.

While I began working on *Listen, World!* with increasing intensity in 2011, my obsession with Elsie began that day in 1996, and unfortunately for those closest to me, they haven't stopped hearing about her, and my discoveries, since. Many also agreed to read early drafts of this book and offer important feedback. To my dearest friends Tracy Costigan, Janet Rossbach, Deniz Ayaz Mullis, Nancy Friedman, Betsy Cadel, Holly Rosen Fink, Kristin Brandt, Tanya Hunt, Jenifer Ross, and Carley Knobloch, thank you for your patience and sharing my enthusiasm. Rob Johnson, I am indebted to you for helping Julia and me understand the dangers of mining. To Christina Baker Kline and Lisa Belkin, you are the kind of writers and human beings I aspire to be, and Pamela Redmond, I remain so very grateful that you came to my rescue during the earliest iterations of this book.

And to my family, Jay (again) and Randi Coen Gilbert, Cheryl Gilbert, Yelena and Ryan Hughes, Marsha and John Jewczyn, Leah and Merritt Johnson, Diana Flanagan, Marilyn Weintraub, Sandy Weintraub, Debra and Chris McGrath, Barry and Ruby Weintraub, Lani Mustacchi, and Steven and Julie Aibel, I am blessed to be surrounded by so much love.

To my son, Jake, and my daughter, Lexi, who endured me working long hours and weekends (even holing up in a hotel room for days while we were on vacation), I adore and love you. Just as Elsie inspired millions of Americans, including me, I hope she'll now do her magic on you. My greatest wish is that you live your lives just as courageously, and that you never stop pursuing what makes you feel happy and whole.

And finally to my husband, Mark Weintraub, who has lived Elsie's story with me for nearly thirty years. You've been my best friend since we met as teenagers, and I still feel that ridiculous rush when I look at you. Thank you for reading every page of this biography multiple times with affection and an unparalleled eye for detail. The book is better because you touched it early and often. I am also grateful that you're the kind of book widower who graciously picks up the household and parenting slack. You're the exact partner I imagine Elsie would have wanted for me—a husband who makes my life bigger. We've no doubt landed in many mudholes over the years, but our love always manages to bring us back to that cherished mountaintop.

RESEARCH NOTE

This book is based on more than eleven years of reporting and research. Because it is the first biography of Hearst syndicated newspaper columnist Elsie Robinson, there was no birth-to-death accounting of her life to follow as a roadmap. It fell to us to fact-check her version of events and fill in the tremendous number of gaps. We're sharing our extensive list of source documents and interviews here in case they can be useful to future historians.

Details of Elsie's life and career were challenging to uncover because so little of her writing has been digitized. Instead of Googling, we exhumed her body of work by combing through microfilm and library offsite storage facilities. This list, for now, is the only complete paper trail of her life and accomplishments. We hope that by presenting this breadth of information, Elsie will be discovered by a new generation of readers and scholars.

NOTES

INTRODUCTION

1. To read Elsie Robinson's March 4, 1940, letter see William Randolph Hearst Papers, MSS 77/121 c, Bancroft Library, University of California, Berkeley. For the reach of Elsie's nationally syndicated column via the Hearst Corporation read David Nasaw, *The Chief: The Life of William Randolph Hearst* (New York: Houghton Mifflin, 2000), xiv, 322–323.

2. For details about Hearst's creation of the world's first media conglomerate see Nasaw, *The Chief*, xiii. For the quantitative analysis of Hearst's vast holdings see Ben Procter, *William Randolph Hearst: The Later Years, 1911–1951* (New York: Oxford University Press, 2007), vii. For specifics about *Good Housekeeping* and *Cosmopolitan* see Kenneth Whyte, *The Uncrowned King: The Sensational Rise of William Randolph Hearst* (Berkeley: Counterpoint, 2009), 463. For specifics about Robinson's salary and readership see Campbell Watson, "Elsie Robinson Began Brilliant Newspaper Career at Age of 35," *Editor & Publisher*, May 11, 1940; Virginia Irwin, "Elsie Robinson—Study in Contrasts," *St. Louis Post-Dispatch*, June 9, 1940; "Elsie Robinson Buried in Family Plot in Benicia," *Benicia Herald*, September 13, 1956; Campbell Watson, "Brilliant Newspaper Career; Elsie Robinson, Listen, World Columnist, Dies," *San Francisco Examiner*, September 9, 1956.

3. To read Elsie's letter to William Randolph Hearst see William Randolph Hearst Papers, BANC MSS 77/121 c, Bancroft Library, University of California, Berkeley.

4. On Robinson's landing at the *Oakland Tribune* see Elsie Robinson, *I Wanted Out!* (New York: Farrar & Rinehart, 1934); "Elsie Robinson, Columnist, Dies," *New York Times*, September 9, 1956; "Kiddies, Look Here!," *Oakland Tribune*, December 19, 1918. Regarding the formation of Aunt Elsie clubs across California, the authors reviewed photographs, articles, and notices in the *Oakland Tribune* from 1919 to 1935. Robinson's first two advice columns were "Cheer Up," launched in the *Oakland Tribune* January 20, 1919, and "Cry on Geraldine's Shoulder," also launched in the *Oakland Tribune*, September 6, 1920. See also "Elsie Robinson Dead at 73," *New York Herald Tribune*, September 9, 1956. Robinson's first "Tell It to Elsie" column was published in the *San Francisco Call and Post*, September 10, 1923.

5. Concerning gold mine specifics, see the September 1909 and March 1921 "Report on Ruth Pierce Mine," MC252, Special Collections, UC Davis Library.

6. Robinson's age and birthdate noted on her death certificate from September 8, 1956, file no. 6771, State of California Department of Public Health, City and County of San Francisco, copy in possession of authors. On Hearst's castle see Oliver Carlson and Ernest Sutherland Bates, *Hearst: Lord of San Simeon* (New York: Viking Press, 1936), 308; Procter, *William Randolph Hearst*, 203.

7. For correspondence between Robinson and Hearst and Robinson and Hearst's private secretary Joseph Willicombe pertaining to editorial assignments for July 18–July 31, 1940, see William Randolph Hearst papers, BANC MSS 91/2 c, Bancroft Library, University of California, Berkeley. The luncheon was covered as news in "Honor Elsie Robinson," *Editor & Publisher*, June 15, 1940.

8. To arrive at approximately nine thousand, the authors examined Robinson's "Listen, World!" columns and news reporting between 1921 and 1956, though Elsie's writing career picked up steam as early as 1916. To do this, columns were examined in the following intervals: 1921, 1923, 1933, 1943, 1950, 1953, and 1956. Running daily from 1921 to 1953, "Listen, World!" appeared as often as six days a week, sometimes less than five. The column was published on a limited basis or not at all, depending on a newspaper's backlog of columns, between February and March 1942, due to an accident she suffered, and they took another dip in mid-1950. In 1953 and 1956, through her death, there were an average of one to four pieces per week. The authors also conducted a review of Robinson's news reporting for the same periods, as well as her "Tell It to Elsie" and "Cry on Geraldine's Shoulder" columns. For Elsie as the most-read woman writer see Howard Beaufait, "Elsie Robinson 'Symbol of West,'" *Cleveland News*, July 27, 1938. See Marc Tracy, "The Times Hits Its Goal of 10 Million Subscriptions with

the Addition of The Athletic," Februrary 2, 2022, https://www.nytimes
.com/2022/02/02/business/media/nyt-earnings-q4-2021.html. For Elsie
as pioneering writer and editorial cartoonist see Jenny Robb, curator at the
Billy Ireland Cartoon Library and Museum at the Ohio State University,
email correspondence with authors, January 3, 2022; Dave Astor, archivist at
the National Society of Newspaper Columnists, phone interview and email
correspondence with authors, December 23, 2021–January 12, 2022.

9. For Robinson's writing on gender differences see "Listen, World!,"
April 1, 1922; on racism "Listen, World!," August 18, 1947; on capital pun-
ishment "Listen, World!," September 10, 1925. For columns urging the
US to support Jews fleeing Nazi Germany, the authors reviewed "Listen,
World!" columns between December 24, 1938, and November 17, 1948.

10. Review of George Crowell's date of death on his death certificate,
January 23, 1926, file no. 653, California State Board of Health, City and
County of San Francisco, copy in possession of authors. See also "Elsie Robinson, 'Listen World' Columnist Dies," *San Francisco Examiner*, September
9, 1956; Beaufait, "Elsie Robinson 'Symbol of West.'"

11. Christie Burnham Crowell and Elsinore Justinia Robinson, marriage
certificate, March 20, 1903, certificate no. 9-2247, State of Vermont, Town
of Brattleboro.

CHAPTER 1: BENICIA

1. To learn more about F Street see "Interview: Former Mayor Jerry
Hayes on Benicia's Fascinating History," *Benicia Magazine*, accessed December 3, 2021, https://www.beniciamagazine.com/interview-former-mayor
-jerry-hayes-on-benicias-fascinating-history/. According to Benicia Historical Museum in Benicia, California, the dividing line has also been reported
as D Street, depending on the year. See also Earl Bobitt, "Looking Back with
Earl Bobitt: A New Century," *Benicia Herald*, August 19, 1983.

2. For Elsie's understanding of women see Robinson, *I Wanted Out!*,
8–9, 57.

3. For late nineteenth-century Benicia population statistics see "Bay
Area Census, City of Benicia, Solano County," accessed October 22, 2021,
http://www.bayareacensus.ca.gov/cities/Benicia50.htm#1940.

4. On the early development of Benicia, including details of the Patwin
tribe and revelations of gold discovery, see exhibition, *The History of Benicia
Is Written in the History of California*, Benicia Historical Museum, Benicia,
California.

5. To read more about Benicia's early days see Kevin Starr, *California:
A History* (New York: Modern Library, 2005). On the region's military

operations see Kristin Delaplane, "Benicia Grew as Arsenal, Building Flourished," *Vacaville Reporter*, April 10, 1995; Robert Bruegmann, *Benicia: Portrait of an Early California Town; An Architectural History* (101 Productions, 1980), 150–153; Richard Dillon, *Great Expectations: The Story of Benicia* (Fresno, CA: Thomas Lithograph and Printing Company, 1980).

6. United States Federal Census, 1860, Solano County, California, town of Benicia, NARA microfilm publication M653, roll 69, pp. 281–318.

7. See Elsie's reflections of Benicia in Robinson, *I Wanted Out!*, 100.

8. On the relationship between gender and fashion protocols see Jane H. Hunter, *How Young Ladies Became Girls: The Victorian Origins of American Girlhood* (New Haven: Yale University Press, 2003), 141.

9. To read Elsie's full column on the original woman see Robinson, "Listen, World!," March 11, 1921.

10. Details about women's restrictive dress can be found in Helene E. Roberts, "The Exquisite Slave: The Role of Clothes in the Making of the Victorian Woman," *Signs: Journal of Women in Culture and Society* 2, no. 3 (Spring 1977): 554–569; Hannah Aspinall, "The Fetishization and Objectification of the Female Body in Victorian Culture," *BrightONLINE: Journal of Literary Criticism and Creativity from the Students of the University of Brighton* (August 10, 2012), accessed May 23, 2021.

11. For her reflections on the arduous process of getting dressed see Robinson, *I Wanted Out!*, 85–88.

12. Elsie writes about the burden of housework in Robinson, "Listen, World!," March 16, 1921; and about the limiting expectations of motherhood, "Listen, World!," December 31, 1923.

13. For details of First Street see Earl Bobitt, "Looking Back with Earl Bobitt: That's Progress," *Benicia Herald*, September 9, 1983; Bobitt, "Looking Back with Earl Bobitt: Easy on Robins," *Benicia Herald*, September 16, 1983.

14. Information on 1890s etiquette can be reviewed by reading John F. Kasson, *Civility and Rudeness: Urban Etiquette and the Bourgeois Social Order in Nineteenth-Century America* (Cambridge: Cambridge University Press, 2009), 168–216; John F. Kasson, "Civility and Rudeness: Urban Etiquette and the Bourgeois Social Order in Nineteenth-Century America," *Prospects: An Annual of American Cultural Studies* 9 (October 1984): 143–167.

15. More on early prostitution in California may be found by reading Angela C. Fitzpatrick, "Women of Ill Fame: Discourses of Prostitution and the American Dream in California, 1850–1890" (PhD diss., Bowling Green State University, 2013).

16. On watching the sordidness of Benicia unfold see Robinson, *I Wanted Out!*, 43.

17. On remembrances of Benicia's sex workers see Robinson, *I Wanted Out!*, 7–8.

18. On Benicia's nightlife see Robinson, *I Wanted Out!*, 16.

19. For Elsie's reflections on her childhood in Benicia see Robinson, "Listen, World!," May 19, 1947.

20. For the scholar's view of Benicia see William Kirk Woolery, "The Educational Resources of Benicia: A Community Survey" (master's thesis, University of California, 1915).

21. On the diversity of people who informed Elsie's worldview see Robinson, "Listen, World!," January 10, 1924.

CHAPTER 2: HOME

1. For Elsie's childhood home address see A. Kingsbury, *Kingsbury's 1904–5 Directory of Vallejo City and Solano County, California* (Vallejo, CA, 1904), 147.

2. For the depiction of the American home in the late nineteenth century see Robinson, *I Wanted Out!*, 23–24.

3. At the time of Elizabeth Pearson's birth, birth records in Ireland were not consistent, yet all available documents point to Donegal, Ireland, as the location of her birth, including her death certificate (State of California, Department of Public Health Vital Statistics, Certificate of Death, 1933, no. 799, Elizabeth Robinson, January 15, 1933). Her sister's birth is recorded at Glenties in County Donegal, Ireland, in 1865 (Ireland Civil Registration Indexes, 1845–1913, County Donegal, Ireland, vol. 121, p. 92, entry for Cathrine Emily Pearson, August 3, 1865; General Register Office, Custom House, Dublin). Census enumerations provide evidence of the year of her immigration and the length of marriage to Alexander Robinson (Alexander Robinson household, 1900 US census, Solano County, California, population schedule, Benicia township, Benicia City, enumeration district 138, p. 26A, dwelling 536, family 582, digital image, Ancestry.com, accessed September 8, 2011, citing NARA microfilm publication T623, roll 113; and Alexander Robinson household, 1880 US census, Alameda County, California, population schedule, Eden township, enumeration district 22, p. 42B, dwelling 358, family 363, Alexander Robinson, digital image, Ancestry.com, accessed September 7, 2011).

4. For Alexander Robinson's work history see "Death Calls Prominent Resident of Solano: Alexander Robinson Passes Away at His Home After a Fit of Coughing," *San Francisco Call*, January 20, 1907, 40.

5. On the injury to Alexander Robinson's finger and years of poverty see Elsie Robinson's poem, "My Father's Hand," in *Listen World!* (Boston: Chapman & Grimes, 1934), 56–59.

6. On Elsie Robinson's four siblings see Paul Robinson gravestone, Benicia City Cemetery, Benicia, California; Alexander Robinson household, 1880 US census; Alexander Robinson household, 1900 US census; World War I draft registration card, Philip Archibald Robinson, serial no. 4059, Local Board, Contra Costa County, California; "California Death Index, 1940–1997," database, FamilySearch (accessed January 3, 2022), entry for Mardele Robinson, December 25, 1946; Department of Public Health Services, Sacramento.

7. See Elsie's remembrance of her mother's internal struggles, this quote and previous one, in Robinson, *I Wanted Out!*, 25.

8. The Robinson yard when the house was purchased is described in Robinson, *I Wanted Out!*, 24.

9. See examples of seed catalogs such as from Vaughan's Seed Company preserved online by New York Botanical Garden Mertz Digital Collections, accessed January 5, 2022, http://mertzdigital.nybg.org/digital/collection/p15121coll8/id/33438/.

10. For Elsie's perspective on how individuals find solace see Robinson's poem, "Love Is—What Have You?," in *Listen World!*, 21–23.

11. For this quote and more details on the expected roles of young women see Hunter, *How Young Ladies Became Girls*, 100.

12. On what gardens meant to girls in the 1800s see Robinson, *I Wanted Out!*, 27–28.

13. On the cultural landscape of boys see Peter N. Stearns, *American Cool: Constructing a Twentieth-Century Emotional Style* (New York: New York University Press, 1994), 33.

14. To review Elsie's childhood reading habits see Robinson, *I Wanted Out!*, 38–39.

15. For Jo March on wanting to be a boy see Louisa May Alcott, *Little Women* (New York: Signet Classics, 2004), 3.

16. On Elsie's wish to be attractive to men see Robinson, *I Wanted Out!*, 47.

17. For the effect of "sensational" fiction on Victorian girls, see Washington Gladden, "The Home: Girls and Their Mothers," in *Library of Inspiration and Achievement* (University Society, 1900), 131.

18. On the oversight of reading materials see Hunter, *How Young Ladies Became Girls*, 60.

19. For Elsie's reflections on looking inside a Benicia saloon see Robinson, *I Wanted Out!*, 14.

20. On the beginning of Elsie's passion for writing and drawing see Robinson, *I Wanted Out!*, 39–40.

21. On Winifred's education see Beatrice Winifred Robinson, "Diploma," Bachelor of Philosophy (University of California, 1898). On Harvard's admission of women see David A. Campbell, "College Honors 25 Years of Yard Co-Residency," October 6, 1997, https://www.thecrimson.com/articles /1997/10/6/college-honors-25-years-of-yard/. On women entering college in the West see Heather R. Johnson, "UC Berkeley Trailblazers: Recognizing Cal's First Women Scholars, 1870–1900," Cal Alumni Association, September 10, 2018, https://alumni.berkeley.edu/announcements/caa-announcements /womenatcal.

22. To learn more about early beliefs regarding Easter clothes see Leigh Eric Schmidt, "The Easter Parade: Piety, Fashion, and Display," *Religion and American Culture: A Journal of Interpretation* 4, no. 2 (1994): 135–164.

23. Elsie's reflections on her Easter dress were included in a piece she wrote on her mother's death; see Elsie Robinson, "A Tribute to Her Mother," *Hayward Daily Review*, April 19, 1939, 4.

24. On concerns stirring about her future see Robinson, *I Wanted Out!*, 55.

25. On Elsie's sister Winnie's graduation from college see "Degrees for Over Three Hundred," *San Francisco Call*, May 18, 1898.

26. On the class of 1900 roster and graduation details see *Benicia High School Graduation Program* (Benicia, CA: Benicia Historical Museum, 1900); Earl Bobitt, *Visiting Around Benicia* (bound volume, exact date of publication unknown, available at the Benicia Public Library and Benicia Historical Museum). For perceptions of women's ability to marry and procreate see Hunter, *How Young Ladies Became Girls*, 315–367.

27. For Elsie's take on "good" versus "bad" women see Robinson, *I Wanted Out!*, 57.

28. On married women having control over property by 1900, see the website for the National Women's History Alliance, "Timeline of Legal History of Women in the United States," accessed January 5, 2022, https:// nationalwomenshistoryalliance.org/resources/womens-rights-movement /detailed-timeline/.

29. For Elsie's views on the historical status of women see Robinson, "Listen, World!," March 8, 1926.

30. For Elsie's opinions on gender and happiness see Robinson, "Listen, World!," May 5, 1939.

31. Elsie reflects on taking her case to God in Robinson, *I Wanted Out!*, 51.

32. Elsie considers that a fulfilling life isn't promised in Robinson, *I Wanted Out!*, 51.

CHAPTER 3: ROMANCE

1. For details about the Congressional Church see "Community Congregational Church, United Church of Christ of Benicia, California: History Outline," Community Congregational Church, UCC, accessed December 5, 2021, http://cccucc.org/bridge/historyoutline.3.1.P.pdf. On the differences in church participation between Elsie's parents see Northfield Mount Hermon Archives, Student Files, Northfield, Robinson #2959N. On the church membership number, see Congregational Church, "Community Congregational Church, United Church of Christ of Benicia: History Outline," 8. For details about Reverend Palmer see Northfield Mount Hermon Archives, Student Files, Mount Hermon, Palmer #632MH.

2. Elsie recalls how her classmates regarded her in Robinson, *I Wanted Out!*, 58–60.

3. For Christie's age at the time of meeting Elsie see Christie B. Crowell, birth registration, January 24, 1873, Page 17, Record 1, Town of Brattleboro, copy in possession of authors.

4. For Elsie's recollections of meeting Christie Crowell for the first time see Robinson, *I Wanted Out!*, 61.

5. For descriptions of Lindenhurst mansion see "From Mansion to Skate Park," *Brattleboro Historical Society Newsletter*, March 2012; "Lindenhurst: The Elegant Family Mansion," *Vermont Phoenix*, February 28, 1890, 2.

6. For details regarding established courting rituals see Julie Golia, *Newspaper Confessions: A History of Advice Columns in a Pre-Internet Age* (New York: Oxford University Press, 2021). For details on courtship expectations see Beth L. Bailey, *From Front Porch to Back Seat: Courtship in Twentieth-Century America* (Baltimore: Johns Hopkins University Press, 1989).

7. For Elsie's views on the changing nature of male-female friendship see Robinson, "Listen, World!," December 11, 1922.

8. Information about Christie's first wife was gathered from Northfield Mount Hermon Archives, Student Files, Northfield, Van Arsdale, #1338N. The description of Louisa Van Arsdale was taken from her 1894 graduation portraits, Northfield Mount Hermon Archives, Classes Images, Series I Northfield, Box 1, Folder 27. For details of Christie's first wedding see "Crowell–Van Arsdale: A Wedding Celebrated at Hackensack, N.J., June 1," *Vermont Phoenix*, June 10, 1898; "Mrs. Christie B. Crowell," *Vermont Phoenix*, April 14, 1899.

9. For details of Louisa Van Arsdale's treatment and death see Louisa Van Arsdale Crowell, Report of Death, April 8, 1899, State of New Jersey; Dr. David St. John, founder of Hackensack Hospital, taken from *Hackensack*

Medical Center: The First One Hundred Years (Hackensack: Hackensack Medical Center, 1988).

10. On the transport of Louisa Van Ardsdale's body from New Jersey to Vermont, author interview with Steve Person, funeral director and expert in Victorian funeral practices, email correspondence and phone call, October 29–30, 2020. On funeral traditions in the late 1800s and early 1900s see David E. Stannard, *The Puritan Way of Death: A Study in Religion, Culture, and Social Change* (New York: Oxford University Press, 1977); Robert W. Habenstein and William M. Lamers, *The History of American Funeral Directing* (Milwaukee: Bulfin Printers, 1955).

11. On the death of Christie's eleven-month-old brother Ralph Crowell, see death registration, April 26, 1883, Page 146, Record 30, Town of Brattleboro, copy in possession of authors. For details regarding Herbert Crowell see note 12.

12. On the suicide of Christie's brother Herbert Crowell, see death registration, May 6, 1896, Page 244, Record 41, Town of Brattleboro, copy in possession of authors; "Mount Hermon School Principal's Report 1895–1896," and "Death of Herbert S. Crowell," *Vermont Phoenix*, May 8, 1896; "A Sad Case: Herbert S. Crowell Shoots Himself at Northfield—Questions Whether Accident or Suicide," *Windham County Reformer*, May 8, 1896.

13. Elsie addressed the driving forces behind her and Christie's growing feelings for each other in Robinson, *I Wanted Out!*, 62, 66–67.

14. Elsie celebrates getting engaged in Robinson, *I Wanted Out!*, 63.

15. Elsie's mother reacts to Elsie's engagement in Robinson, *I Wanted Out!*, 62.

16. On mail delivery service timing see Steve Kochersperger, "Mail by Rail: History of the Transcontinental Railroad and US Mail," United States Postal Service, accessed December 7, 2021, https://uspsblog.com/transcontinental-railroad-and-mail/.

17. For details of Elsie's Northfield application see Elsie Robinson Northfield Application, Northfield Mount Hermon Archives, Student Files, Northfield, Robinson #2959N.

CHAPTER 4: NORTHFIELD

1. For Elsie's memories of listening to the sound of train whistles see Robinson, *I Wanted Out!*, 13.

2. For Elsie's reflections on Benicia's changing culture see Robinson, *I Wanted Out!*, 56. Elsie's train route from California to Massachusetts

was recreated with expertise from Lisa Borok, California State Railroad Museum Library & Archives, email to authors, August 11, 2018; and Bill Howes, author of *The American Railroad*, *Travel by Pullman*, and *The Cars of Pullman*, multiple interviews with authors, December 2021–February 2022. To arrive at Elsie's itinerary and travel times, we relied on "The Official Standard Time of the Railways and Steam Navigation Lines of the United States, Porto Rico, Canada, Mexico, and Cuba," *National Railway Publication Co.*, February 1901.

3. Elsie remarks on the differences between California and Vermont in Robinson, *I Wanted Out!*, 67.

4. For descriptions of Elsie's first moments on the train see Robinson, *I Wanted Out!*, 70.

5. Details of food that travelers packed for long-distance rail travel were provided by James D. Porterfield, author of *Dining by Rail: The History and Recipes of America's Golden Age of Railroad Cuisine*, phone interview and email correspondence with authors, September 8–10, 2020.

6. For details on bedding and lighting see Joseph Husband, *The Story of the Pullman Car*, (Chicago: A. C. McClurg, 1917), 42–58. Porter assignments varied, but for those related to unaccompanied women and children see *Promotional Flyer for Rock Island Route*, Pullman State Historic Site (Illinois Digital Archives), accessed December 6, 2021, http://www.idaillinois.org /digital/collection/pshs/id/17080.

7. Elsie muses about the "highbinder" on the train in Robinson, *I Wanted Out!*, 71.

8. On the population of Chicago see "Twelfth Census of the United States," Census Bureau, No. 21, Washington, DC, December 15, 1900. For details about getting off the train in Chicago see Robinson, *I Wanted Out!*, 72.

9. For the description of Elsie's arrival in Northfield see Robinson, *I Wanted Out!*, 72.

10. On Northfield under quarantine see *Vermont Phoenix*, Friday, September 13, 1901. For background on the scarlet fever outbreak see Charles A. Lindsley (Charles Augustus), "Precautions Respecting Diphtheria and Scarlet Fever: Issued by Order of the Board of Health of New Haven," New Haven (Conn.) Board of Health, US Library of Medicine, Digital Collections. For the mortality rate of 25 percent see Richard L. Guerrant, David H. Walker, and Peter F. Weller, *Tropical Infectious Diseases: Principles, Pathogens and Practice*, 3rd ed. (Philadelphia: Saunders, 2011), 203–211.

11. For details of the ways mourners responded to the death of McKinley see Marshall Everett, *Complete Life of William McKinley and Story of His*

Assassination (1901). Northfield Seminary's student newspaper, *The Hermonite*, reported campus reaction.

12. To learn about Victorian Gothic style see Virginia and Lee McAlester, *A Field Guide to American Houses* (New York: Alfred A. Knopf, 1984), 268–280. Descriptions of Revell Hall taken from photos supplied to authors by Northfield Mount Hermon Archives.

13. On the number of students living in Revell see *Northfield Seminary Class Catalogue: 1900–1901* (Brattleboro: E. L. Hildreth & Co., 1901), 15. For details on the King's Daughters see Henry W. Rankin, *Hand-Book of the Northfield Seminary and the Mt. Hermon School* (Chicago: Fleming H. Revell, 1889), 77.

14. On the religious goals of Northfield see Rankin, *Hand-Book of the Northfield Seminary*, 14.

15. For Elsie's recollections of her time at Northfield see Robinson, *I Wanted Out!*, 73.

16. For her commentary on women being called the "weaker sex" see Robinson, *I Wanted Out!*, 231.

17. For Elsie's slate of classes we consulted her academic file; see Northfield Mount Hermon Archives, Student Files, Northfield, Robinson #2959N.

18. Elsie describes her growing dismay at Northfield in Robinson, *I Wanted Out!*, 76–77.

19. For details regarding Elsie and Christie's travel between Northfield and Brattleboro see map of New London Northern Railroad, US Geological Survey US Massachusetts–New Hampshire–Vermont Warick Sheet, State of Massachusetts, 1894. Details about the most likely route taken provided by Peter Weis, archivist of the school, Northfield Mount Hermon, email correspondence and phone interviews with authors, November 9–17, 2021.

20. Specifics about the double-decker bridge are from Northfield Mount Hermon Archives, Buildings and Grounds Collection, Series V Northfield Inn and Birnam House, Box 10, Folder 21.

21. For information on Brattleboro at the turn of the twentieth century in this and the preceding paragraph see Brattleboro Historical Society, "Brattleboro's Main Street Through the Years," slideshow, accessed January 5, 2022, https://bhs802.org/2016/02/slideshow-brattleboros-main-street-throughout-the-years/.

22. On Christie and his first wife's commitment to church see "Mrs. Christie B. Crowell," *Vermont Phoenix*, April 14, 1899.

23. For background of Christie's father see "Geo E. Crowell Dead," *Vermont Phoenix*, October 20, 1916; Mary R. Cabot, *Annals of Brattleboro, 1681–1895* (Brattleboro: E. L. Hildreth & Co., 1922); Harold A. Barry,

Before Our Time: A Pictorial Memoir of Brattleboro, Vermont, from 1830 to 1930 (Brattleboro: Stephen Greene Press, 1974).

24. Descriptions of George Crowell's publication *The Household* 14, no. 1 (January 1881).

25. On number of subscribers see Fran Lynggaard Hansen, *Brattleboro: Historically Speaking* (Charleston, SC: History Press, 2009), 12.

26. "Crowell House Being Wrecked," *Brattleboro Reformer*, November 30, 1936.

27. Elsie describes the social protocols at Lindenhurst in Robinson, *I Wanted Out!*, 109.

28. The strained relationship between Elsie and her in-laws is in Robinson, *I Wanted Out!*, 77.

29. On the sexual slavery of young girls see Julia Flynn Siler, *The White Devil's Daughters: The Women Who Fought Slavery in San Francisco's Chinatown* (New York: Alfred A. Knopf, 2019).

30. Writing becomes Elsie's door to healing in Robinson, *I Wanted Out!*, 136.

CHAPTER 5: MARRIAGE

1. Elsie explains the pressure to get married in Robinson, *I Wanted Out!*, 78–79.

2. "Off for the East to Become a Bride," *San Francisco Bulletin*, March 12, 1903.

3. For recollections of Elsie and Christie's reunion in Brattleboro see Robinson, *I Wanted Out!*, 91–92.

4. Reflections on putting on her wedding dress are in Robinson, *I Wanted Out!*, 95.

5. On her sister's wedding day see Robinson, *I Wanted Out!*, 95.

6. On her final moments alone before marrying Christie see Robinson, *I Wanted Out!*, 95–96.

7. For the interior details of Lindenhurst, including the "Welcome" carving on the mantel, see "The Elegant Family Mansion," *Vermont Phoenix*, February 28, 1890, 2.

8. See Elsie's description of her marriage ceremony in Robinson, *I Wanted Out!*, 96, 101–102.

9. On perceptions of sex among girls see John D'Emilio and Estelle B. Freedman, *Intimate Matters: A History of Sexuality in America*, 2nd ed. (Chicago: University of Chicago Press, 1988). On disbelief in genital differences see Sylvanus Stall, DD, *Purity and Truth: What a Young Husband*

Ought to Know (London: Vir Publishing Company, 1897), 41–52. On concerns about masturbation see Myer Solis-Cohen, MD, *Women in Girlhood, Wifehood, Motherhood: Her Responsibilities and Her Duties at all Periods of Life; A Guide in the Maintenance of Her Own Health and That of Her Children* (Philadelphia: John C. Winston Company, 1906), 114.

10. On worries about sex dampening intellect and depleting health see Stall, *Purity and Truth.*

11. For details related to Clelia Mosher and her research see James MaHood and Kristine Wenberg, eds., *The Mosher Survey: Sexual Attitudes of 45 Victorian Women* (New York: Arno Press, 1980), 328.

12. On Ida Craddock's perspectives on sexual pleasure see Ida C. Craddock and Paul Royster (ed.), *The Wedding Night* (self-published, 1902), 3, 10.

13. "Ban on Evil Pictures: America Will Ask France to Stop Mailing of Them," *San Francisco Call,* February 7, 1905, 14.

14. Elsie seeks information and advice from her mother in Robinson, *I Wanted Out!,* 80–81.

15. For customs surrounding death, grief, and mourning see Habenstein and Lamers, *History of American Funeral Directing,* 397–398.

16. On Christie's accomplishments as a Mount Hermon baseball player see *The Hermonite* 7, no. 18 (June 19, 1894). For Louisa's post-Northfield involvement see NMHA, Alumnae/i and Philanthropy, Series II Northfield Alumnae Association, Box 1, Folder 5 Alumnae Association Minute Book 1884–1906. For details of Louisa and Christie's wedding see "Crowell-Van Arsdale: A Wedding Celebrated in Hackensack, N.J., June 1," *Vermont Phoenix,* June 10, 1898, and "Mrs. Christie B. Crowell," *Vermont Phoenix,* April 14, 1899.

17. Elsie muses about the inner workings of other married couples in Robinson, *I Wanted Out!,* 108.

18. Elsie begins to wonder if her marriage will ever satisfy her in Robinson, *I Wanted Out!,* 100–101, 107.

19. Elsie tries to embrace domestic life at 13 Myrtle Street in Robinson, *I Wanted Out!,* 109–110.

20. On the transformation of American households see Carol Hymowitz and Michaele Weissman, *A History of Women in America: From Founding Mothers to Feminists—How Women Shaped the Life and Culture of America* (New York: Bantam, 1984), 221.

21. Elsie wonders why she and Christie aren't developing an intimate bond in Robinson, *I Wanted Out!,* 110–111.

22. On Christie singing in a men's quartet see *Vermont Phoenix,* June 9, 1905, and June 21, 1907; on playing in a baseball league *Vermont Phoenix,*

June 28, 1901; on participating in poultry shows *Vermont Phoenix*, September 27, 1900. Christie was an active Mason, rising to Grand Master, Grand Lodge of Vermont, between 1924 and 1925, "Proceedings of the Supreme Council," 114th Annual Meeting, Buffalo, New York, September 23, 1926.

23. For popular advice columnists on wifehood see Ruth Ashmore, *Side Talks with Girls* (New York: Charles Scribner's Sons, 1896), 231.

24. Elsie urges women to demand fulfillment outside the home in Robinson, "Listen, World!," December 31, 1923.

25. The emotional downturn Elsie experiences is all-encompassing in Robinson, *I Wanted Out!*, 139.

26. Details on neurasthenia are drawn from Tom Lutz, *American Nervousness, 1903: An Anecdotal History* (Ithaca: Cornell University Press, 1991).

27. Elsie goes to a doctor in Boston in Robinson, *I Wanted Out!*, 140.

CHAPTER 6: AWAKENING

1. Judith Walzer Leavitt, "Under the Shadow of Maternity: American Women's Responses to Death and Debility Fears in Nineteenth-Century Childbirth," *Feminist Studies* 12, no. 1 (Spring 1986): 129–154.

2. Robinson, *I Wanted Out!*, 141.

3. Judith Walzer Leavitt, *Brought to Bed: Childbearing in America, 1750–1950* (New York: Oxford University Press, 2016), 28–29.

4. Solis-Cohen, *Women in Girlhood, Wifehood, Motherhood*, 165.

5. Carolyn Skinner, "The Purity of Truth: Nineteenth-Century American Women Physicians Write About Delicate Topics," *Rhetoric Review* 26, no. 2 (2007): 103–119.

6. Alice B. Stockham, *Tokology: A Book for Every Woman* (Chicago: Sanitary Publishing Company, 1883), 188. On the widespread popularity of *Tokology* see Marsha Silberman, "The Perfect Storm: Late Nineteenth-Century Chicago Sex Radicals: Moses Harman, Ida Craddock, Alice Stockham and the Comstock Obscenity Laws," *Journal of the Illinois State Historical Society* 102, no. 3/4 (Fall–Winter 2009): 324–367.

7. Elsie recounts not being able to discuss her pregnancy in Robinson, *I Wanted Out!*, 143.

8. On her experience of isolation during pregnancy see Robinson, *I Wanted Out!*, 142.

9. On her expectations that married life would improve see Robinson, *I Wanted Out!*, 123.

10. On Elsie's lack of communication with her mother see Robinson, *I Wanted Out!*, 144.

11. For Christie's response to Elsie's pregnancy see Robinson, *I Wanted Out!*, 144–145.

12. For Elsie's experiences of joy during pregnancy see Robinson, *I Wanted Out!*, 145. The passage in the next paragraph continues with the same citation.

13. On the presence of midwives at births and medicine available in 1900 see Richard W. Wertz and Dorothy C. Wertz, *Lying-In: A History of Childbirth in America*, expanded ed. (New Haven: Yale University Press, 1989).

14. On the desire of women for their mothers at first birth see Leavitt, "Under the Shadow of Maternity," 129–154.

15. For Elsie's description of the midwife see Robinson, *I Wanted Out!*, 146.

16. On Elsie giving birth see Robinson, *I Wanted Out!*, 147.

17. For Elsie's elation at George's birth see Robinson, *I Wanted Out!*, 147, 150.

18. Asthma and Allergy Foundation of America, "Asthma in Infants," accessed November 5, 2021, https://www.aafa.org/asthma-in-infants/; Michael Stephen, MD, author of *Breath Taking: The Power, Fragility, and Future of Our Extraordinary Lungs*, phone interviews and email correspondence, May 20–November 9, 2021; Robinson, *I Wanted Out!*, 156–157.

19. Robinson, *I Wanted Out!*, 156–157.

20. For leading causes of death in the United States see "Deaths and Death Rates for Leading Causes of Death: Death Registration States, 1900–1998," https://www.cdc.gov/nchs/data/dvs/lead1900_98.pdf, accessed December 8, 2021.

21. For early understandings of asthma, symptoms, and treatment see L. Emmett Holt, *Diseases of Infancy and Childhood* (New York: D. Appleton and Company, 1908), 527.

22. On Christie's promise to Elsie about ranching see Robinson, *I Wanted Out!*, 157.

23. Elsie contemplates leaving Vermont in Robinson, *I Wanted Out!*, 157.

24. Christie and Elsie reach an impasse in Robinson, *I Wanted Out!*, 158.

25. Elsie recognizes Christie's love for George in Robinson, *I Wanted Out!*, 157.

26. For their different approaches to managing George's illness see Robinson, *I Wanted Out!*, 166.

27. Elsie's resolve comes into focus in Robinson, *I Wanted Out!*, 166–167.

28. Elsie explores the library holdings in Robinson, *I Wanted Out!*, 169.

29. Elsie begins to analyze people and her surroundings in Robinson, *I Wanted Out!*, 168.

30. On discovering the power of writing see Robinson, *I Wanted Out!*, 169.

31. Elsie keeps the details of her marriage from family in Robinson, *I Wanted Out!*, 158.

32. Her goal of returning to California intensifies in Robinson, *I Wanted Out!*, 159.

33. On the death of Alexander Robinson see "A Bereaved Family," *Rapid City Journal* (South Dakota), January 16, 1907, with another obituary in the *San Francisco Call* on January 20, 1907. On the death of Elsie's brother see "Engineer Paul Robinson Dies in Carson," *Nevada State Journal*, June 8, 1907.

34. Reflections of her childhood home getting electricity for the first time are in Robinson, *I Wanted Out!*, 52–53.

35. George's attendance records and teacher assignment are on file at "Vermont School Register for 1911–1912," High Street School, Brattleboro Town Clerk, Brattleboro, VT.

36. Martin Gardner, "John Martin's Book: An Almost Forgotten Children's Magazine," *Children's Literature* 18 (1990): 145–159; "John Martin Papers," Biographical Sketch, de Grummond Children's Literature Collection, University of Southern Mississippi, accessed July 6, 2018, https://www.lib.usm.edu/legacy/degrum/public_html/html/research/findaids/martin.htm.

37. Elsie's first story for *John Martin's Letters* was published in 1911. This passage is taken from that letter. See note 38 for archive details.

38. While Elsie revealed in her memoir, *I Wanted Out!*, that her work appeared in *John Martin's Letters*, she did not disclose the stories she contributed or that she wrote under the pseudonym "Comfy Lady." To arrive at this determination, the authors worked with a forensic handwriting expert to compare Elsie's cursive lettering in her application to Northfield Seminary in 1901 with the multitude of handwritten stories that appeared in *John Martin's Letters* between 1909 and 1911. Volumes of these letters are available online and at the Library of Congress.

39. Elsie urges married women to have lives as full as married men in Robinson, *I Wanted Out!*, 59.

40. Elsie's performance in a show, listed as Mrs. C. B. Crowell, is mentioned in "The Cast in First Regiment Band's Play, 'A Night Off,'" *Vermont Phoenix*, May 10, 1912. Elsie describes permissible clothing in Robinson, *I Wanted Out!*, 127–128. Elsie remarks on feeling overjoyed by her new outfit in Robinson, *I Wanted Out!*, 128.

41. Federation of Women's Clubs, "History and Mission," accessed May 14, 2021, https://www.gfwc.org/about/history-and-mission/.

42. Elsie recalls her awakening in Robinson, *I Wanted Out!*, 169–170.

43. Elsie describes confinement within her home in Robinson, *I Wanted Out!*, 170–171.

CHAPTER 7: ART

1. For details regarding Robert Wallace and his social habits see "Miss Melusina Marx Wants $15,000 for Loss of Organ Caused by Accident During Auto Ride," *Philadelphia Inquirer*, June 2, 1907, 11.

2. For biographical details see Robert Wallace, Brattleboro Retreat Case File #7568A, Brattleboro Retreat (with permission of the Wallace family); Robert Wallace, registry of birth, November 23, 1870, no. 140, Town of Pittsfield, State of Massachusetts; written history of Robert Wallace's daughter, Janet, shared with the authors nearly eighty years after his death by his great-granddaughter. For age at time of immigration for Andrew Brabner Wallace Jr., father of Robert Wallace, see Reverend John H. Lockwood and Ernest Newton Bagg et al., *Western Massachusetts, a History, 1636–1925*, vol. 3 (New York: Lewis Historical Publishing Company, 1926), 400–401. For a description of Wallace's childhood home see Derek Strahan, "Foot-Wallace House, Springfield, Mass.," *Lost New England*, December 21, 2017, https://lostnewengland.com/2017/12/foot-wallace-house-springfield-mass/. For his affiliation with the Masons see "Membership Card," Springfield Lodge, Initiated September 16, 1896, with full membership February 3, 1897; and Walter H. Hunt, Grand Historian, Grand Lodge of Massachusetts, interview and email correspondence with authors, August 3 and 6, 2018, and February 25, 2021. For Robert Wallace's residence with his wife and children see 1900 United States Federal Census, Hampden County, Massachusetts, Springfield Ward 4, enumeration district 583, sheet 2B, dwelling 42, family 44, lines 95–99; NARA microfilm publication T623, roll 652. For his age at the time of losing his mother see Massachusetts Vital Records, Deaths, 1881, Springfield, vol. 328, p. 385, no. 212; State Archives, Boston. On his aborted plans to attend college and details of substance use see "Intake Report," Brattleboro Retreat Case File, September 19, 1911. For reports of his employment status see "Robert M. Wallace Leaves Consolidated Dry Goods Co.," *North Adams Transcript*, April 15, 1907, 5.

3. For the history of Brattleboro Retreat see Esther Munroe Swift and Mona Beach, *Brattleboro Retreat: 1834–1984, 150 Years of Caring* (Brattleboro: Book Press, 1984).

4. See Wallace, Brattleboro Retreat Case File.

5. Robert Wallace, *Behind the Garden Wall* (San Francisco: Paul Elder and Co., 1913).

6. Christopher C. Wright, "Masonic Principles, Revisited," Petaluma Masons' website, accessed January 5, 2022, http://masons180.org.

7. Elsie's initial thoughts on meeting and collaborating with Robert Wallace are in Robinson, *I Wanted Out!*, 171–172.

8. Gossip swirls around Elsie and Robert Wallace in Robinson, *I Wanted Out!*, 173.

9. "1601 Perished at Sea," *Vermont Phoenix*, April 19, 1912.

10. To live a richer life, Elsie urges readers to be proactive in Robinson, "Listen, World!," January 16, 1924.

11. For reflections on Robert Wallace see Robinson, *I Wanted Out!*, 172.

12. Elsie asks readers to consider who is really to blame for their unhappiness in Robinson, "Listen, World!," December 15, 1937.

13. Julian Weaver Farnsworth, "Worries Drive Man to Suicide," *San Francisco Call*, March 26, 1912, 3. For her brother Phil's graduation from Stanford see *Alumni Directory and Ten-Year Book II, 1891–1910* (Palo Alto, CA: Stanford University, 1910), 222.

14. Robert Wallace and Elsie hatch a plan in Robinson, *I Wanted Out!*, 175–176.

15. Elsie attempts to act indifferently to Robert Wallace's plan in Robinson, *I Wanted Out!*, 176.

16. Robert Wallace, "Petition and Citation for Guardian of Insane," October 14, 1912, Probate Court, Brattleboro, Vermont, Vermont State Archives and Records Administration. On the role and responsibilities of the guardian see "The Public Statues of Vermont: 1906" (1907).

17. For discharge papers with doctor notes see Wallace, Brattleboro Retreat Case File.

18. Robinson, *I Wanted Out!*, 177.

19. On the Robinson family living in Berkeley see Polk-Husted Directory Company's Oakland, Berkeley, Alameda Directory, 1913 (Oakland, CA: Polk-Husted Directory Company, 1913), 210.

20. Robert Wallace, *Within the Deep Dark Woods* (San Francisco: Blair-Murdock Company, 1913).

21. Elsinore Robinson Crowell illustrated Charles E. Little (advisory ed.), *Primer: Life and Literature Readers* (San Francisco: Doub & Company, 1914) and *First Reader: Life and Literature Readers* (San Francisco: Doub & Company, 1914).

22. California Historical Society exhibit, "Panama-Pacific International Exhibit," 1915–2015; "A Curious Story of the 14-Ton Underwood

Master Typewriter," *Red Letter Day Zine*, accessed January 5, 2022, https://
redletterdayzine.wordpress.com/2015/06/23/giant-typewriters-at-the
-panama-pacific-expo-1915/.

23. Christie implores Elsie to return to Vermont in Robinson, *I Wanted
Out!*, 181–182.

24. George's condition worsens in Robinson, *I Wanted Out!*, 181. On pop-
ular treatments for asthma at the turn of the twentieth century see Mark
Jackson, "Divine Stramonium: The Rise and Fall of Smoking for Asthma,"
Medical History 54, no. 2 (April 2010): 171–194.

25. "Berkeley Man's Mine Yields Rich Ore Pocket," *San Francisco Call*,
August 27, 1915.

26. Elsie urges readers to take risks in Robinson, "Listen, World!," February 10, 1939; Robinson, "Listen, World!," February 16, 1939; Robinson,
"Listen, World!," May 9, 1939.

CHAPTER 8: HORNITOS

1. On the early development of Hornitos, California, see Newell
D. Chamberlain, *The Call of Gold: True Tales on the Gold Road to Yosemite* (Mariposa, CA: Gazette Press, 1936). On Hornitos as the most prolific mining district in California see "Volume III—Technical Background
Report," Mariposa County Wide General Plan, Cultural and Historic Resources, 11-8. From Mariposa County, https://www.mariposacounty.org
/DocumentCenter/View/3103/Volume-III—11-Cultural—Historic
?bidId=, accessed May 21, 2021.

2. On bandits and their narrow escapes from law enforcement see
"Ghost Towns on '49 Tour," *San Francisco Call*, May 12, 1922.

3. On the mechanics of selling gold see James J. Rawls and Richard J.
Orsi, eds., *A Golden State: Mining and Economic Development in Gold Rush
California* (Berkeley: University of California Press, 1999). On protection
offered by riflemen see John Boessenecker, "Shotguns and Outlaws," *True
West Magazine*, May 2022. On stores and shopping in Hornitos see Judge
Thomas Coakley, "Life in a Mining Town—Hornitos, California, Oldtim-
ers of Hornitos," oral history interview conducted January 24, 1954, Re-
gional Oral History Office, University of California, Berkeley, Bancroft
Library; "San Nicholas Saloon," *Mariposa Gazette*, November 13, 1860.

4. On mayhem and justice in the early days of Hornitos see Chamberlain, *Call of Gold*. For reference to ending disputes with gunfire see "Murders Miner in Drunken Quarrel: Harry Collis Kills Thomas Lynn Without
Cause in Mariposa," *Madera Mercury*, November 12, 1915. Description of

jail derived from author interviews with Hornitos residents in Hornitos, California, June 11–12, 2021.

5. "Fourteenth Census of the United States: 1920: Bulletin: Population: California," Table 3—Population of Incorporated Places: 1920, 1910, and 1900, Department of Commerce.

6. Information about the iron door to the defunct opium den comes from author visits and interviews with Hornitos residents in Hornitos, California, June 12–13, 2021.

7. Dame Shirley wrote, "Gold mining is Nature's great lottery scheme." Louise A. K. S. Clappe, *The Shirley Letters* (Peregrine, 1970).

8. Elsie recalls arriving in Hornitos in Robinson, *I Wanted Out!*, 188.

9. Robinson, *I Wanted Out!*, 190.

10. George's condition improves in Robinson, *I Wanted Out!*, 191.

11. For how puberty impacts lung development see author interviews and email correspondence about lung development with Dr. Michael Stephen, May 20–November 9, 2021.

12. On Robert Wallace's claim to Duncan Mine see "Find Gold in Mine Long Inactive: Rich Pocket of Precious Metal Rewards Efforts to Revive Mining Activity at Hornitos," *Merced County Sun*, August 27, 1915; "News Around the Loop," *San Joaquin Light and Power*, June 1915, 338. For location and size of Duncan Mine see Olaf P. Jenkins, *California Journal of Mines and Geology* (San Francisco, CA: State Mineralogist Report, Department of Natural Resources, Division of Mines, State of California, vol. 53, nos. 1–2, 1957). On production of Duncan Mine see "Duncan Mine," Hudson Institute of Mineralogy, accessed August 3, 2021, https://www.mindat.org/loc-82114.html.

13. On living in a rented house see Elsinore Robinson Crowell, "Statement by Mrs. C. B. Crowell: Reviews Events Leading Up to Beginning of Divorce Proceedings," *Brattleboro Reformer*, November 19, 1917.

14. Description of Hornitos School is based on photos held at Mariposa Museum and History Center, Mariposa, California.

15. Elsie encourages readers to think about unobvious drivers of happiness in Robinson, "Listen, World!," January 21, 1924.

16. "Ruth Pierce: Spontaneous News Items from Ruth Pierce Mine and Vicinity," *Mariposa Gazette*, November 22, 1919.

17. Andrew J. Cherlin, "American Marriage in the Early Twenty-First Century," *Future of Children* 15, no. 2 (Autumn 2005): 33–35.

18. Elsie states George's health is the only reason for going to Hornitos in Robinson, *I Wanted Out!*, 191.

19. Elsie reflects on her growing financial desperation in Robinson, *I Wanted Out!*, 194.

20. Analysis of surviving mines in Mariposa County between 1915 and 1918 was conducted on behalf of the authors by Brenda Callen, senior engineering geologist, and Fred Gius, supervising engineering geologist, California Geological Survey, State of California, March–April 2021. See also *Mariposa Gazette*, September 21, 1912; Lloyd L. Root, "Mining in California" (San Francisco: Division of Mines and Mining, State of California, 1928); "Report on Ruth Pierce Mine," MC252, Special Collections, UC Davis Library.

21. On the role of women in the mining camp see Nancy J. Taniguchi, "Weaving a Different World: Women and the California Gold Rush," *California History* (Summer 2000): 141–168. On the dangers of mining see İpek Özmen and Emine Aksoy, "Respiratory Emergencies and Management of Mining Accidents," *Turkish Thoracic Journal* 16, no. 1 (April 2015); "Milford Mine Memorial Park," background on drowning of miners, accessed January 5, 2021, https://www.crowwing.us/294/Milford-Mine-Memorial-Park.

22. On the Speculator Mine disaster in Butte, Montana, see "The Granite Mountain Speculator Mine Memorial," accessed January 5, 2021, http://www.minememorial.org/history/intro.htm.

23. On the fatal accident involving a teen boy see "Miner Meets Death," *Mariposa Gazette*, June 6, 1914.

24. On the reaction to Elsie's decision to work at the Ruth Pierce Mine see Robinson, *I Wanted Out!*, 194–195.

25. Elsie recalls asking for a job at the mine in Robinson, *I Wanted Out!*, 195.

26. For tunnel and shaft configuration see Fletcher Hamilton, *Report XVII of the State Mineralogist* (San Francisco: California State Mining Bureau, 1921); "Report on Ruth Pierce Mine," UC Davis Library.

27. Elsie describes working in the Ruth Pierce Mine in Robinson, *I Wanted Out!*, 189, 195, 197, 199, 200–201, 205.

28. Elsie reflects on finding freedom in the mines in Robinson, *I Wanted Out!*, 196, 219.

29. On meeting a murderer and how it shaped Elsie's worldview see Robinson, "Listen, World!," May 7, 1921.

30. On Hornitos as a place of transformation and peace in Elsie's life see Robinson, *I Wanted Out!*, 184.

31. On Christie's meeting another woman see "Crowell-Burnett," *Brattleboro Reformer*, March 5, 1926. On the first woman doctor see "Happy Birthday, Brattleboro!," Brattleboro Area Chamber of Commerce, accessed December 11, 2021, https://www.brattleborochamber.org/happy-birthday-brattleboro/.

32. Elsie's response to Christie's request for divorce is in Robinson, *I Wanted Out!*, 159.

33. "100 Years of Marriage and Divorce Statistics, United States, 1867–1967," Table 1, National Vital Statistics System, National Center for Health Statistics; Kristin Celello, *Making Marriage Work: A History of Marriage and Divorce in the Twentieth-Century United States* (Chapel Hill: University of North Carolina Press, 2009).

34. Joanna L. Grossman, Ellen K. Solender Endowed Chair in Women and the Law, Southern Methodist University, Dedman School of Law, and coauthor of *Inside the Castle: Law and the Family in 20th Century America*, interviews and email correspondence with authors, February–December 2021.

35. Joseph Clement Bates, *History of the Bench and Bar of California* (San Francisco: Bench and Bar Publishing Co., 1912), 520; "Elsinore Robinson Crowell, plaintiff vs. Christie B. Crowell," Superior Court of the State of California, in the County of Mariposa, December 1, 1916; "Superior Court Notes: The Week's Record of Judicial Proceedings," *Mariposa Gazette*, December 16, 1916; "Summons," *Mariposa Gazette*, December 30, 1916.

36. "Elsinore Robinson Crowell, plaintiff vs. Christie B. Crowell," Superior Court of the State of California, in the County of Mariposa, October 10, 1917.

37. "Christie B. Crowell v Elsinore R. Crowell, Petition for Divorce," Windham County Court, State of Vermont, September Term, 1917.

38. Elsie reflects on the shame she faced in Robinson, *I Wanted Out!*, 190. On adultery in colonial New England see Deborah L. Rhode, *Adultery: Infidelity and the Law* (Cambridge: Harvard University Press, 2016). On laws pertaining to adultery, including prison terms and fines, see "The General Laws of Vermont: 1917," Legislative Reference Bureau, Montpelier, Vermont. For Vermont adultery prosecutions see "Windham County's Good Rank: Only Two Other Counties of the State Show Smaller Number of Criminal Prosecutions," *Vermont Phoenix*, October 7, 1910. On sentencing for adultery see "Girl Sent to Windsor: Hilda Elo of Worcester, Mass., to Serve a Year for Adultery," *Brattleboro Reformer*, February 16, 1916, 2; "Harvie S. Hill and Maude E. Scoville of Rochester, Charged with Adultery," *Brattleboro Reformer*, February 28, 1916, 5.

39. "Jury Acquitted Smith: Acted in Self Defense When He Shot Clark Mundell," *Vermont Phoenix*, June 9, 1911, 4.

40. "Elsinore Robinson Crowell, plaintiff vs. Christie B. Crowell," Superior Court of the State of California, in the County of Mariposa, October 5, 1917.

41. Answer and Cross-Complaint, Divorce, Elsinore Robinson Crowell, Plaintiff, vs. Christie B. Crowell, Defendant, filed April 30, 1917, Mariposa Superior Court.

42. Elsie recounts her feelings toward Christie during divorce proceedings in Robinson, *I Wanted Out!*, 199–200.

CHAPTER 9: TYPEWRITER

1. Authors' visit to Hornitos, California, and interviews with residents, June 12–13, 2021.

2. For biographical details of Luola and Moses Rodgers see US census 1880, Hornitos, Mariposa, California, Roll 68, Family History film 1254068, page 160A, Enumeration District 39, image 0316; Delilah L. Beasley, *The Negro Trail Blazers of California* (Fairfield: James Stevenson Publisher, 2004 [1919]), 105, 113–115; "Rodgers, Moses L. October 27, 1900," *Mariposa Gazette*, October 27, 1900; Rudolph M. Lapp, *Blacks in Gold Rush California* (New Haven: Yale University Press, 1977), 92–93. On the liberation of Black slaves in California see Chamberlain, *Call of Gold*. On the Washington Mine see Jenkins, *California Journal of Mines and Geology*, 179; *Mariposa Gazette*, March 18, 1876; *Sacramento Daily Union*, July 13, 1869.

3. Beasley, *Negro Trail Blazers of California*, 114–115; 1880 census. On Luola Rodgers living with the Olcese family see US Census, 1910, Township 1, Mariposa, California, Roll T624_87, page 6B, Enumeration District 0093, image 1177, FHL number 1374100. On the population of Stockton see "Twelfth Census of the United States." On Olcese as postmaster of Hornitos see "Register of Officers and Agents, Civil Military, and Naval in the Service of the United States, 1877," Secretary of the Interior, Government Printing Office, 1878.

4. "Rodgers, Moses L. October 27, 1900," *Mariposa Gazette*; State Board of Health (San Joaquin County, California), death certificate (1910), Sarah Jane Rodgers, local register no. 371; "150 Years of Women at Berkeley," UC Berkeley Chancellor's Immediate Office, accessed March 2, 2021, https://150w.berkeley.edu/part-2-first-graduate; "Death Summons Vivian Rodgers," *Evening Mail*, August 6, 1914.

5. Luola's connection with children in Hornitos comes from authors' interviews with Hornitos residents in Hornitos, California, June 11–12, 2021. On exhibiting her work at the 1915 World's Fair see Beasley, *Negro Trail Blazers of California*, 114.

6. On the golden age of American magazines see Frank Luther Mott, *A History of American Magazines 1885–1905*, vol. 4 (Cambridge: Harvard

University Press, 1957). On the creation of brand-name products see The-odore Peterson, *Magazines in the Twentieth Century* (Urbana: University of Illinois Press, 1956). On the rise of the packaged goods economy see William M. O'Barr, "A Brief History of Advertising in America," *Advertising & Society Review* 11, no. 1 (2010).

7. On the changing finances of magazine ads over subscriptions see Quint Randle, "A Historical Overview of the Effects of New Mass Media," *First Monday* 6, no. 9 (September 2001). On raising circulation to boost ad revenue see David E. Sumner, *The Magazine Century: American Magazines Since 1900* (New York: Peter Lang Publishing, 2010). On the decrease in pricing driving circulation see Sumner, *The Magazine Century*.

8. On success for writers who published in national magazines see S. S. McClure, *My Autobiography* (New York: Frederick A. Stokes Co., 1914).

9. Elsie recounts the encouragement she received from Luola Rodgers in Robinson, *I Wanted Out!*, 222.

10. Information on the mechanics of early typewriters and the Smith Premier No. 2 is from Jay Schweitzer, Gramercy Typewriter Co., email correspondence and phone conversations with authors, June 29–30, 2020; Paul Robert, Virtual Typewriter Museum, email correspondence with authors, April 16–June 12, 2021; Alan Seaver, Machines of Loving Grace, email correspondence with authors, April 16–July 9, 2021; Richard Polt, the Classic Typewriter Page, email correspondence with authors, June 21, 2021. See also "Instruction Book: The Smith Premier Typewriter, Manual of Operating and Instructions for Machines No. 2, 3, 4, 5 and 6," circa 1896–1914; Rupert P. SoRelle and Ida McLenan Cutler, *Rational Typewriting*, revised ed. (New York: Gregg Publishing Co., 1916).

11. Remembrances of learning how to type and making time for writing are in Robinson, *I Wanted Out!*, 220, 223.

12. Elsie reflects on trying to sell her first story in Robinson, *I Wanted Out!*, 222.

13. For the process by which Luola weighed mail see "Triner Scale & MFG Co., est. 1903," Made in Chicago Museum, accessed January 5, 2021, https://www.madeinchicagomuseum.com/single-post/triner/.

14. "Lewis A. Browne, a Writer, Was 61," *New York Times*, May 25, 1937.

15. Edwin Wildman, *Writing to Sell* (New York: Wildman Magazine & News Service 1914), 108.

16. To see how *Black Cat* billed itself see *Black Cat Magazine*, March 1915.

17. Jack London's tribute to Herman Umbstaetter is in Mott, *History of American Magazines*, 429–430.

18. Elsinore Robinson Crowell, "The Little Maverick," *Black Cat*, July 1918.

19. Elsinore Robinson Crowell, "Buck Calhoun's Woman," *Breezy Stories*, February 1919.

20. Elsie Robinson, "Shall the Woman Tell?," *McClure's*, July 1927.

21. Robinson, *I Wanted Out!*, 219.

22. Musings about the life she left behind are in Robinson, *I Wanted Out!*, 166.

23. For her belief that other women would relish the chance to live as she did see Robinson, *I Wanted Out!*, 197.

24. For an analysis of the "tender years" doctrine we relied on Grossman, interviews and email correspondence with authors, February–December 2021.

25. "Statement by Mrs. C. B. Crowell," *Brattleboro Reformer*, 5.

26. "Geo. E. Crowell Dead: Proprietor of Water System, Former Household Publisher," *Brattleboro Reformer*, October 10, 1916.

CHAPTER 10: SAN FRANCISCO

1. "Superior Court Notes: The Week's Record of Judicial Proceedings," *Mariposa Gazette*, January 19, 1918.

2. Elsie reflects on the divorce proceedings and the impact on George in Robinson, *I Wanted Out!*, 192–193.

3. Descriptions of courtroom are from authors' visit on June 10, 2021.

4. "Affidavit of Position, in the matter of the estate of George Alexander Crowell," February 7, 1918; "Superior Court Notes: The Week's Record of Judicial Proceedings," *Mariposa Gazette*, March 9, 1918; "Mrs. Crowell Gets Custody of Child: No Contest Was Made or Filed in Superior Court in Mariposa, Calif., by Christie Crowell," *Brattleboro Reformer*, March 20, 1918.

5. Elsie writes about the importance of not holding on to hate in Robinson, "Listen, World!," January 23, 1945. On the need to move forward see Robinson, "Cheer-Up," *Oakland Tribune*, October 24, 1919.

6. See Elsie's reflections on the changing postwar economy in Robinson, *I Wanted Out!*, 224.

7. Analysis of mine production between 1915 and 1918 was conducted on behalf of the authors by Brenda Callen and Fred Gius, California Geological Survey, State of California. In 1916, 3,300 fine ounces of gold were produced; in 1918, the amount was 842.02 ounces.

8. *Amador Ledger-Dispatch*, February 16, 1917.

9. The residents of Hornitos crafted a monument in their honor, and the inlaid brass plaque reads, "A loving tribute to Eugenia Gagliardo (1869–1960) and Luola L. Rodgers (1879–1955). In appreciation of a lifetime of dedication to community service and good will."

10. On leaving Hornitos see Robinson, *I Wanted Out!*, 224–225.

11. Women should not make their relationships with men their entire existence. See Robinson, "Listen, World!," April 17, 1922.

12. On the final years in the life of Robert Wallace see Robert M. Wallace household, 1920 United States Federal Census, San Diego County, California, City of San Diego, enumeration district 293, sheet 3A, dwelling 38, family 83, NARA microfilm publication T625, roll 131; Coley E. Kellie household, 1930 United States Census, Panola County, Texas, town of Carthage, enumeration district 183-12, sheet 14A, dwelling 304, family 354, NARA microfilm publication T626, roll 2382; Texas, Death Certificates, Panola County, 1939, no. 52430, Robert M. Wallace; Texas Department of State Health Services, Austin, Texas; "Robert M. Wallace Dies Thursday in Carthage," *Marshall News Messenger*, December 1, 1939. For a description of Carthage, Texas, see https://www.carthagetexas.us, accessed January 15, 2022.

13. On San Francisco during and after World War I see Oscar Lewis, *San Francisco: Mission to Metropolis* (Berkeley: Howell North Books, 1966); John B. McGloin, *San Francisco: The Story of a City* (San Raphael: Presidio Press, 1978). On bodies moved to Colma see John Branch, "The Town of Colma, Where San Francisco's Dead Lives," *New York Times*, February 5, 2016.

14. Elsie experiences postwar San Francisco in Robinson, *I Wanted Out!*, 229–230, 235–236.

15. On women's work in World War I see https://www.striking-women.org/module/women-and-work/world-war-i-1914-1918, accessed February 22, 2022.

16. On social and economic changes for women see Lucy Adlington, *Great War Fashion: Tales from the History Wardrobe* (Gloucestershire: History Press, 2014); Lucy Adlington, *Fashion: Women in World War One* (London: Pitkin Publishing, 2014); Victoria Sherrow, *For Appearance' Sake: The Historical Encyclopedia of Good Looks, Beauty, and Grooming* (Phoenix: Oryx Press, 2001).

17. Elsie experiences postwar San Francisco in Robinson, *I Wanted Out!*, 230–231.

18. 1920 US census, San Francisco County, California, population schedule, San Francisco Assembly District 26, p. 15B, lines 53–54, Elsinore R. Crowell, digital image, Ancestry.com (http://www.ancestry.com, accessed October 29, 2011), citing NARA microfilm publication T625, roll 134.

19. Elsie recalls George's symptoms returning in Robinson, *I Wanted Out!*, 236.

20. I. Ziment and D. P. Tashkin, "Alternative Medicine for Allergy and Asthma," *Journal of Allergy and Clinical Immunology* 106, no. 4 (October

2000); Dr. Michael Stephen, interviews and email correspondence, May 20–November 9, 2021.

21. "Influenza Encyclopedia: The American Influenza Epidemic of 1918–1919," University of Michigan Center for the History of Medicine, University of Michigan Library, accessed January 9, 2021, https://www.influenza archive.org/cities/city-sanfrancisco.html#; "Influenza Pandemic," University Libraries, University of Washington, accessed December 14, 2021, https://content.lib.washington.edu/exhibits/WWI/influenza.html.

22. Elsie grows increasingly alarmed about George's well-being in Robinson, *I Wanted Out!*, 238.

23. Elsie leaves George to look for work in Robinson, *I Wanted Out!*, 236.

24. *San Francisco Chronicle*, October 21, 1918, 10; "Age Discrimination," US Department of Labor, accessed October 2, 2021, https://www.dol.gov/general/topic/discrimination/agedisc.

25. Elsie considers employment opportunities in Robinson, *I Wanted Out!*, 236.

26. Robinson, *I Wanted Out!*, 237.

27. Robinson, "I Wanted Out!," *Hearst's International combined with Cosmopolitan*, July 1934.

28. Elsie tries her first newspaper and gets turned away in Robinson, *I Wanted Out!*, 237–238.

29. Robinson, "I Wanted Out!," *Hearst's International combined with Cosmopolitan*, July 1934.

30. Desperation grows as Elsie fails to find full-time work in Robinson, *I Wanted Out!*, 238.

31. "Announcements," *Vermont Phoenix*, August 24, 1906, 4.

32. Elsie recalls the night she hit rock bottom in Robinson, *I Wanted Out!*, 240–245.

33. Ruth Rosen, *The Lost Sisterhood: Prostitution in America, 1900–1918* (Baltimore: Johns Hopkins University Press, 1982).

34. "History of California Minimum Wage," California Department of Industrial Relations, State of California, accessed November 1, 2021; Norris C. Hundley Jr., "Katherine Philips Edson and the Fight for the California Minimum Wage, 1912–1923," *Pacific Historical Review* 29, no. 3 (August 1960); Sears, Roebuck and Co., *1918 Catalogue*, 163; Peter C. Hennigan, "Property War: Prostitution, Red-Light Districts, and the Transformation of Public Nuisance Law in the Progressive Era," *Yale Journal of Law and the Humanities* 16, no. 1 (2004).

35. "Pay Girls a Living Wage and Vice Evil Will Cure Itself Cries Mrs. Gamble," *San Francisco Chronicle*, January 26, 1917.

36. Elsie considers prostitution in Robinson, *I Wanted Out!*, 244–246.

CHAPTER 11: OAKLAND

1. Elsie regroups and reconsiders the possibility of writing in Robinson, *I Wanted Out!*, 249.

2. Leonard S. Marcus, *Minders of Make-Believe: Idealists, Entrepreneurs, and the Shaping of American Children's Literature* (Boston: Houghton Mifflin, 2008); Miranda McDermott, "Children's Literature @NYPL," New York Public Library, May 1, 2015, https://www.nypl.org/blog/2015/05/01/childrens-book-week; "John Newbery Medal," American Library Association, accessed November 8, 2021, https://www.ala.org/alsc/awardsgrants/bookmedia/newbery; Jacalyn Eddy, *Bookwomen: Creating an Empire in Children's Book Publishing, 1919–1939* (Madison: University of Wisconsin Press, 2006).

3. "A New Feature in the Tribune," *National Tribune*, August 1, 1880, 61; "The Children's Page," 63.

4. Elsie thinks about trying the Oakland market in Robinson, *I Wanted Out!*, 249.

5. On the population of Oakland see *Oakland, Berkeley, and Alameda Directory 1916*. For the description of the *Oakland Tribune* see *Tribune Tower Under Construction*, photo circa 1920, Oakland History Center, Oakland Public Library, Oakland, California. For details of interiors and workspaces see "The New Tribune Building: Eight Floors Devoted Entirely to a Newspaper," *The Oakland Tribune Yearbook*, January 1919.

6. "Tribune's Leo S. Levy Dies at 75: Veteran Managing Editor Started His Career Here in 1909," *Oakland Tribune*, April 23, 1961; "Death of a Friend," *Oakland Tribune*, April 24, 1961; "Private Rites Set for Editor Leo S. Levy," *Oakland Tribune*, April 24, 1961.

7. Elsie recalls her interview with the *Oakland Tribune* in Robinson, *I Wanted Out!*, 250–251.

8. Brady Schwind, "Neill or Not," *The Lost Art of Oz*, September 28, 2020, https://www.lostartofoz.com/lost-art-of-oz-blog/neill-or-not. To read Elsie's philosophy on writing for children, quoted on page 192, read "Aunt Elsie to Tell of Past: Tribune Writer Knows History," *Oakland Tribune*, May 7, 1919.

9. Launch of *Aunt Elsie's Magazine for the Kiddies of the Oakland Tribune* was on May 11, 1919.

10. Aunt Elsie's playful mailing address was routinely featured in the paper, and her illustrated "Tribune House" stationery was used at least until January 27, 1960. The Aunt Elsie brand endured four years after her death and more than thirty years after leaving the *Tribune*. Copies of her letters are in possession of the authors. See Elsie's encouragement to girls in "And Here Is 'Jewel Box,'" *Oakland Tribune*, May 11, 1919.

11. News of clubs forming was printed regularly in the *Oakland Tribune*, with mentions of students who joined and the names of teachers and community leaders who served as organizers. The paper also routinely ran notices for member-only special events.

12. Membership card for *Oakland Tribune* Aunt Elsie Club, Collection of the Oakland Museum of California, Gift of Ms. Patricia Monaco, 1945; Aunt Elsie Club membership pin is in possession of the authors.

13. Early examples appeared on the *Tribune's* front page. "Aunt Elsie Entertains Youngsters and They Haven't Stopped Giggling Yet," *Oakland Tribune*, June 14, 1919. See also "Aunt Elsie Club to Hold Theater Party," *Oakland Tribune,* April 21, 1933; "Christmas Entertainment Given by Tribune Set for December 21," *Oakland Tribune*, December 16, 1922.

14. *San Francisco Chronicle* copy cat: "The Chronicle's Kiddies' Corner, Conducted by Aunt Dolly," *San Francisco Chronicle*, July 2, 1922.

15. Elsie's fame skyrockets and captures the attention of parents in Robinson, *I Wanted Out!*, 256.

16. "Curtains, Collars, and Cutlets: Cheer-Up Column" debuted in the *Oakland Tribune* on January 20, 1919. It morphed into a column targeting male readers, too, sometimes appearing with only Elsie's byline and without "Cheer-Up" branding. An example of this approach appeared in the *Oakland Tribune* on May 22, 1919.

17. "Cry on Geraldine's Shoulder" launched in the *Oakland Tribune* on September 6, 1920.

18. On Nellie Bly and the early history of women in journalism see Julie Golia, *Newspaper Confessions: A History of Advice Columns in a Pre-Internet Age* (New York: Oxford University Press, 2021); Brooke Kroeger, *Nellie Bly: Daredevil, Reporter, Feminist* (New York: Crown, 1994); Ishbel Ross, *Ladies of the Press: The Story of Women in Journalism by an Insider* (New York: Harper, 1936).

19. Elsie recounts her work schedule in Robinson, *I Wanted Out!*, 258.

20. Elsie urges readers to consider how working mothers benefit children in Robinson, "Listen, World!," January 20, 1937.

21. Elsie Robinson, "Just All of a Piece," *Quad-City Times*, January 24, 1921; "Listen, World," *Modesto Morning Herald*, January 23, 1921.

22. Elsie recounts her rising pay and George's ongoing illness in Robinson, *I Wanted Out!*, 252, 258–260, 262.

23. Dr. Abelson Epsteen, *Alumni-Faculty Association Bulletin* (San Francisco: School of Medicine, University of California, Fall 1955); Guthrie McClain, "Out of the Past in California Chess," *California Chess Journal* 1, no. 13 (October 1987).

24. Elsie remembers Dr. Epsteen in Robinson, *I Wanted Out!*, 252.

25. George is sent to live in Mariposa, California, in Robinson, *I Wanted Out!*, 260–261.

26. "The Candy Pull That Wouldn't Pull," *Mariposa Gazette*, December 17, 1921; "Press Club Organized by Mariposa High School Students," *Mariposa Gazette*, December 17, 1921; "A Bang! A Red Ford Climbs Chaparral Bush!," *Mariposa Gazette*, December 17, 1921.

CHAPTER 12: LISTEN, WORLD!

1. Ross, *Ladies of the Press*; Fremont Older, *My Own Story* (New York: Macmillan, 1926); Guide to the Fremont Older papers, 1907–1941, Fremont Older Papers, Bancroft Library, University of California, Berkeley.

2. John Bruce, *Gaudy Century, 1848–1948: San Francisco's One Hundred Years of Robust Journalism* (New York: Random House, 1948); Older, *My Own Story*.

3. Elsie's letter to Fremont Older at *The Call* dated April 10, 1929, Fremont Older papers, BANC MSS C-B 376, Bancroft Library, University of California, Berkeley.

4. *American Newspaper Annual and Directory* (Philadelphia: N. W. Ayer and Sons, 1923).

5. "Brilliant Woman Opens Heart, Mind to Readers of the Call," *San Francisco Call and Post*, September 5, 1923.

6. "Tell It to Elsie" column launched in the *San Francisco Call and Post* on September 10, 1923.

7. Academic transcript for George Crowell, California Polytechnic School, January 1923–October 1924; *The Polygram*, April 12, June 7, November 23, December 7, December 14, 1923; October 16, 1924.

8. On the close relationship between Arthur Brisbane and William Randolph Hearst see Nasaw, *The Chief*; Procter, *William Randolph Hearst*. On circulation of the *Evening Journal* see N. W. Ayer & Sons, *American Newspaper Annual & Directory* (Philadelphia, 1925).

9. Brisbane writes Elsie about her column in Robinson, *I Wanted Out!*, 265.

10. Brisbane leaves Pulitzer for Hearst in James McGrath Morris, *Pulitzer: A Life in Politics, Print, and Power* (New York: Harper Perennial, 2010), 334; Nasaw, *The Chief*; Whyte, *The Uncrowned King*; Procter, *William Randolph Hearst*.

11. On one in four Americans see Whyte, *The Uncrowned King*, 464. On adding millions more readers with syndication see Nasaw, *The Chief*, 322–323. On additional Hearst media holdings, including International News Service, see Carlson and Bates, *Hearst: Lord of San Simeon*, 185–186. On ownership of national magazines see Nancy Frazier, *William Randolph Hearst: Modern Media*

Tycoon (Woodbridge, CT: Blackbirch Press, 2001), 95; John K. Winkler, *W. R. Hearst: An American Phenomenon* (New York: Simon & Schuster, 1928), 245.

12. Judith Gura and Kate Wood, *Interior Landmarks: Treasures of New York* (New York: Monacelli Press, 2015); "Hotels with a Past: The Plaza Hotel New York," Historic Hotels of America, accessed February 26, 2022, https://www.historichotels.org/us/hotels-resorts/the-plaza/history.php.

13. Elsie recounts her stay at the Plaza and her meeting with Arthur Brisbane in Robinson, *I Wanted Out!*, 265–266.

14. Details of Brisbane's career are in W. A. Swanberg, *Citizen Hearst* (New York: Scribner, 1961). For the description of Brisbane's desk from a photo see Brisbane Family Papers, Special Collections Research Center, Box 11, Syracuse University Libraries.

15. "Transcription of Elsie Robinson interview," September 17, 1937, Brisbane Family Papers, Special Collections Research Center, Box 3 (2001 addition), Syracuse University Libraries; Robinson, *I Wanted Out!*, 266–267.

16. On Brisbane's success see Whyte, *The Uncrowned King*, 351. For Elsie's salary within the Hearst organization see Ross, *Ladies of the Press*, 384, and Watson, "Began Brilliant Career at 35," 7; "Transcription of Elsie Robinson interview."

17. Elsie reflects on her successful meeting with Arthur Brisbane in Robinson, *I Wanted Out!*, 268.

CHAPTER 13: ST. LUKE'S

1. Eric K. Chu and Jeffrey M. Drazen, "Asthma: One Hundred Years of Treatment and Onward," *American Journal of Respiratory and Critical Care Medicine* 171, no. 11 (2005); Arlene Shaner, Historical Collections librarian, New York Academy of Medicine, email correspondence with authors, December 3, 2021. Elsie is optimistic about George's future in Robinson, *I Wanted Out!*, 273.

2. Elsie recalls celebrating with George at the train station in Robinson, *I Wanted Out!*, 274–275.

3. Academic transcript for George Crowell, California Polytechnic School, January 1923–October 1924; *The Polygram*, October 16, 1924.

4. San Francisco Sales Ledgers: Years 1914–1967, Parcel number 2641-021; "Country Home in City," *San Francisco Chronicle*, July 3, 1924, 17; "A Country Home in the City," *San Francisco Chronicle*, March 2, 1924, 20.

5. George's attendance at Sacramento Junior College was recorded in the campus newspaper, *The Blotter*, November 6, 1925, and February 19, 1926.

6. *The Polygram*, October 2, 1924; George Crowell death certificate, January 23, 1926, file no. 653, California State Board of Health, City and County

of San Francisco, copy in possession of authors. Elsie reflects on George's new health concern in Robinson, *I Wanted Out!*, 275.

7. Elsie writes about fear and resilience in Robinson, "Listen, World!," January 13, 1926.

8. "The Influenza Epidemic of 1926: A Preliminary Note on Certain Epidemiological Indications," *Public Health Reports (1896–1970)* 41, no. 34 (August 1926); Department of Commerce, Bureau of the Census, *Mortality Statistics 1926: Twenty-Seventh Annual Report, Part 1* (1929), 110.

9. St. Luke's Hospital *Annual Report* (San Francisco: St. Luke's Hospital, October 1, 1925–September 30, 1926); Jeffrey M. Bender et al., "Parapneumonic Empyema Deaths During Past Century, Utah," *Emerging Infectious Diseases* 15, no. 1 (January 2009); Dr. Michael Stephen, interviews and email correspondence, May 20–November 9, 2021.

10. "Large S. F. Gin Source Traced," *Oakland Tribune*, January 23, 1926, 1.

11. Elsie reveals her grief in Robinson, *I Wanted Out!*, 276.

12. George Crowell death certificate, copy in possession of authors.

13. N. Gray and Company Funeral Home (San Francisco, California), Funeral Record, 1926, p. 558, for George Alexander Crowell, January 25, 1926; digital image, Ancestry.com (http://www.ancestry.com, accessed December 20, 2021), "California, U.S., San Francisco Area Funeral Home Records, 1895–1985," microfilm publication (Researchity, San Francisco, California).

CHAPTER 14: SONORA

1. On her column about women who are too attached to their mothers see Robinson, "Listen, World!," January 25, 1926.

2. On her column about separating work from personal life see Robinson, "Listen, World!," December 21, 1933.

3. On her column and editorial cartoon about resilience see Robinson, "Listen, World!," August 31, 1927.

4. "A Monument to Love," Robinson, *Listen World!*, 45–48.

5. Elsie's letter to Fremont Older at the *Call* dated April 10, 1929, Fremont Older papers, BANC MSS C-B 376, Bancroft Library, University of California, Berkeley.

6. For the volume of fan mail, there are numerous references. For one, see Watson, "Began Brilliant Career at 35," 7.

7. Tuolumne County, California, Deed Book "A" 94: 18, Fred J. Grundell to Elsinore Robinson, March 4, 1929, County Recorder, Sonora.

8. On the history of Sonora see Pat Perry, "Queen of the 'Southern Mines' Still Reigns," City of Sonora, accessed January 11, 2022, https://www.sonoraca.com/downtown-sonora/sonora-california-history/.

9. Exterior and interior details of Elsie's cabin in Sonora are from Jessica Hewitt, director of Foothill Horizons Outdoor School, interviews and email correspondence with authors, August 2–5, 2021.

10. Elsie's reflections on finding comfort in nature are in Robinson, *I Wanted Out!*, 28.

11. Elsie begins writing about her life in Robinson, *I Wanted Out!*, 1.

12. Reflections of George and her enduring grief are in Robinson, "Listen, World!," January 9, 1945; Robinson, *I Wanted Out!*, 277.

13. Elsie recalls working with Fremont Older on the story of her life in Robinson, *I Wanted Out!*, 290.

14. Her final words land on the page in Robinson, *I Wanted Out!*, 64, 299.

15. Elsie urges readers to stop skirting risk to live fully engaged lives in Robinson, *I Wanted Out!*, 46.

EPILOGUE

1. *Cosmopolitan* magazine publishes Elsie's serial over seven months in Robinson, "I Wanted Out!," *Hearst's International combined with Cosmopolitan*, February 1934–August 1934.

2. Elsie's memoir receives favorable reviews on November 5, 1934, accessed January 13, 2022, https://www.kirkusreviews.com/book-reviews/a/elsie-robinson/i-wanted-out/; "A Girl of the 90s," *New York Times*, January 6, 1935; Elizabeth Young, "A Columnist Reveals Life," *Washington Post*, December 23, 1934.

3. On the expansion of the Sonora property see "History of Camp Property," Girl Scouts of Northern California Heritage Committee, unpublished narrative in possession of authors.

4. Elsie explains why she only hires men to be secretaries in Irwin, "Elsie Robinson—Study in Contrasts."

5. Elsie wrote prolifically about hot-button topics. There are many more articles and columns for interested readers to explore. These are just a sampling: in support of labor unions, "The Truth About California," *San Francisco Examiner*, January 14, 1940; against Prohibition, "Listen, World!," June 16, 1926, and "Listen, World!," May 27, 1932; against the death penalty, "Listen, World!," March 17, 1922, and "Listen, World!," May 25, 1923; and in defense of Jews, "Listen, World!," December 24, 1938; July 19, 1939; May 6, 1940; March 7, 1944; August 9, 1946; November 17, 1948.

6. For writing that takes aim at racism see Robinson, "Listen, World!," October 16, 1946. For the column about Paul Robeson and the DAR see Robinson, "Listen, World!," August 18, 1947.

7. For her column about the murder of a Black man see Robinson, "Listen, World!," May 28, 1930.

8. For her coverage of the Lindbergh baby kidnapping see Robinson, "10 Million Sympathetic Mothers Weep with Anne," *Austin Statesman*, March 3, 1932. For her Bonus March reporting see Robinson, "Stink of Ashes in the Air" (draft of story, July 29, 1932) and "Bill Hushka's Dead" (draft of story, July 30, 1932), William Randolph Hearst Papers, BANC MSS 77/121 c, Bancroft Library, University of California, Berkeley; Robinson, "Elsie Robinson Gives Graphic Description of B.E.F. Tragedy," *San Francisco Examiner*, September 18, 1932. For Elsie on the 1940 Democratic National Convention see Robinson, "Listen, Neighbor" (draft of story, August 16, 1940), William Randolph Hearst Papers, BANC MSS 77/121 c, Bancroft Library, University of California, Berkeley.

9. On Elsie launching into NBC radio see Emil Brisacher, "The Regional Success of S&W Food: Extensive Promotion and Good Scripts Are Secrets," *Broadcasting and Broadcast Advertising*, May 1, 1938.

10. This new feature began December 1936 and ran for more than a decade. For a good overview, readers may want to read Robinson, "Listen, World!," December 14, 1936, "Listen, World!," September 26, 1937, and "Aims and Ambitions of Young America," June 9, 1940. For an example of the Young America clubs that formed see "Wise Words, Saves Clippings," *San Francisco Examiner*, October 3, 1937. Elsie's letter to William Randolph Hearst was written on February 27, 1940. William Randolph Hearst Papers, BANC MSS 77/121 c, Bancroft Library, University of California, Berkeley.

11. Elsie is celebrated at the Warwick Hotel in Manhattan in "Honor Elsie Robinson," *Editor & Publisher*, June 15, 1940.

12. State of California, Department of Public Health Vital Statistics, Certificate of Death, 1933, no. 799, Elizabeth Robinson, January 15, 1933. On the agony she must endure for the rest of her life see Robinson, "My Crucifix," *Listen World!*, 85–88.

13. For her recipe for resilience see Robinson, "Go On—Make the Gestures!," *Listen World!*, 74–77.

14. For her lessons on tragedy see Robinson, "Don't Try to Forget," *Listen World!*, 78–80.

15. On Elsie's writing and her appeal see Ray Long, "Elsie Robinson," *Cosmopolitan*, March 1924.

16. For Elsie on the so-called mother instinct see Robinson, "Listen, World!," January 15, 1924.

17. For her reflections on the need for women to take care of their own needs for the sake of their children see Robinson, "Listen, World!," December 31, 1923.

18. On urging women to consider love as part of their lives, not the sole objective, see Robinson, "Listen, World!," April 17, 1922.

19. Henry Ford Imprints and Reprints Collection, 1850–1950 (Bulk 1935–1944), Box 2, 4, 5, Finding Aid Published: November 2011. Ann Landers quotes Elsie on September 3, 1984. Elsie was entered into *Congressional Record* on March 13, 1945, when Congressman James Trimble of Arkansas read a poem of hers as part of his argument in support of H.R. 2013, the Lend-Lease Bill.

20. To put Elsie's art into historical context see Martha H. Kennedy, *Drawn to Purpose: American Women Illustrators and Cartoonists* (Jackson: University Press of Mississippi, in association with the Library of Congress, 2018).

21. For Elsie as pioneering writer and editorial cartoonist see Jenny Robb, curator at the Billy Ireland Cartoon Library and Museum at the Ohio State University, email correspondence with authors, January 3, 2022; Dave Astor, archivist at the National Society of Newspaper Columnists, phone interview and email correspondence with authors, December 23, 2021–January 12, 2022.

22. On response to "Listen, World!" by some male readers see Fred D. Harbaugh, "Reader's Forum: Listen, Elsie!," *News-Journal* (Mansfield, OH), December 1, 1954.

23. On annulment of her second marriage see Robinson, *I Wanted Out!*, 286. On Christie's second divorce see "Mrs. C. B. Crowell Granted Divorce: Local Woman Physician Obtains Decree on Grounds of Intolerable Severity," *Brattleboro Reformer*, May 5, 1933. On Benton and Elsie's marriage see Francis Townsend Benton Fremont and Elsinore Crowell Demoro, marriage license, June 14, 1933, Book 10 of Marriage Licenses on page 174, State of California, County of Tuolumne; "Fremont's Grandson Married in Sonora," *Oakland Tribune*, June 15, 1933.

24. On Elsie's marriage and relationship to Benton Fremont see Robinson, *I Wanted Out!*, 298. On Benton's son see "Father Winner in Fight for Custody of His Boy," *Trenton Evening Times*, September 21, 1932; "History of Camp Property," Girl Scouts of Northern California Heritage Committee, unpublished narrative in possession of authors.

25. On Benton Fremont's political ambitions see "Sonora Man to Run for Congress Post," *Mountain Democrat*, June 18, 1936; "Bourbons Lead GOP Slightly in California," *Weekly Adin Argus*, September 3, 1936.

26. On Benton Fremont's campaign for family property see "One-Man War Ends: Benton Fremont, Ft. Mason 'Owner,' Dies a Pauper," *San Francisco Examiner*, October 9, 1960; "Fremont Heir Dies Pauper," *San Bernardino Sun-Telegram*, October 9, 1960.

27. United Press covered Elsie's overdose and recovery, including on May 30 and June 1, 1936. Reports are held in the archives of the Hayward Area Historical Society in Hayward, California. News of her overdose made headlines in newspapers and trade publications: "Phone Operator Traces Cry, Aids Elsie Robinson," *Chicago Daily Tribune*, May 31, 1936; "Elsie Robinson Recovering," *Editor & Publisher*, June 6, 1936. Elsie jokes about her medical scare in Irwin, "Elsie Robinson—Study in Contrasts."

28. Readers miss Elsie's column and write her letters in "Elsie Robinson Will Resume Column Monday," *Wilkes-Barre Record*, April 24, 1942.

29. Elsie breaks both hips in a fall and becomes bedridden in "Listen World Columnist, 73, Dies in S.F.," *Editor & Publisher*, September 15, 1956. On recovering at her Sonora home see "Elsie Robinson Resumes," *Editor & Publisher*, May 2, 1942.

30. Elsie reflects on World War II casualties and the loss of George in Robinson, "Listen, World!," April 29, 1942.

31. A final column written about letting go of anger in Robinson, "Listen, World!," September 5, 1956.

32. Robinson, death certificate, September 8, 1956, file no. 6771, State of California Department of Public Health, City and County of San Francisco, copy in possession of authors.

33. Burial arrangements are revealed in "Elsie Robinson Buried in Family Plot in Benicia," *Benicia Herald*, September 13, 1956.

34. Obituaries that ran in the days following her death include Associated Press, "Famed Woman Columnist Dies at 73," *Santa Cruz Sentinel*, September 9, 1956; "TIME Milestones: September 17, 1956," *Time Magazine*, September 17, 1956; "Elsie Robinson, Columnist, Dies," *New York Times* via Associated Press, September 9, 1956.

35. On Elsie's finances after death see Superior Court of the State of California, in and for the City and County of San Francisco, "In the Matter of the Estate of Elsie Fremont, also known as Elsie Robinson," No. 140104, Dept. 9. A former secretary accuses Benton Fremont of misusing funds in "History of Camp Property," Girl Scouts of Northern California Heritage Committee, unpublished narrative in possession of authors. On use of Fort Mason today see National Park Service, US Department of the Interior, *Cultural Landscape Report for Fort Mason: Golden Gate National Recreation Area*, vol. 1, September 2004; "About Fort Mason Center," Fort Mason Center for Arts and Culture, accessed January 17, 2022, https://fortmason.org/about/.

36. For sale of Sonora property see Tuolumne County, California, Deed Book 58: 231, Elsinore Robinson Fremont and Benton Fremont to North San Mateo County Girl Scout Council, May 7, 1953; County Recorder, Sonora; "Girl Scout Camp Site Acquired," *San Mateo Times*, May 13, 1953;

Tuolumne County, California Deed Book 420: 430, San Francisco Bay Girl Scout Council to Stanislaus County Department of Education, September 5, 1974; County Recorder, Sonora.

37. Examples of columns that published after Elsie's death include Robinson, "Listen, World!," October 24, 1956, and November 6, 1956.

38. The last iteration of "Cry on Geraldine's Shoulder" was titled "Letters to Geraldine" and published November 12, 1961, in the *Oakland Tribune*.

39. Howard Gardiner, phone interview with authors, September 7, 2020. Other examples of "Aunt Elsie" fans who became writers include Ron Genini, email correspondence with authors, May 14, 2021; Evie (Evelyn) Lederer, email correspondence with authors, May 28, 2021; Patty (Patricia) Hall, phone interview and email correspondence with authors, October 8–14, 2021.

40. Elsie invites readers to write their own column in Robinson, "Listen, World!," October 21, 1937.

41. Elsie recounts why being a columnist made her feel whole in Robinson, "Listen, World!," January 18, 1950.

REMEMBERING ELSIE

1. For the study showing the number of historical figures taught in US schools who are women see "Where Are the Women? Summit," National Women's History Museum, February 13, 2021; see findings and video of summit at https://unladylike2020.com.

2. On the best strategies for learning new histories see Martha S. Jones, "Keynote Address," reflections offered during "Where Are the Women? Summit," National Women's History Museum, February 13, 2021.

3. On the current framework for teaching social studies see Alexander Cuenca, "Panel Discussion," reflections offered during "Where Are the Women? Summit," National Women's History Museum, February 13, 2021.

4. Canceled copyright renewal registration for *I Wanted Out!*, United States Copyright Office, Catalog of Copyright Entries (CCE), July–December 1962 volume for Books, page 1990; no copyright renewal registration on file for *Listen World!*, United States Copyright Office letter to authors dated January 13, 2015.

INDEX

© *Davia Rose-Scheeres*

Julia Scheeres is the author of the *New York Times*–bestselling memoir *Jesus Land* and the award-winning *A Thousand Lives: The Untold Story of Jonestown*. She lives in Northern California.

Allison Gilbert is an award-winning journalist and author of numerous books including *Passed and Present* and *Parentless Parents*. She lives outside New York City.

© *Elena Seibert*